AF841016

Insurance Law in Germany

Insurance Law in Germany

Robert Koch

This book was originally published as a monograph in the International Encyclopaedia of Laws/Insurance Law.

Founding Editor: Roger Blanpain
General Editor: Frank Hendrickx
Volume Editor: Herman Cousy

Wolters Kluwer

Published by:
Kluwer Law International B.V.
PO Box 316
2400 AH Alphen aan den Rijn
The Netherlands
E-mail: international-sales@wolterskluwer.com
Website: lrus.wolterskluwer.com

Sold and distributed in North, Central and South America by:
Wolters Kluwer Legal & Regulatory U.S.
7201 McKinney Circle
Frederick, MD 21704
United States of America
Email: customer.service@wolterskluwer.com

Sold and distributed in all other countries by:
Air Business Subscriptions
Rockwood House
Haywards Heath
West Sussex
RH16 3DH
United Kingdom
Email: international-customerservice@wolterskluwer.com

DISCLAIMER: The material in this volume is in the nature of general comment only. It is not offered as advice on any particular matter and should not be taken as such. The editor and the contributing authors expressly disclaim all liability to any person with regard to anything done or omitted to be done, and with respect to the consequences of anything done or omitted to be done wholly or partly in reliance upon the whole or any part of the contents of this volume. No reader should act or refrain from acting on the basis of any matter contained in this volume without first obtaining professional advice regarding the particular facts and circumstances at issue. Any and all opinions expressed herein are those of the particular author and are not necessarily those of the editor or publisher of this volume.

ISBN 978-94-035-0520-6

e-Book: ISBN 978-94-035-0521-3
web-PDF: ISBN 978-94-035-0522-0

© 2018, Kluwer Law International BV, The Netherlands

All rights reserved. No part of this publication may be reproduced, stored in a retrieval system, or transmitted in any form or by any means, electronic, mechanical, photocopying, recording, or otherwise, without the prior written permission of the publisher.

Permission to use this content must be obtained from the copyright owner. More information can be found at: lrus.wolterskluwer.com/policies/permissions-reprints-and-licensing

The Author

Dr Robert Koch is Professor at the University of Hamburg. He holds the chair of Private Law and Insurance Law. He is the director of the Institute of Insurance Law, which was founded in 1916, and the director of the LLM programme on insurance law. He is the chairman of the Hamburg Association of Insurance Science and chairman of the International Insurance Law Association's Working Party on Financial Lines. In the latter capacity he is a member of the Presidential Council of the International Insurance Law Association (AIDA). His special interests lie in liability insurance with a focus on financial lines. He is the author of numerous articles and books on insurance law, especially on liability insurance, fidelity insurance and cyber risk insurance. He is the managing editor of the Bruck/Moeller, the most comprehensive commentary on German insurance law, which consist of 12 volumes, where he comments *inter alia* on all classes of liability insurance and on motor insurance.

The Author

Table of Contents

List of Abbreviations

ABL	*Allgemeine Bedingungen fuer die Sachversicherung landwirtschaftlicher Betriebe, Wirtschaftsgebaeude und deren Inhalt sowie Wohngebaeude* (GDV Model Terms and Conditions for Agricultural Insurance)
ABBL	*Allgemeine Bedingungen für die Versicherung von Bauleistungen* (GDV Model Terms and Conditions for Construction Insurance)
ABBV	*Allgemeine Bedingungen für die Baubestandsversicherung* (GDV Model Terms and Conditions for Business Building Stock Insurance)
ABE	*Allgemeine Bedingungen für die Elektronikversicher*ung (GDV Model Terms and Conditions for Electronic Equipment Insurance)
ABMG	*Allgemeine Bedingungen für die Maschinen- und Kaskoversicherung von fahrbaren oder transportablen Geraeten* (GDV Model Terms and Conditions for Mobile Machines Machinery Breakdown Insurance)
ADHGB	*Allgemeines Deutsches Handelsgesetzbuch* (German General Commercial Law of 1869)
AG	*Aktiengesellschaft* (Stock Corporation)
AHagB	*Allgemeine Versicherungsbedingungen für die Hagelversicherung* (GDV Model Terms and Conditions for Hail Insurance)

List of Abbreviations

AHB	*Allgemeine Versicherungsbedingungen für die Haftpflichtversicherung* (GDV Model Terms and Conditions for Liability Insurance)
AKB	*Allgemeine Bedingungen für die Kfz-Versicherung* (GDV Model Terms and Conditions for Motor Vehicle Insurance)
AktG	*Aktiengesetz* (Stock Corporations Act)
ALB	*Allgemeine Bedingungen für die kapitalbildende Lebensversicherung* (GDV Model Terms and Conditions for Endowment Policies)
ALR	*Allgemeines Landrecht fuer die Preußischen Staaten* (General Land Law for the Prussian States); *Allgemeine Bedingungen für die Risikolebensversicherung* (GDV Model Terms and Conditions for Term Life Policies)
AltZertG	*Altersvorsorgevertraege-Zertifizierungsgesetz* (Pension Provision Agreements Certification Act)
AMB	*Allgemeine Bedingungen für die Maschinenversicherung von stationaeren Maschinen* (GDV Model Terms and Conditions for Machinery Breakdown Insurance)
AMBUB	*Allgemeine Bedingungen für die Maschinen-Betriebsunterbrechungsversicherung* (GDV Model Terms and Conditions for Machinery Loss of Profits nsurance)
AmtsG	*Amtsgericht* (Local Court)
ARB	*Allgemeine Bedingungen für die Rechtsschutzversicherung* (GDV Model Terms and Conditions for Legal Expenses Insurance)
Art.	Article
Arts	Articles
ATB	*Allgemeine Bedingungen für die Terrorversicherung* (Standard Terms and Conditions for Terror Insurance)

AtG	*Atomgesetz* (Atomic Energy Act)
AUB	*Allgemeine Bedingungen für die Unfallversicherung* (GDV Model Terms and Conditions for Accident Insurance)
AuslPflVG	*Gesetz ueber die Haftpflichtversicherung fuer auslaendische Kraftfahrzeuge und Kraftfahrzeuganhaenger* (German Act on Obligatory Insurance for Motor Vehicles and trailers Registered Abroad)
AuslKfzPflVV	*Verordnung ueber die Kraftfahrzeug-Haftpflichtversicherung auslaendischer Kraftfahrzeuge und Kraftfahrzeuganhaenger* (Ordinance on Compulsory Liability Insurance for Motor Vehicles and Trailers Registered Abroad)
AVB-AVG	*Allgemeine Versicherungsbedingungen für die Vermoegensschaden-Haftpflichtversicherung von Aufsichtsraeten, Vorstaenden und Geschaeftsfuehrern* (GDV Model Terms and Conditions for D&O-Liability Insurance)
AVB BHV	*Allgemeine Versicherungsbedingungen für die Betriebs- und Berufshaftpflichtversicherung* (GDV Model Terms and Conditions for Commercial General Liability)
AVB/BT	*Allgemeine Versicherungsbedingungen für den Basistarif* (PKV Model Terms and Conditions for the Basic Tariff in Health Insurance)
AVB Cyber	*Allgemeine Versicherungsbedingungen fuer die Cyberrisiko-Versicherung* (GDV Model Terms and Conditions for Cyberrisks)
AVB PHV	*Allgemeine Versicherungsbedingungen fuer die Privathaftpflichtversicherung* (GDV Model Terms and Conditions for Private Liability Insurance)
BaFin	*Bundesanstalt fuer Finanzdienstleistungsaufsicht* (Federal Financial Supervisory Authority)

List of Abbreviations

BAG	*Bundesarbeitsgericht* (Federal Labour Court)
BB	*Betriebs-Berater* (law journal, Deutscher Fachverlag)
Bd.	Band (volume)
BdV	*Bund der Versicherten e.V.* (German Registered Association of the Insured)
BDVM	*Bundesverband Deutscher Versicherungsmakler e.V.* (German Registered Association of Brokers)
BeckRS	*Beck online Rechtsprechung* (Beck Online Case Journal, Verlag C.H. Beck)
BerVersV	*Verordnung ueber die Berichterstattung von Versicherungsunternehmen gegenueber der Bundesanstalt fuer Finanzdienstleistungsaufsicht* (Regulation on Reporting by Insurance Undertakings to the BaFin)
BetrAVG	*Gesetz zur Verbesserung der betrieblichen Altersversorgung* (Act to Improve Occupational Pension Schemes)
BFH	*Bundesfinanzhof* (Federal Finance Court)
BGB	*Buergerliches Gesetzbuch* (German Civil Code)
BGBl.	*Bundesgesetzblatt* (Federal Law Gazette)
BGH	*Bundesgerichtshof* (Federal Court of Justice on Civil and Criminal Matters)
BGHZ	*Entscheidungssammlung des Bundesgerichtshofes in Zivilsachen* (Federal Court of Justice on Civil Matters Law Reports, Carl Heymanns Verlag)
BKV	*Berufskrankheiten-Verordnung*
BNotO	*Bundesnotarordnung* (Federal Public Notaries Ordinance)
BSG	*Bundessozialgericht* (Federal Social Court)
BRAO	*Bundesrechtsanwaltsordnung* (Federal Lawyers' Act)
BR-Drucks.	*Bundesratsdrucksache* (Official Records of the Bundesrat)
BT-Drucks.	*Bundestagsdrucksache* (Official Records of the Bundestag)

BUV	*Allgemeine Bedingungen für die Berufsunfaehigkeitsversicherung* (GDV Model Terms and Conditions on Occupational Disability Insurance)
BVerfG	*Bundesverfassungsgericht* (Federal Constitutional Court)
BVerwG	*Bundesverwaltungsgericht* (Federal Administrative Court)
BVK	*Bundesverband Deutscher Versicherungskaufleute e.V.* (German Registered Association of Self-Employed Insurance Agents)
BVVB	*Bundesverband der Versicherungsberater e.V.* (German Registered Association of Insurance Advisers)
BWE	*Besondere Bedingungen für die Versicherung weiterer Elementarschaeden* (GDV Model Terms and Conditions for Natural Hazard Insurance)
BZA	*Bundeszentralamt fuer Steuern* (Federal Central Tax Office)
BZRG	*Gesetz über das Bundeszentralregister* (Federal Register of Criminal and Court Records)
DB	*Der Betrieb* (law journal, Verlag Handelsblatt Fachmedien)
DeckRV	*Deckungsrueckstellungsverordnung* (Regulation on the Principles Underlying the Calculation of the Premium Reserve)
DfVW	*Deutscher Verein fuer Versicherungswissenschaft e.V.* (German Insurance Science Association)
DIHK	*Deutscher Industrie- und Handelskammertag e.V.* (Registered Association of German Chambers of Commerce and Industry)
DVO	*Durchfuehrungsverordnung* (Delegated Regulation 2015/35/EU)

List of Abbreviations

DVStB	*Verordnung zur Durchfuehrung der Vorschriften ueber Steuerberater, Steuerbevollmaechtigte und Steuerberatungsgesellschaften* (Regulation Implementing the Tax Consultants' Act)
cf.	confer (compare)
EC	European Community
EEA	European Economic Area
EEC	European Economic Community
e.g.	exempli gratia (for example)
EGHGB	*Einfuehrungsgesetz zum Handelsgesetzbuch* (Introductory Act to the German Commercial Code)
EhfG	*Entwicklungshelfer-Gesetz* (Development Workers Act)
EStG	*Einkommensteuergesetz* (Income Tax Act)
et al.	et alii (and others)
etc.	et cetera
EU	European Union
e.V.	*eingetragener Verein* (Registered Asscociation)
FamGKG	*Gesetz ueber Gerichtskosten in Familiensachen* (Court Costs Family Matters Act)
FeuerschStG	*Feuerschutzsteuergesetz* (Fire Protection Insurance Act)
FZV	*Fahrzeug-Zulassungsverordnung* (German Vehicle-Admission-Ordinance)
GbR	*Gesellschaft buergerlichen Rechts* (Non-registered Unlimited Civil Partnership)
GDV	*Gesamtverband der Deutschen Versicherungswirtschaft e.V.* (German Insurance Registered Association)
GewO	*Gewerbeordnung* (German Trade, Commerce and Industry Regulation Act)
GewStDV	*Gewerbesteuer-Durchfuehrungsverordnung* (Ordinance on the Trade Tax Implementation)
GewStG	*Gewerbesteuergesetz* (Trade Tax Act)
GG	*Grundgesetz* (Basic Law (German Constitution))

GKG	*Gerichtskostengesetz* (Court Costs Act)
GmbH	*Gesellschaft mit beschraenkter Haftung* (Limited Liability Company)
GmbHG	*Gesetz ueber die Gesellschaften mit beschraenkter Haftung* (Limited Liability Companies Act)
GRV	*Gesetzliche Rentenversicherung* (Mandatory Public Retirement Insurance)
GVG	*Gerichtsverfassungsgesetz* (German Courts Act)
GvKostG	*Gerichtsvollzieherkostengesetz* (Bailiffs' Costs Act)
GVNW	*Gesamtverband der versicherungsnehmenden Wirtschaft e.V.* (Association Representing the Insured Businesses and Inhouse brokers)
HGB	*Handelsgesetzbuch* (German Commercial Code)
i.e.	id est (that is)
IHK	*Industrie- und Handelskammer(n)* (Chamber(s) of Commerce and Industry)
InsO	*Insolvenzordnung* (German Insolvency Act)
jurisPR-VersR	*juris PraxisReport Versicherungsrecht* (online case law journal, juris GmbH)
JVEG	*Justizverguetungs- und –entschaedigungsgesetz* (Judicial Remuneration and Compensation Act)
KapAusstV	*Verordnung ueber die Kapitalausstattung von Versicherungsunternehmen* (Capital Resources Regulation)
KfzPflVV	*Kraftfahrzeug-Pflichtversicherungsverordnung* (Ordinance on Compulsory Liability Insurance for Motor Vehicle Keepers)
KG	*Kammergericht* (Berlin Court of Appeal)
KG	*Kommanditgesellschaft* (Registered Limited Commercial Partnership)
KOM	European Commission

KStDV 1994	*Koerperschaftsteuer-Durchfuehrungsverordnung 1994* (Ordinance on the Corporate Tax Implementation)
KStG	*Koerperschaftsteuergesetz* (German Corporate Tax Act)
LG	*Landgericht* (District Court)
LHB	*Luftfahrt-Haftpflichtversicherungs-Bedingungen für Luftfahrzeughalter und Luftfrachtführer* (Aviation Liability Insurance Conditions for Aircraft Operators and Carriers)
LKB	*Luftfahrt-Kaskoversicherungs-Bedingungen* (Aviation Hull Insurance Conditions)
LUB	*Luftfahrt-Unfallversicherungs-Bedingungen* (Aviation Accident Insurance Conditions)
LuftVG	*Luftverkehrsgesetz* (Air Traffic Act)
LuftVZO	*Luftverkehrszulassungsordnung* (Air Traffic Licensing Ordinance)
LVRG	*Gesetz zur Absicherung stabiler und fairer Leistungen fuer Lebensversicherte (Lebensversicherungsreformgesetz* (Life Insurance Reform Act))
MB/KK	*Musterbedingungen fuer die Krankheitskosten- und Krankenhaustagegeldversich*erung (PKV Model Terms and Conditions for Comprehensive Health Insurance and Daily Hospital Allowance Insurance)
MB/KT	*Musterbedingungen 2009 für die Krankentagegeldversicherung* (PKV Model Terms and Conditions for Daily Sickness Allowance Insurance)
MCR	Minimum Capital Requirement
MGar	*Allgemeine Bedingungen für die Garantieversicherung* (GDV Model Terms and Conditions for Warranty Insurance)
n.	note (in German: Randnummer)
NJOZ	*Neue Juristische Online-Zeitschrift* (case law journal, Verlag C.H.Beck)

NJW	*Neue Juristische Wochenschrift* (law journal, Verlag C.H.Beck)
NJW-RR	*Neue Juristische Wochenschrift Rechtsprechungs-Report Zivilrecht* (case law journal, Verlag C.H.Beck)
no.	number
nos	numbers
ns	notes
NVersZ	*Neue Zeitschrift fuer Versicherung und Recht* (law journal, Verlag C.H.Beck)
NZA	*Neue Zeitschrift fuer Arbeitsrecht* (law journal, Verlag C.H.Beck)
oHG	*Offene Handelsgesellschaft* (Registered Unlimited Commercial Partnership)
O.J.	Official Journal of the European Union
OLG	*Oberlandesgericht* (Court of Appeal)
OVG	*Oberverwaltungsgericht* (Administrative Court of Appeal)
para.	paragraph
paras	paragraphs
PartG	*Partnerschaftsgesellschaft* (Registered Professional Partnership)
PartGG	*Partnerschaftsgesellschaftsgesetz* (Registered Professional Partnership Act)
PFAV	*Verordnung betreffend die Aufsicht ueber Pensionsfonds und ueber die Durchfuehrung reiner Beitragszusagen in der betrieblichen Altersversorgung* (Regulation on the Supervision of Pensions Fund)
PflVG	*Gesetz ueber die Pflichtversicherung fuer Kraftfahrzeughalter* (German Act on Obligatory Insurance for Motor Vehicle Keepers)
PKV	*Verband der Privaten Krankenversicherung e.V.* (Association of Private Health Insurers)
ProdhaftG	*Produkthaftungsgesetz* (Product Liability Act)

ProdHM	*Besondere Bedingungen und Risikobeschreibungen für die Produkthaftpflichtversicherung von Industrie- und Handelsbetrieben (Produkthaftpflicht-Modell)* (Special Terms and Conditions for Product Liability Insurance)
RDG	*Rechtsdienstleistungsgesetz* (Legal Services Act)
RDV	*Verordnung zum Rechtsdienstleistungsgesetz* (Ordinance on the Legal Service Act)
RechVersV	*Versicherungsunternehmens-Rechnungslegungsverordnung* (Regulation on the Accounting of Insurance Undertakings)
RGZ	*Entscheidungen des Reichsgerichts in Zivilsachen* (Imperial Court of Justice on Civil Matters Law Reports, Verlag DeGruyter)
RuS	*Recht und Schaden* (law journal, Verlag C.H.Beck)
RVG	*Rechtsanwaltungsverguetungsgesetz* (Lawyers' Remuneration Act)
SchauHV	*Schaustellerhaftpflichtverordnung* (Ordinance on the Liability of Fairground Workers)
SCR	Solvency Capital Requirement
SE	Societas Europaea (European Stock Corporation)
SG	Sozialgericht (Social Court)
SGB	*Sozialgesetzbuch* (German Social Code)
SGG	*Sozialgerichtsgesetz* (German Social Courts Act)
SolZG	*Solidaritaetszuschlaggesetz* (Solidarity Tax Act)
StBerG	*Steuerberatungsgesetz* (Tax Advisers Act)
StGB	*Strafgesetzbuch* (German Criminal Code)
StVG	*Straßenverkehrsgesetz* (Road Traffic Act)
SvEV	*Sozialversicherungsentgeltverordnung* (Ordinance on Social Security Compensation)

TK	*Technische Klausel*
TranspR	*Transportrecht* (law journal, Wolters Kluwer)
UklaG	*Gesetz ueber Unterlassungsklagen bei Verbraucherrechts- und anderen Verstoeßen* (Act on Injunction Relieve)
UmweltHG	*Umwelthaftungsgesetz* (Environmental Liability Act)
UmweltHM	*Besondere Bedingungen und Risikobeschreibungen für die Versicherung der Haftpflicht wegen Schaeden durch Umwelteinwirkung (Umwelthaftpflicht-Modell)* (Special Terms and Conditions for E Liability Insurance)
UmwG	*Umwandlungsgesetz* (German Transformation Act)
USchadG	*Umweltschadensgesetz* (German Environmental Damage Act)
UstG	*Umsatzsteuergesetz* (Value-Added Tax Act)
USV	*Allgemeine Versicherungsbedingungen für die Umweltschadensversicherung* (General Terms and Conditions for Environmental Damage Insurance)
v.	versus
VAG	*Versicherungsaufsichtsgesetz* (German Insurance Supervision Act)
VermVO	*Verfahrensordnung fuer Beschwerden im Zusammenhang mit der Vermittlung von Versicherungsvertraegen* (Rules of Procedure for the Out-of-Court Settlement of Claims against Insurance Intermediaries)
VersR	*Versicherungsrecht* (law journal, *Verlag Versicherungswirtschaft*)
VersStG	*Versicherungssteuergesetz* (Insurance Tax Act)
VersVermV	*Versicherungsvermittlerverordnung* (Ordinance on Insurance Mediation)
VG	*Verwaltungsgericht* (Administrative Court)

VGB	*Allgemeine Wohngebaeude Versicherungsbedingungen* (GDV Model Terms and Conditions for Building Insurance)
VHB	*Allgemeine Hausrat Versicherungsbedingungen* (GDV Model Terms and Conditions for Comprehensive Household Insurance)
VomVO	*Verfahrensordnung des Versicherungsombudsmanns e.V.* (Rules of Procedure of the Insurance Ombudsman Registered Association for the Out-of-Court Settlement of Claims against Insurers)
VVaG	*Versicherungsverein auf Gegenseitigkeit* (Mutual Insurance Association)
VVG	*Versicherungsvertragsgesetz* (German Insurance Contract Act)
VVG-InfoV	*Verordnung ueber Informationspflichten bei Versicherungsvertraegen* (Ordinance on the Obligation to Supply Information Pertaining to Insurance Contracts)
VoeV	*Verband oeffentlicher Versicherer* (Association of Public Sector Insurers)
VW	*Versicherungswirtschaft* (insurance journal, Verlag VW GmbH)
VwGO	*Verwaltungsgerichtsordnung* (German Administrative Courts Act)
WM	*Wertpapier-Mitteilungen* (law journal, Verlag Herausgebergemeinschaft WERTPAPIER-MITTEILUNGEN)
WPO	*Wirtschaftsprueferordnung* (Public Accountants Act)
zfs	*Zeitschrift fuer Schadensrecht* (law journal, Deutscher Anwaltverlag)
ZfU	*Zeitschrift fuer Umweltpolitik & Umweltrecht* (*Verlag dfv Mediengruppe*)
ZGR	*Zeitschrift fuer Unternehmens- und Gesellschaftsrecht* (law journal, Verlag DeGruyter)
ZIP	*Zeitschrift fuer Wirtschaftsrecht* (law journal)

ZPO	Zivilprozessordnung (German Code of Civil Procedure)
ZVersWiss	*Zeitschrift fuer die gesamte Versicherungswissenschaft* (law journal; Verlag Springer)

List of Abbreviations

General Introduction

§1. General Background Information

1. Germany is a federal state made up of 16 constituent states – the Laender, namely Baden-Wuerttemberg, Bayern, Berlin, Brandenburg, Bremen, Hamburg, Hessen, Mecklenburg-Vorpommern, Niedersachsen, Nordrhein-Westfalen, Rheinland-Pfalz, Saarland, Sachsen, Sachsen-Anhalt Schleswig-Holstein und Thueringen. The capital is Berlin. Germany occupies about 357,137 square kilometres and has a population of some 82.8 million people (about 230 inhabitants per square kilometre).[1] Each 'Land' has a parliament, a government and (except in Berlin and Schleswig-Holstein) a constitutional court.

I. Political and Legal System

A. *Constitution*

2. The Basic Law (*Grundgesetz*, hereafter 'GG') is the constitution of Germany. It lays down the basic human rights (Articles 1–19 and 101–104 GG), the principle of democracy, the rule of the law including the principle of separation of powers (Article 20 GG), and divides the tasks and the powers between the constitutional organs of Germany, i.e., the Parliament (*Bundestag*) (Articles 38–48), the Council of the Laender (*Bundesrat*) (Articles 50–53 GG), the President (*Bundespraesident*) (Articles 54–61 GG), the Federal Government (*Bundesregierung*) (Articles 62–69 GG) and the judiciary including the Federal Constitutional Court (*Bundesverfassungsgericht*, hereafter 'BVerfG') (Articles 92–100 GG).

B. *Legislation*

1. Federal Level

3. Federal legislative power is vested in the Bundestag and in the Bundesrat. The Bundestag is supposed to have 598 members. Half of them are elected directly in

1. *See* https://www.destatis.de/Europa/EN/Country/EUMemberStates/Germany.html (accessed 28 Mar. 2018).

the 299 constituencies on the basis of the first of two votes cast by each voter. Further 299 members are elected on the basis of the second vote, which is cast in favour of one of the lists of candidates put forward by the political parties in each of Germany's Laender. The second vote is decisive for the composition of the Bundestag. There is a five percent threshold for representation of a party in the Bundestag. In fact, the Bundestag has always more Members due to what are called 'overhang' seats (*Ueberhangmandante*). Whenever a party wins more direct constituency seats in a single Land than the number to which it would be entitled based on its share of the second votes, all of the party's successful constituency candidates take up their seats in the Bundestag. In order to restore the balance between the parties on the basis of the second votes extra 'balance seats' are allocated to the other parties.[2] At present, the Bundestag is composed of 709 members (598 statutory seats, plus overhang and balance seats).[3]

4. The Bundesrat enables the governments of the 16 Laender to participate directly in the legislation and administration of the Federation and in matters concerning the EU. The members must be members of the government in their Land (e.g., minister). The number of members and votes allocated to each federal state is determined by the number of inhabitants in that Land.

2. Laender Level

5. There are federal laws that apply to the whole territory of Germany, and Laender laws that only have validity in the 'land' in question. The division of constitutional legislative powers between the Federation and the Laender is regulated in detail by Articles 71–75 GG. Insurance law is not included in Article 73 GG as a matter under exclusive legislative power of the Federation. Article 74 paragraph 1 no. 11 GG rather provides only for concurrent legislative power in insurance matters. In fields subject to concurrent legislation, however, the Laender have the right to adopt legislation only if the Federation has made no use of its legislative powers in the same field. Since the Federation has in fact pre-empted the entire field of insurance law, there is hardly any room left for Laender legislation. At the Laender law level, there is legislation on compulsory liability insurance e.g., for architects, dog owners, hunters.

C. Court System

6. The judicial system in Germany is made of ordinary courts, specialized courts and constitutional courts.

---

2. For further general details, *see* Linn/Sobolewski, The German Bundestag Functions and procedures 18th electoral term, 2015, Verlag NDV GmbH, https://www.btg-bestellservice.de/pdf/10041000.pdf (accessed 28 Mar. 2018); Election of Members and the allocation of seats, https://www.bundestag.de/en/parliament/elections/arithmetic (accessed 28 Mar. 2018).
3. *See* http://www.bundestag.de/en (accessed 28 Mar. 2018).

1. Constitutional Courts

7. There are constitutional courts at the state level (*Verfassungsgerichte der Laender*) empowered to review state law, and there is the *Bundesverfassungsgericht*, which is the highest court in the German judicial system. It is not only a court but also a constitutional organ (*see* paragraph 2). The *Bundesverfassungsgericht's* function is to ensure that the Basic Law (*see* paragraph 2) is obeyed. As a constitutional organ the *Bundesverfassungsgericht* is not subject to the administrative supervision of a ministry.[4] Its decisions are final and binding upon the constitutional organs of the Federation and of the Laender, as well as on all courts and the authorities (Article 31 paragraph 1 Act on the Federal Constitutional Court (*Bundesverfassungsgerichtsgesetz*, hereafter 'BVerfGG')). Generally, the binding effect is limited to the case at hand.

8. It is to be noted that the *Bundesverfassungsgericht* is not part of the avenue of appeal from ordinary courts or specialized courts. Since the *Bundesverfassungsgericht* only examines whether specific constitutional law was violated, a constitutional complaint (*Verfassungsbeschwerde*) against a decision of an ordinary court or a specialized court is only admissible on the basis of an alleged breach of the basic law (e.g., a violation of the right to be heard (Article 103 paragraph 1 GG)).[5] Generally, the constitutional complaint is only admissible if all legal remedies before the ordinary courts or specialized courts have been exhausted. With regard to insurance law the *Bundesverfassungsgericht* had to deal several times with constitutional complaints against decisions of the *Bundesgerichtshof* (hereafter 'BGH') on the validity of surrender value provisions in life insurance policies.[6]

2. Ordinary Courts and Specialized Courts

9. The ordinary courts deal with civil and criminal matters (*Zivilgerichte*, *Strafgerichte*). The specialized courts are divided into labour courts (*Arbeitsgerichte*), tax courts (*Finanzgerichte*), administrative courts (*Verwaltungsgerichte*) and social courts (*Sozialgerichte*). The courts are all organized hierarchically. In civil matters, if there is a claim of the policyholder for coverage against the insurer, depending on the value of the matter, the Court of First Instances are local courts (*Amtsgerichte*) or district courts (*Landgerichte*). Claims worth less than EUR 5,000 have to be filed with local courts (*see* § 23 no. 1 of the German courts act (*Gerichtsverfassungsgesetz*, hereafter 'GVG')). Appeals from local courts are heard by the district courts and appeals from the district courts are heard by the Court of Appeals (*Oberlandesgericht*). Against their decisions an appeal on points of law is possible only before the BGH. The same is true for appeals on points of law in cases heard before the

4. For further information, *see* http://www.bundesverfassungsgericht.de/EN/Das-Gericht/Gericht-und-Verfassungsorgan/gericht-und-verfassungsorgan_node.html (accessed 28 Mar. 2018).
5. Further details are provided in Art. 93 para. 1 nos 4a and 4b GG.
6. For example, BGH, 17 Feb. 2017 – 1 BvR 781/15, NJW 2017, p. 1593; BVerfG, 26 Jul. 2005 – 1 BvR 80/95, NJW 2005, p. 2376.

local court or district court (*Sprungrevision*). It is to be noted that in disputes regarding long-term care insurance the social courts are competent, no matter whether the long-term care insurance is based on statute (*Sozialversicherung*) (*see* paragraphs 678, 682) or on private contract (*see* § 51 paragraph 1 no. 2 of the social courts act (*Sozialgerichtsgesetz*, hereafter 'SGG')). They have three levels (*Sozialgericht – Landessozialgericht – Bundessozialgericht*). Administrative law courts, which too have three levels (*Verwaltungsgericht – Oberverwaltungsgericht – Bundesverwaltungsgericht*), hear cases against administrative acts of the federal financial supervisory authority (*Bundesanstalt fuer Finanzdienstleistungsaufsicht*, hereafter 'BaFin').

3. No Doctrine of Stare Decisis

10. Germany follows the civil law tradition.[7] The legal system is based on the basic law and on statutory law. Court decisions have effect only between the parties. There is no doctrine of stare decisis. Neither are courts bound by their own previous decisions in similar cases, nor should they make their decisions consistent with previous decisions of higher courts.[8] In practice, however, especially judgments by the highest courts enjoy high persuasive authority from which lower courts will only depart from for good reason. Whenever the BGH – its Fourth Civil Senate is competent for disputes between policyholders and insurers, the Third Civil Senate is competent for claims of policyholders against insurance intermediaries – finds for the invalidity of e.g., an exclusion clause, not only the insurer in question but all other the insurance companies respond to the ruling and will replace this clause in their policies. It is to be noted that when a court hearing an appeal on points of law refers the case back to a court of lower instance, the lower court, must base its new decision on the legal assessment on which the reversal of its previous judgment was based (*see* § 538 and § 563 of the German code of civil procedure (*Zivilprozessordnung*, hereafter 'ZPO')).

II. Commerce and Industry

11. Germany is the largest national economy in Europe, and it is a founding member of the EU. According to the International Monetary Fund (IMF), in 2017, the country accounted for 28% of the Euro area economy.[9] Its economic model is based on the concept of the social market economy. On the world scale, it ranks as

7. For further information, *see* Law – Made in Germany, https://web.archive.org/web/20150416094948/http://www.bmjv.de/SharedDocs/Downloads/DE/pdfs/Law_Made_in_Germany.pdf?__blob=publicationFile (accessed 28 Mar. 2018).
8. For further information, *see* http://www.bundesgerichtshof.de/EN/Home/home_node.html (accessed 28 Mar. 2018).
9. *See* http://www.imf.org/en/News/Articles/2017/07/05/na070717-germany-spend-more-at-home (accessed 28 Mar. 2018).

the fourth largest economy in terms of nominal GDP. As reported by recent statistics of the IMF, the size of German's nominal GDP is USD 3.42 billion, while its GDP in terms of purchasing power parity is USD 4.13 trillion. Germany's GDP per capita is USD 49,814.[10]

12. Germany exported goods to the value of EUR 1,279,066 million and imported goods to the value of EUR 1,034,323 million in 2017. The top ten exports of Germany are motor vehicles, machinery and equipment, chemicals and chemical goods, computer, electronic and optical products, pharmaceuticals, transport equipment, basic metals, food products, and rubber and plastics.[11]

III. Financial Institutions

13. Germany's financial institutions are made up of the commercial banks, investment banks and insurance companies. The commercial banking system can be divided into private banks (e.g., Deutsche Bank AG, Commerzbank AG), cooperative banks ('Volksbanken und Raiffeisenbanken'), public banks (e.g., 'Landesbanken') and public saving banks ('Sparkassen'). The Deutsche Bank AG is the biggest German investment bank and belongs to the world's top ten investment banks. Allianz SE and Munich Reinsurance belong to the largest insurance companies in the world.

IV. Currency Legislation and Monetary Regulations

14. Germany is a member of the Eurozone. Up to the end of 1998, the Deutsche Bundesbank, based in Frankfurt/M., was responsible for ensuring price stability in Germany. With the launch of the European Monetary Union and the introduction of the Euro at the beginning of 1999, this task was transferred to the Euro system. Since then, the European Central Bank (ECB), also based in Frankfurt/M., together with all national central banks of the EU Member States, which have adopted the Euro, have constituted the Euro system. The ECB *inter alia* sets the *interest rates* at which it lends to commercial banks in the *Eurozone*, manages the Eurozone's foreign currency reserves and the buying or selling of currencies to balance exchange rates, and authorises production of Euro banknotes by Eurozone countries

---

10. *See* https://www.investopedia.com/articles/investing/022415/worlds-top-10-economies.asp (accessed 28 Mar. 2018).
11. For further information, *see* https://www.destatis.de/EN/FactsFigures/NationalEconomyEnvironment/ForeignTrade/Tables/ImportsExports.html (accessed 28 Mar. 2018).

V. Insurance Business, General Organization and Special Features

A. German Insurance Association

15. The private insurance industry is represented by the German Insurance Association (*Gesamtverband der Deutschen Versicherungswirtschaft e.V.*, hereafter 'GDV'), based in Berlin. According to the GDV its about 450 member companies offer comprehensive insurance coverage to private and corporate customers through their 431 million insurance contracts. The premium income amounts to EUR 194 billion.[12] The GDV plays an important role in the development of model terms and conditions for almost all kinds of insurance except for private healthcare insurance.[13]

B. Association of Private Health Insurers

16. Model terms and conditions for private health insurance are provided by the Association of Private Health Insurers (*Verband der Privaten Krankenversicherung e.V.*, hereafter 'PKV').[14] According to the PKV there are forty-one ordinary and seven extraordinary member companies as of August 2017.[15]

C. Association of Public Sector Insurers

17. The association of public sector insurers (*Verband oeffentlicher Versicherer*, hereafter 'VoeV') is the umbrella organization of the German public insurance companies, and a corporation established under public law. Founded in 1911, it represents 11 primary insurer groups across Germany that are embedded in their Laender/regions. According to VoeV, the group is the second largest primary insurance provider in the German market with EUR 123 billion of investments under management. The group has 50 million insurance contracts and pays out EUR 18 billion each year to its clients. The public insurers employ 30,000 people. Through 3,700 own branches and more than 15,000 offices of their partners (savings banks and further affiliated partners), they offer advice and protection across most insurance sectors (health, life, pension, motor vehicle, indemnity, fire, etc.) for retail clients of all income groups and for professional clients with a specific focus on small and medium sized companies.[16]

---

12. For details about the number of insurance companies, premium income, insurance density and insurance penetration, etc., *see* Statistical Yearbook of German Insurance, https://www.en.gdv.de/resource/blob/31008/4b8253fd8687f0f071e318bf42112353/download-statistical-yearbook-2017-data.pdf (accessed 28 Mar. 2018).
13. *See* https://www.gdv.de/de/ueber-uns/unsere-services/musterbedingungen-23924 (accessed 28 Mar. 2018).
14. *See* www.pkv.de/service/rechtsquellen/musterbedingungen (accessed 28 Mar. 2018).
15. For further information, *see* www.pkv.de (accessed 28 Mar. 2018).
16. For further information, *see* www.voev.de (accessed 28 Mar. 2018).

D. *Association of German Chambers of Commerce and Industry*

18. The Association of German Chambers of Commerce and Industry (*Deutscher Industrie- und Handelskammertag e.V.*, hereafter 'DIHK') is the central organization for 79 Chambers of Commerce and Industry (*Industrie- und Handelskammer*, hereafter 'IHK') in Germany.[17] All companies registered in Germany, with the exception of handicraft businesses, the free professions and farmers, are required by law to join a chamber. The local IHKs play an important role not only for insurance intermediaries such as agent, brokers but also to insurance advisers since according to § 34d and § 34e of the German trade, commerce and industry regulation act (*Gewerbeordnung*, hereafter 'GewO') they need authorization for their activities from their local IHK (for more details *see* paragraph 760).

E. *Associations of Insurance Intermediaries*

19. The (self-employed) insurance agents, insurance brokers and insurance advisers have their own professional bodies such as the *Bundesverband Deutscher Versicherungskaufleute e.V.* (hereafter 'BVK'),[18] the *Bundesverband Deutscher Versicherungsmakler e.V.* (abbreviated 'BDVM'),[19] and the *Bundesverband der Versicherungsberater e.V.* (hereafter 'BVVB').[20]

F. *Associations of the Policyholders*

20. Stakeholders of the policyholders are the Association representing the insured businesses and in-house brokers (*Gesamtverband der versicherungsnehmenden Wirtschaft e.V.*, hereafter 'GVNW'), based in Bonn,[21] and the German Association of the Insured (*Bund der Versicherten e.V.*, hereafter 'BdV')[22] representing the rights of insured individuals.

G. *Insurance Science Associations*

21. There are a number of Insurance Science Associations in Germany. The oldest institutions are the German Insurance Science Association (*Deutscher Verein fuer Versicherungswissenschaft e.V.*, hereafter 'DfVW')[23] established in 1899, and the Hamburg Insurance Science Association (*Versicherungswissenschaftlicher*

17. For further information, *see* https://www.dihk.de/en (accessed 28 Mar. 2018).
18. For further information, *see* https://www.bvk.de (accessed 28 Mar. 2018).
19. For further information, *see* https://vdvm.de/en (accessed 28 Mar. 2018).
20. For further information, *see* http://www.bvvb.de/Content.aspx?content=12 (accessed 28 Mar. 2018).
21. For further information, *see* www.gvnw.de (accessed 28 Mar. 2018).
22. For further information, *see* https://www.bundderversicherten.de/english (accessed 28 Mar. 2018).
23. For further informaton, *see* www.dvfvw.de (accessed 28 Mar. 2018).

Verein in Hamburg e.V.)[24] established in 1916. The DfVW has around 1,200 corporate and personal members and offers numerous academic conferences. The DfVW publishes the journal 'Zeitschrift fuer die gesamte Versicherungswissenschaft' which covers insurance science related fields, not only law but also business management, actuarial mathematics und medicine. The Hamburg Insurance Science Association has more than 500 corporate and personal members and is linked to the Institute of Insurance Science (*Seminar fuer Versicherungswissenschaft*) at the University of Hamburg, which was also established in 1916 and is the German oldest existing insurance law institute.[25]

§2. Historical Background of Insurance and Insurance Legislation[26]

I. Pre-codification Period

22. The oldest preserved insurance contract was concluded in Hamburg in 1588. It was a marine insurance contract based on Dutch law in form of the Antwerp policy brought to Hamburg by merchants who fled the Dutch-Spanish war. Again in Hamburg, in 1591, approximately 100 so-called brewery heirs signed the first 'Hamburg Fire Contract'. Already in the beginning of the fifteenth century fire guilds, as sort of mutual fire insurance associations had evolved in Schleswig-Holstein.[27] Early in the seventeenth century, fire insurance institutions comparable to those in Schleswig Holstein and Hamburg were also established in Eastern Prussia.

23. Various German states identified the availability of fire insurance as an important public good and set up numerous public fire insurance companies in the late seventeenth and during the eighteenth century. They were founded as non-profit organizations with the purpose to serve a certain region or administrative district and were equipped with monopoly authorization to offer fire insurance coverage for buildings in their district.[28] Furthermore, in regions served by a public insurance company, it was usually compulsory for owners of buildings to purchase fire insurance coverage from these companies. The first insurance undertaking of

24. For further information, *see* www.versicherungswissenschaftlicherverein.de (accessed 28 Mar. 201 8).
25. For further information, *see* www.jura.uni-hamburg.de/einrichtungen/institute-seminare/seminar-versicherungswissenschaft/ueber-uns.html.
26. For a detailed overview of the development of insurance law in Germany, *see* Beckmann, in: Bruck/Moeller Großkommentar zum Versichungsvertragsgesetz, 9 ed., vol. 1, DeGruyter 2008, Einf. A n. 27 et seq.
27. For further details, *see* Evenden, Deutsche Feuerversicherungs Schilder/German Fire Insurance Signs, Verlag Versicherungswirtschaft 1989.
28. Wende/Berry-Stoelzle/Lai, The Effect of Regulation on Comparative Advantages of Different Organizational Forms: Evidence from the German Property-Liability Insurance Industry, p. 4, https://mafiadoc.com/the-effect-of-regulation-on-comparative-advantages-of-different-_59f5bb681723dd4e505a2b95.html (accessed 28 Mar. 2018).

that kind was the Hamburg Fire Office (*Hamburger Feuerkasse*) founded in 1676. The Hamburger Feuerkasse, which still exists, is the oldest insurance company in the world.

II. Codification Efforts

24. In 1731, the City of Hamburg adopted the 'Hamburgische Assecuranz- und Havereiordnung' as legal basis for marine insurance contracts. In the following decades, types of insurance other than marine and fire evolved (transport, life, hail, pension, accident, gals). In 1794, the General Land Law for the Prussian States (*Allgemeines Landrecht fuer die Preussischen Staaten*, hereafter 'ALR') codified the insurance law for indemnity insurance contracts closely following the Hamburgische Assecuranz- und Havereiordnung of 1731, thereby extending the principles of marine insurance to all fields of indemnity insurance.

25. In the course of the codification of the commercial law in the nineteenth Century it became apparent for the Prussian states that the different fields of insurance are too diverse to be able to apply marine insurance principles as a uniform standard. As a consequence there was only a chapter on marine insurance (Articles 782–905) while the non-marine insurance was classified as a commercial transaction (Article 271 paragraph 3) in the General Commercial Law of 1869 (*Allgemeines Deutsches Handelsgesetzbuch*, hereafter 'ADHGB') that was later replaced by the commercial code (*Handelsgesetzbuch*. hereafter 'HGB') (§§ 778–900 and 905 HGB). The HGB came into force together with the civil code (*Buergerliches Gesetzbuch*, hereafter 'BGB') on 1 January 1900. By that time, the preparatory work for the introduction of a code on non-marine insurance had already begun which led to the adoption of the insurance contract act (*Versicherungsvertragsgesetz*, hereafter 'VVG') in 1908.[29]

III. End of Codification

26. The VVG was modified a number of times. The most important legislative changes were made in 1939 (introduction of rules on compulsory liability insurance), 1990 (introduction of rules on legal expense insurance) and 1994 (introduction of rules on health insurance). A major revision of the VVG took effect in 2008.

27. The main objective of the 2008 reform was to adapt the insurance contract law to the factual and legal developments in the field of insurance law. In the absence of any pre-existing statutory provisions dealing with general insurance contract law, the general terms and conditions of insurance in use at the end of the nineteenth century and the provisions on marine insurance, which were part of the

29. For further details, *see* Ralph Neugebauer, Versicherungsrecht vor dem Versicherungsvertragsgesett, 1st ed., Klostermann 1990.

German commercial code, served as a model for the VVG 1908.[30] Policyholder protection was only realized by making provisions serving that aim cogent to the extent that derogation to the detriment of policyholders was not permitted (semi-mandatory rules). Not surprisingly, the VVG 1908 contained a number of provisions favouring the interest of the insurer over that of the policyholder. For example, while the policyholder had to disclose all material facts and circumstances in order to enable the insurer to make objective risk assessment there was no equivalent obligation for the insurer. The insurer was not required to give advice that takes into account the demands and needs of the policyholder.

28. Under the § 16 paragraph 1 sentence 1 VVG 1908, the policyholder had to disclose all relevant information about the insured risk irrespective of whether the insurer had made enquiries in that regard. There was no obligation on insurers to advice policyholders of the extent of their duty of disclosure. The risk arising from any failure to recognise which facts and circumstances not queried by the insurer were of relevance to him therefore laid with the policyholder. Whenever the contract was terminated by insurer due to e.g., an increase of a risk, the insurer was nevertheless entitled to the premium to the end of the insurance period (*Grundsatz der Unteilbarkeit der Praemie*).

29. It is important to note, that the reform was aimed at the protection of the policyholder as such (or such third persons for whose benefit the insurance is taken out) no matter whether it is a natural or legal person or, if it is a natural person, whether he/she is concluding the insurance contract for private or business purposes. The reformed VVG, as was the case under the VVG 1908, only makes a difference with regard to policies covering large risks[31] in that § 210 VVG exempts them from the restraints of the (semi-)mandatory VVG provisions on contractual freedom.

30. During the course of the reform of the VVG, the chapter on marine insurance in the HGB, in a move that was welcomed by the market, was abolished. In the legislator's not-well-thought through view there was no need to maintain or modernize the marine insurance rules because in practice the marine insurance business would be dominated by market practice and standards.[32] As consequence, whenever the contract of marine insurance is subject to German law, the HGB and the BGB apply which have no special rules designed for insurance contracts.

30. *See* R. Koch, German Reform of Insurance Contract Law, European Journal of Commercial Contract Law 2010–3, pp. 163–171; Roemer, Die Reform des Versicherungsvertragsrechts, in Humboldt Forum Recht 2009, pp. 176, 177, http://www.humboldt-forum-recht.de/deutsch/13-2009/beitrag.html (accessed 28 Mar. 2018).
31. The definition of large risks is determined by Art. 5 lit. d) of Directive 73/239/EEC (O.J., 16 August 1973, L 228/3) as amended by Directive 88/357/EEC (O.J., 4 July 1988, L 172/1). There are three type of large risks defined under § 210 para. 2 VVG, namely: (1) broadly, risks of the transport and liability insurance; (2) risks of the credit and suretyship insurance; or (3) risks of the property, liability and other indemnity insurance, where the policy holders exceed at least two of the following characteristics: (a) EUR 6,200,000 balance sheet total; (b) EUR 12,800,000 net turnover; (c) an average of 250 employees per fiscal year.
32. BT-Drucks. 16/3945, p. 120.

§3. SOURCES OF INSURANCE LAW[33]

I. International Law

31. Germany has ratified a number of international treaties which provide for the introduction of compulsory liability insurance only (e.g., European Convention on Compulsory Insurance against Civil Liability in respect of Motor Vehicles of 1959;[34] Montreal Convention for the Unification of Certain Rules for International Carriage by Air of 1999[35]) or as alternative to other forms of financial security such as bank guarantees or special funds with public participation (e.g., Convention on Civil Liability for Bunker Oil Pollution Damage of 2001,[36] Convention on Liability and Compensation for Damage in Connection with the Carriage of Hazardous and Noxious Substances by Sea of 1996 (HNS Convention),[37] Protocol of 2002 to the Athens Convention relating to the Carriage of Passengers and their Luggage by Sea of 1974,[38] Nairobi International Convention on the Removal of Wrecks of 2007[39]).

II. EU Law

A. Primary Law

32. At the European primary law level, the rules on freedom of establishment (Articles 49–55 TFEU) and freedom to provide services (Articles 56–62 TFEU) apply to the insurance businesses. The prohibition of discriminatory practices because of nationality (Article 18 TFEU) is also of relevance to the insurance industry.

33. For a detailed overview of the sources of insurance law, *see* Beckmann, in: Bruck/Moeller, Großkommentar zum Versichungsvertragsgesetz, 9 ed., vol. 1, DeGruyter 2008, Einf. A n. 112 et seq.
34. 'Europaeisches Uebereinkommen ueber die obligatorische Haftpflichtversicherung fuer Kraftfahrzeuge' as of 20 Apr. 1959, BGBl. II 1965 p. 282.
35. 'Gesetz zu dem Uebereinkommen zur Vereinheitlichung bestimmter Vorschriften ueber die Befoerderung im internationalen Luftverkehr (Montrealer Uebereinkommen)' as of 28 May 1999, BGBl. 2004 II p. 458.
36. 'Gesetz zu dem Internationalen Uebereinkommen von 2001 ueber die zivilrechtliche Haftung fuer Bunkeroelverschmutzungsschaeden (Bunkeroel-Uebereinkommen)' as of 8 Jul. 2006, BGBl. II 2006 p. 578.
37. 'Internationales Uebereinkommen ueber Haftung und Entschaedigung fuer Schaeden bei der Befoerderung gefaehrlicher und schaedlicher Stoffe auf See (HNS-Uebereinkommen)' as of 3 May 1996, O.J., 13 December 2002, L 337/57.
38. 'Bekanntmachung ueber das Inkrafttreten des Protokolls von 1996 zur AEnderung des Uebereinkommens von 1976 ueber die Beschraenkung der Haftung fuer Seeforderungen' as of 23 Nov. 2004, BGBl. II 2004, p. 1793.
39. 'Gesetz zu dem Internationalen Uebereinkommen von Nairobi von 2007 ueber die Beseitigung von Wracks' as of 29 May 2013, BGBl. II 2013, p. 530.

B. Secondary Law

1. Regulations

a. Compulsory Liability Insurance

33. At the European secondary law level, the Regulation 785/2004/EC of 21 April 2004 on insurance requirements for air carriers and aircraft operators introduces compulsory insurance covering their aviation-specific liability in respect of passengers, baggage, cargo and third parties.[40] The Regulation 1371/2007/EC of 23 October 2007 on rail passengers' rights and obligations[41] requires a railway undertaking to be adequately insured or to make equivalent arrangements for cover of its liabilities with regard to passengers and their luggage, and the Regulation 1013/2006/EC of 14 June 2006 on the transboundary shipments of waste,[42] too, provides for compulsory liability insurance.

b. Private International Law

34. The Regulation 593/2008/EC of 17 June 2008 on the law applicable to contractual obligations (Rome I)[43] determines the applicable law to all insurance contracts covering a large risk (*see* paragraph 29) whether or not the risk covered is situated in a Member State, and to all other insurance contracts covering risks situated inside the territory of the Member States. It does not apply to reinsurance contracts (Article 7 Rome I).

c. Jurisdiction

35. The Regulation 1215/2012/EU of 12 December 2012 on jurisdiction and the recognition and enforcement of judgments in civil and commercial matters (Brussels I Recast)[44] determines the jurisdiction in matters relating to insurance (Articles 10–16) whenever a claim is brought against a defendant domiciled within the EU. The Lugano Convention governs jurisdiction and the recognition and enforcement of judgments as between the EU and Switzerland, Norway and Iceland (Lugano States) and essentially applies the provisions of the Brussels I Regulation which has been replaced by Brussels I Recast. The Lugano Convention applies to determine the jurisdiction in matters relating to insurance (Articles 8–14) whenever a defendant is domiciled in a Lugano State.[45]

40. O.J., 30 April 2004, L 138/1.
41. O.J., 3 December 2007, L 315/14.
42. O.J., 12 July 2006, L 190/1.
43. O.J., 4 July 2008, L 177/6.
44. O.J., 20 December 2012, L 351/1.
45. O.J., 20 December 2012, L 351/1.

2. Directives

a. First, Second and Third Life and Non-Life Insurance Directives

36. The first, second and third life and non-life insurance directives on insurance as well as the consolidated life directive have been transposed into German law. The same is true with regard to the five directives on compulsory insurance cover for motor vehicles (Directives 72/166/EEC, 84/5/EEC, 90/232/EEC, 2000/26/EC and 2005/14/EC) that have been consolidated into a single instrument by the Directive 2009/103/EC of 16 September 2009.[46] Article 10 paragraph 4 of the Insurance Distribution Directive 2016/97/EU of 20 January 2016 ('IDD')[47] requires all insurance intermediaries to obtain professional indemnification insurance as a pre-condition to be able to provide services. According to the Directive 2004/114/EC on the conditions of admission of third-country nationals for the purposes of studies, pupil exchange, unremunerated training or voluntary service, a third-country national who applies to be admitted for the purpose of study must have health insurance in respect of all risks normally covered for its own nationals in the Member State concerned.

b. Intermediaries Directives

37. The IDD, which replaced the Directive 2002/92/EC on insurance mediation ('IMD'),[48] has been ratified on 29 June 2017 and will enter into force on 23 February 2018.[49] While the IMD was aimed to regulate selling practices by brokers and other intermediaries selling insurance products the IDD regulates the entire distribution chain. It thus applies to all distributors of insurance contracts, not just brokers and tied insurance intermediaries but direct distribution by insurers as well. The transposition of the IDD has required changes to the Insurance Supervision Act (*Versicherungsaufsichtsgesetz*, hereafter 'VAG'), the VVG and the Trade, Commerce and Industry Regulation Act (*Gewerbeordnung*, hereafter 'GewO').

c. Unfair Contract Terms Directive

38. Indirectly, the unfair contract terms Directive 93/13/EEC of 5 April 1993[50] has an effect on insurance contracts with consumers since it requires contract terms to be drafted in plain, intelligible language and not to cause a significant imbalance in the parties' rights and obligations to the detriment of the private costumers. The directive is particularly of importance as regards to exclusions from coverage.

---

46. O.J., 7 October 2009, L 263/11.
47. O.J., 2 February 2016, L 26/19.
48. O.J., 15 January 2003, L 9/3.
49. BT-Drucks. 18/13009, pp. 1 et seq.
50. O.J., 21 April 1993, L 95/29.

III. German Law

A. *Insurance Contract Law*

1. Legislation

a. Insurance Contract Act

39. The VVG is the most important piece of legislation governing the relationship between the parties to a contract of insurance. As indicated, the VVG does not apply to marine insurance or reinsurance contracts (*see* § 209 VVG).

40. The VVG is divided into three parts. There is a 'General Part' that contains a Chapter 1 on all kinds of insurance (§§ 1–73). Chapter 2 provides for general rules for all indemnity insurance contracts (*Schadensversicherung*), comprising property and liability insurance as well as those forms of personal insurance where cover is granted in accordance with the principles of indemnity insurance) (§§ 74–87), and rules dealing with property insurance (§§ 88–99). Part 2 contains chapters on specific kinds of insurance: liability, legal expenses, transportation, fire, life, occupational disability insurance, accident, and health insurance. Part 3 includes final provisions (§§ 209–216) relating *inter alia* to the scope of application of the VVG, to large risks, to conciliation and the place of jurisdiction in respect of claims against the insurer, policyholder and intermediaries such as agents or brokers arising out of the insurance contract or the intermediation.

b. German Social Code

41. The rules on private long-term care insurance are not included in the VVG but can be found in the German Social Code (*Sozialgesetzbuch*, hereafter 'SGB'). The SGB, in principle, deals with statutory insurances (health, retirement, accident, long-term care) only. The rules on private long-term care insurance, however, are included in Book XI ('SGB XI') (*see* paragraph 682).

c. Act on Compulsory Liability Insurance for Motor Vehicle Keepers

42. The statutes concerning obligatory liability insurance for keepers of motor vehicles and motor vehicle trailers are not contained in the VVG but in the act on obligatory insurance for motor vehicle keepers (*Gesetz ueber die Pflichtversicherung fuer Kraftfahrzeughalter*, hereafter 'PflVG'). It was first enacted in 1939 and revised and re-enacted in 1965 to comply with the European Convention on Compulsory Insurance against Civil Liability in respect of Motor Vehicles of 1959.[51] The PflVG applies to all motor vehicles (trailers) registered in Germany (*see* paragraph 574). The administrative enforcement of the insurance requirement by the licensing authorities is not regulated by the PfIVG but by the German vehicle-admission-ordinance (*Fahrzeug-Zulassungsverordnung*, hereafter 'FZV'),

---

51. 'Gesetz zu dem Uebereinkommen vom 20. April 1959 ueber die obligatorische Haftpflichtversicherung fuer Kraftfahrzeuge', BGBl. II 1965, p. 281.

which transposes the Directive 1999/37/EC of 29 April 1999 on the registration documents for vehicles into German law.[52]

d. Act on Compulsory Liability Insurance for Foreign Motor Vehicle Keepers

43. The statutes concerning obligatory liability insurance for keepers of motor vehicles and motor vehicle trailers registered outside of Germany are contained in the act on compulsory liability insurance for foreign motor vehicle keepers (*Gesetz ueber die Haftpflichtversicherung fuer auslaendische Kraftfahrzeuge und Kraftfahrzeuganhaenger*, hereafter 'AuslPflVG').

2. Governmental Regulations

44. In accordance with § 7 paragraph 2 VVG the German Federal Ministry of Justice and Consumer Protection has determined the information the insurers are required to provide to the insured in the ordinance on the obligation to supply information pertaining to insurance contracts (*Verordnung ueber Informationspflichten bei Versicherungsvertraegen*, hereafter 'VVG-InfoV') (*see* paragraph 300), which transposes the Directives 97/48/EEC,[53] 73/239/EEC,[54] 2002/65/EC,[55] 90/619/EEC,[56] 97/7/EC[57] and 2002/93/EC[58] into German law.

45. In accordance with § 4 paragraph 1 and 2 PflVG the German Federal Ministry of Justice and Consumer Protection has determined the scope of coverage of the contract on compulsory liability insurance for motor vehicle keepers and the minimum amount of the insured sum for bodily injuries, property damage and pecuniary loss in two ordinances (*Kraftfahrzeug-Pflichtversicherungsverordnung*, hereafter 'KfzPflVV', and *Mindestversicherungssummenverordnung*) (for details *see* paragraph 586).

B. Private Law

1. Commercial Code

a. Re-/Insurance Contracts

46. Although the HGB is applicable to insurance contracts since insurers always qualify as merchants in terms of § 6 HGB, it is virtually of no importance for the relationship between the parties to a primary insurance contract since it does not

52. O.J., 1 June 1999, L 138/57.
53. O.J., 12 August 1997, L 222/10.
54. O.J., 16 August 1973, L 228/3.
55. O.J., 9 October 2002, L 271/16.
56. O.J., 29 November 1990, L 330/50.
57. O.J., 4 June 1997, L 144/19.
58. O.J., 7 December 2002, L 331/27.

contain specific rules dealing with the rights and obligations of the insurer or the policyholder. In the reinsurance business there are general principles (*see* paragraph 175) that apply to reinsurance contracts as commercial usage in the sense of § 346 HGB.

b. Self-employed Insurance Agents

47. The HGB is of relevance, however, for the relationship between the insurer and self-employed agents. § 92 HGB provides that the agency contract between the insurance agent and the insurer is subject to the provisions applicable to the agency contract between the commercial agent and the principal (§§ 84 to 92c HGB). In practice, the most important is § 89b paragraph 5 HGB, which gives the insurance agent the right to compensation from the insurer upon termination of the agency contract. The compensation shall amount to not more than three years' worth of commissions or annual remunerations. Compensation is excluded, however, if the insurance agent has terminated the contract himself, or if the insurer has terminated the contract and the agent has given sufficient cause by misconduct to terminate the contract prematurely (§ 89b paragraph 3 no. 1 and 2 HGB).[59]

48. It is to be noticed that the right of the insurance agent to compensation against the insurer remains unaffected when the insurance company transfers the agency relationship by means of a spin-off to another company (§ 131 paragraph 1 no. 1 in connection with § 123 paragraph 3 no. 1 German Transformation Act (*Umwandlungsgesetz*, hereafter 'UmwG')) and the agency relationship is only terminated after the spin-off has become effective.[60]

49. The agent's right to compensation cannot be excluded in advance (*see* § 89b paragraph 4 HGB), nor can it be circumvented by agreement on the law of a non-EU Member State where there is no such right to compensation and a non-EU place of jurisdiction or arbitration. Whenever such agreement on the applicable law and on the choice of forum/arbitration may cause a detriment to the insurance agent, a German court will declare it null and void.[61]

c. Insurance Brokers

50. There are a few provision concerning commercial brokers which include insurance brokers (*see* §§ 93–104 HGB). In fact, however, these rules have no importance because they have been replaced by local custom. Most notably, contrary to § 99 HGB not the insured but the insurer who pays the commission to the broker.

---

59. For details in English, *see* Wendler/Tremler/Buecker, Key Aspects of German Business Law, 4th ed., Springer 2008, pp. 170 et seq.
60. BGH, 13 Aug. 2015 – VII ZR 90/14, NJW 2015, pp. 3373, 3374.
61. OLG Muenchen, 17 May 2006 – 7 U 1781/06, WM 2006, p. 1556.

d. Accounting Rules

51. Finally, §§ 341–341p HGB contain provisions dealing with insurance companies' accounting.

2. Civil Code

a. First Party Non-marine Insurance Contracts

52. The VVG contains numerous references to the BGB,[62] and some provisions of the BGB deal specifically with insurance contract law.[63] In the absence of such references, as a general rule, it follows from the general principles of law that specific rules take precedence of general rules that in insurance matters the provisions of the BGB apply only to the extent the VVG does not provide otherwise (*see* Article 2 Introductory Act to the German Commercial Code (*Einfuehrungsgesetz zum Handelsgesetzbuch*, hereafter 'EGHGB').[64] As a consequence the provisions in the BGB, *inter alia*, on capacity, conclusion of a contract and most notably on incorporation, interpretation and control of standard business terms apply to insurance contracts. It needs to be emphasized that, whenever the VVG does not specifically address the issue at hand, resort to the BGB is only permissible if no solution can be found within the VVG itself by (literal, historical, contextual or teleological) means of interpretations, including the use of the methods of analogy to fill gaps in the VVG.

b. Marine Insurance and Reinsurance Contracts

53. Since § 209 VVG expressly states that the VVG does not apply to marine insurance contracts[65] and reinsurance contracts,[66] such contracts are subject of the BGB.

3. Customary Law (*Gewohnheitsrecht*)

54. There are basically two concepts in German insurance law which could be characterised as customary law (some scholars, however, characterize the concepts as 'judge-made law' (*Richterrecht*, *see* paragraph 69)).

---

62. Cf. § 4 para. 1, § 6 para. 6, § 8 para. 3 nos 2, 4, para. 4, § 34 para. 1, § 49 para. 1, § 117 para. 4, § 211 para. 2, § 214 para. 1 no. 1 VVG.
63. *See* §§ 1045, 1046, 1127–1130 BGB.
64. Cf. Beckmann, in: Bruck/Moeller Großkommentar zum Versichungsvertragsgesetz, 9 ed., vol. 1, DeGruyter 2008, Einf. A n. 152.
65. Cf. R. Koch, in: Bruck/Moeller Großkommentar zum Versichungsvertragsgesetz, 9 ed., vol. 11, DeDruyter 2013, § 209 n. 206 et seq.
66. Cf. Echarti/Labes, in: Bruck/Moeller Großkommentar zum Versichungsvertragsgesetz, 9ed., vol. 11, DeGruyter 2013, § 209 n. 35 et seq.

a. Customary Liability for the Performance (*Gewohnheitsrechtliche Erfuellungshaftung*)

55. Prior to the reform of the VVG the jurisprudence had developed the doctrine of the so-called Gewohnheitsrechtliche Erfuellungshaftung, which literally translated means 'customary liability for the performance'. This doctrine applies to a promise made by the insurer's agent prior to the conclusion of the insurance contract which turned out to be wrong after the conclusion of the contract. In this case the policyholder may require the insurer to fulfil the promise unless the policyholder could not have been unaware of the agent's misrepresentation. This doctrine had already been developed by the German Imperial Court (*Reichsgericht*, hereafter 'RG'), the predecessor of the BGH, in order to satisfy the needs of an insured where a claim for damages was not adequate to protect the expectation interest of the policyholder.[67]

56. The judgment of the OLG Frankfurt/M. dated 19 May 2011[68] is a good illustration of the scope of the *Gewohnheitsrechtliche Erfuellungshaftung* doctrine and the consequences following from its application. The case was about life endowment insurance and a loan repayable at maturity. According to the policyholder the insurance agent had orally guaranteed that the pay out on maturity of the life endowment insurance would be sufficient to pay off the loan. On maturity the pay out, however, fell short and the policyholder sued the insurer for balance the short fall. Under a claim for damages, the policyholder could have only sought compensation in the amount of the premiums paid since he would not have been able to prove that no such shortfall would have occurred had he concluded the insurance contract with another insurer. Under the *Gewohnheitsrechtliche Erfuellungshaftung* doctrine, however, the policyholder is entitled to the promised sum because the promise by the insurer's agent is treated as if the insurer has made the promise by itself. Accordingly, the OLG Frankfurt/M. found for the policyholder after taking evidence from witnesses who confirmed that the agent had declared that the pay out on maturity of the endowment insurance would be sufficient to pay off the loan.

57. There is much debate among scholars of whether this doctrine is still applicable after the reform of the VVG.[69] The OLG Frankfurt/M. in its afore-illustrated decision and subsequently the LG Saarbruecken[70] answered this question in the affirmative, and it remains to be seen how the BGH will decide this issue once an appeal on it reaches the BGH.

67. Cf. BGH, 9 May 1951 – II ZR 8/51, BGHZ 2, pp. 87, 92 with further references to judgments of the RG.
68. OLG Frankfurt/M., 19 May 2011 – 7 U 67/08, VersR 2012, pp. 342, 343.
69. For the discussion, *see* R. Koch, in: Festschrift fuer Egon Lorenz, Verlag Versicherungswirtschaft 2014, 199, 212 ff.; Reiff, in: Langheid/Wandt (eds), Muenchener Kommentar zum VVG, 2nd ed., vol. 1, C.H. Beck 2016, § 69 n. 78; Rixecker, in: Rixecker/Langheid (eds), VVG, 5th ed., C.H. Beck 2016, § 6 n. 3; Schwintowski, in: Bruck/Moeller Großkommentar zum Versichungsvertragsgesetz, 9ed., vol. 2, DeGruyter 2010, § 63 n. 6 ff.; Ebers, in: Schwintowski/Broemmelmeyer (eds). Praxiskommentar zum Versicherungsvertragsrecht, 3rd ed., ZAP Verlag 2017, § 6 n. 56 ff.
70. LG Saarbruecken, 5 Aug. 2013 – 14 O 152/12, VersR 2014, pp. 317, 319; for a different conclusion LG Stuttgart, 22 Oct. 2015 – 22 O 113/15, VersR 2016, p. 1235.

b. Imputation of Knowlegde and Conduct to the Policyholder (*Repraesentantenhaftung*)

58. There is another concept of customary insurance law, known as *Repraesentantenhaftung*.[71] It is disputed among scholars whether this concept qualifies as customary law or as 'judge-made law' (*see* paragraph 69).[72] According to this concept, the policyholder is vis-a-vis the insurer accountable for the non-compliance with the terms of the insurance policy or for triggering an exclusion of any person entrusted by the policyholder with the management of the insured risk.[73] For example, if such person, which is called *Repraesentant*, gross negligently failed to comply with the duty to minimise the loss upon occurrence of the insured event, the insurer is entitled to reduce the claim in proportion to the severity of gross negligence (principle of proportionality) (*see* paragraphs 267, 274). Where the *Repraesentant* intentionally caused the insured event (indemnity insurance, *see* § 81 paragraph 1 VVG[74]) or intentionally inflicted damage (liability insurance, *see* § 103 VVG[75]), the insurer is not obliged to make any payment or release the policyholder from the damage claim.

59. The mere possession or custody of property is not sufficient to qualify the possessor/custodian as policyholder's *Repraesentant*.[76] In comprehensive motor vehicle insurance, for instance, driving the insured car alone does not make the driver a 'Repraesentant' of the policyholder/keeper of the car. Only persons who have the authority to act autonomously to a not insubstantial extent, i.e., to somehow step into the shoes of the policyholder are his/her *Repraesentanten* (*Risikoverwaltung*). For example, an employee who uses a company car for his/her daily business is not a 'Repraesentant' of the company/policyholder even if he/she is allowed to take the car home and/or use the car for private purposes. However, if the employee is entitled to a long-term use of the car and is also in charge for its maintenance, he/she becomes a *Repraesentant* of the company/policyholder. Persons who are entrusted by the company/policyholder to manage the insurance contract and all issues related to coverage (*Vertragsverwaltung*) are also considered as *Repraesentant*.[77]

60. It should be noted that the concept of *Repraesentantenhaftung* does not apply to motor vehicle liability insurance because motor vehicle liability insurance shall protect by all means the policyholder against liability risks arising out of the

71. OLG Oldenburg, 18 Jul. 1951 2 U 140/51, VersR 1951, pp. 272, 273.
72. For an overview of the discussion cf. Armbruester, in: Proelss/Martin, VVG, 30 ed., C.H. Beck 2018, § 28 n. 98.
73. BGH, 14 May 2003 – IV ZR 166/02, NJW-RR 2003, p. 1250; BGH, 10 Jul. 1996 – IV ZR 287/95, VersR 1996, p. 1229; BGH, 21 Apr. 1993 – IV ZR 34/92, BGHZ 122, pp. 250, 253.
74. Cf. BGH, 4 May 1994 – IV ZR 298/93, NJW-RR 1994, p. 988; BGH, 8 Feb. 1965 – II ZR 171/62, VersR 1965, pp. 425, 429.
75. R. Koch, in: Bruck/Moeller Großkommentar zum Versichungsvertragsgesetz, 9th ed., vol. 4, DeGruyter 2013, § 103 VVG n. 50 et seq.
76. BGH, 14 May 2003 – IV ZR 166/02, NJW-RR 2003, 1250; BGH, 2 May 1990 – IV ZR 48/89, VersR 1990, p. 736.
77. BGH, 21 Apr. 1993 – IV ZR 34/92, BGHZ 122, pp. 250, 253.

use of his/her car by a third party.[78] Thus, even if the driver qualifies as *Repraesentant* the liability insurer is not exempt from liability towards the injured party in the case the driver inflicted the damage by intention, and the insurer is not released from its obligation to release the policyholder of the car, who is liable in his/her capacity as keeper of the car (§ 7 road traffic act (*Strassenverkehrsgesetz*, hereafter 'StVG'), from the damage claim.

C. *Private International Law*

61. The private international law is subject to the Rome I Regulation (*see* paragraph 34).

D. *Jurisdiction*

1. Civil Courts

62. The jurisdiction of German civil courts is subject to the Brussels I Recast (*see* paragraph 35) or the Lugano Convention (*see* paragraph 35) whenever a suit has been brought against a natural person or a legal person domiciled in another EU Member State or in a Lugano Convention signatory state. Where the Brussels I Recast or the Lugano Convention is not applicable, the place of jurisdiction is subject to the ZPO and § 215 VVG. According to §§ 12, 13 ZPO, as a general principle, the court where the defendant has his/her/its place of residence has jurisdiction. In respect of actions against the insurer or an intermediate, § 215 paragraph 1 sentence 1 VVG provides for an exception to this general principle of *actor sequitur forum rei* and allows not only policyholders but also third party beneficiaries, such as co-insureds (*see* paragraph 308) or beneficiaries in life insurance (*see* paragraph 724) to also sue the insurer or an intermediate before the courts of the place of his/her/its domicile. In its judgment dated 8 November 2017, the BGH held that the scope of § 215 paragraph 1 sentence 1 VVG is not limited to natural persons but also includes legal persons.[79] Therefore also legal entities may sue the insurer before the court where their places of business is situated.

63. By contrast, in respect of actions brought against the policyholder by the insurer, § 215 paragraph 1 sentence 1 VVG states that only the court of the policyholder's domicile has exclusive jurisdiction.

64. Pursuant to § 215 paragraph 3 VVG the parties may only derogate from § 215 paragraph 1 VVG where the policyholder moves his/her domicile or habitual place of residence outside of Germany after signing the contract or where his/her domicile or habitual place of residence is unknown at such time as the action is filed. In addition choice of forum clauses must comply with the requirements set forth in

78. BGH, 20 May 1969 – IV ZR 616/68, NJW 1969, pp. 1387, 1388.
79. BGH, 8 Nov. 2017 – IV ZR 551/15, NJW 2018, pp. 232, 233 et seq.

§ 38 paragraph 3 ZPO (written form) and § 40 paragraph 1 ZPO (reference to a certain legal relationship, e.g., contract, and to the legal disputes arising therefrom).[80]

2. Social Courts

65. The jurisdiction of social courts in disputes on private long-term care insurance is subject to the SGG. Competent is the Sozialgericht where the policyholder has its registered seat or place of residence (§ 57 paragraph 1 SGG).

3. Administrative Courts

66. The jurisdiction of administrative courts is subject to the Administrative Procedure Code (*Verwaltungsgerichtsordnung*, hereafter 'VwGO'). For claims against decisions of the BaFin, the VG Frankfurt/M. is competent (*see* § 52 no. 2 VwGO).[81]

E. Supervisory Law

67. The insurance supervision is divided between the Federation and the Laender. All private insurers and public insurance enterprises, which carry on private insurance business within the scope of the VAG and have their registered office in Germany, are subject to supervision either by the BaFin or by the supervisory authorities of the Laender. Since December 2004 Domestic reinsurance undertakings have also been subject to insurance supervision by BaFin under the VAG. At present, 567 insurance undertakings are supervised by BaFin. Just under 900 undertakings, most of them relatively small, regional mutual insurance associations are supervised by the supervisory authorities of the Laender.[82]

68. The VAG is not a source of insurance contract law. It does not contain provisions creating rights and obligations of the parties to a contract of insurance. There are a few provisions, however, which may affect the relationship between the policyholder and the insurer. For example, § 13 paragraph 5 VAG provides that in case of an insurance portfolio transfer from one insurer (transferor) to another one (transferee) the rights and obligations of the transferor under the insurance contracts, also in relation to the policyholders, are transferred to the transferee. For historical reasons the provision on formation and constitution of mutual insurance associations (§§ 171–210 VAG) are part of the VAG although they are of corporate (private) law

80. Looschelders, in: Langheid/Wandt (eds), Kommentar zum VVG, 2nd ed., C.H. Beck 2017, § 215 n. 60.
81. Cf. VG Frankfurt/M., 23 Jul. 2009 – 1 K 3082/08, VersR 2009, pp. 1389 et seq. (prohibition order against the further use of a standard term clause in a health insurance contract).
82. For further information, *see* www.bafin.de/EN/Aufsicht/VersichererPensionsfonds/versicherer pensionsfonds_node_en.html (accessed 28 Mar. 2018).

nature. Indirectly, the VAG may have an effect on insurance contract because § 298 paragraph 1 VAG authorizes the BaFin to take any measures with regard to the undertaking which are appropriate and necessary to avoid or eliminate activities which conflict with objectives of insurance supervision, i.e., the protection of policyholders and beneficiaries. To this end, the BaFin may prohibit insurers from the use of standard business terms which in BaFin's view unreasonably disadvantage policyholders in terms of § 307 BGB (*see* paragraph 185).[83]

IV. Case Law

69. In Germany case law is not regarded as a formal source of law since the function of the courts is seen in applying the law rather than creating it. As pointed out above (*see* paragraph 10) court decisions generally do not have a binding legal effect. Settled case law, in particular decisions of the BGH, however, plays an important role in supplementing the law by expanding or narrowing the scope of its application. In this respect it is generally accepted that the courts do not simply interpret texts but also entitled to develop the law, if necessary, and insofar as the result is not *contra legem*. This process is called *richterliche Rechtsfortbildung*, and the decisions resulting from this process are considered to be 'judge-made law' (*Richterrecht*).

70. Quite frequently, the German legislator deliberately avoids specific regulation but leaves the development of the law to the courts. For example, when reforming the VVG in 2008, the legislator expressly refrained from codifying the concept of *Repraesentantenhaftung* (*see* paragraph 58) because the legislator was of the opinion that this concept would be more suitable to be dealt with by courts.[84] On the other hand, the legislator may codify settled case law, e.g., for general efficiency of operating the law. A good example is § 90 VVG which obliges the insurer to reimburse the policyholder's expenses incurred in order to avoid an imminent insured event or to minimise its impacts. Prior to the reform of the VVG there was no such explicit rule but 'only' settled case law to that effect. The same is true with regard to the principle that facts communicated to the insurance agent are deemed to be communicated to the insurer. This rule, which bases on the notion that the agents are the insurer's 'eyes and ears'[85] has been codified in § 70 VVG.

83. *See* BVerwG, 21 Mar. 2007 – 6 C 26/06, NJW 2007, p. 2871 (upholding the VG Frankfurt/M. judgment of 23 Jul. 2009 – 1 K 3082/08, VersR 2009, 1389 on the BaFin prohibition order against the further use of a standard term clause in an health insurance contract).
84. BT-Drucks. 16/3945, p. 79.
85. *See* BGH, 18 Dec. 1991 – IV ZR 299/90, BGHZ 116, pp. 387, 390; BGH, 23 May 1989 – Iva ZR 72/88, BGHZ 107, pp. 322, 323; BGH, 11 Nov. 1987 – IVa ZR 240/86, BGHZ 102, 194, 197.

V. Scholarly Writings

71. Scholarly writings alone are never (direct) sources of law. The positions taken by academic scholars, however, have a strong influence not only on the legislator but also on German judges. Whenever a question of law arises for the first time, courts will review and rely on existing legal literature. Whenever decisions of a court (of any instance but in particular of the BGH) on a legal point have caused controversies within the legal literature, the court will address the controversies and deal with counterarguments if it will maintain its line of case law. On the other hand, whenever a court wants to deviate from settled case it will give as a reason that the criticism is well founded. For this reason, there is abundant reference to academic writings in court decisions. In this regard scholars contribute to the consolidation of case law. [86]

§4. Dispute Settlement and Arbitration

I. Dispute Settlement

72. Under § 214 VVG, the German Ministry of Justice has the power to authorise private-law institutions to act as conciliation boards for the extra-judicial settlement of disputes involving insurance agreements with consumers, and for claims made by a policyholder against an insurance intermediary (*see* paragraph 758) or insurance adviser (*see* paragraph 759) with regard to the mediation of insurance or consultation activities. At present, there are two institutions recognized, namely the insurance ombudsman association (*Versicherungsombudsmann e.V.*) and the ombudsman for private health and long-term care insurers (*Ombudsmann Private Kranken- und Pflegeversicherung*, hereafter 'PKV-Ombudsman').

A. Insurance Ombudsman Association

73. The insurance ombudsman was founded as registered association in 2001 and has its office in Berlin. Members of the association are almost all primary insurance companies operating in Germany and the GDV. The average number of yearly complaints amounted to around 20,000 over the last three years (2014–2017). The proceedings before the insurance ombudsman association are free of charge for the policyholders, except for own expenses as, e.g., postage or for their representative.[87] The insurance ombudsman association has two jurisdictions that are based on different procedural rules: First, the insurance ombudsman association is responsible for disputes of the policyholders (or co-insureds or beneficiaries) against

86. *See* Reimann/Zekoll, Introduction to German Law, 2nd ed., C.H. Beck 2006, p. 27 (stating that there is a close cooperation between courts and legal writers in developing the law); Foster/Su, German Legal System and Laws, 4th ed., Oxford University Press 2010, p. 137.
87. For further information in English, *see* www.versicherungsombudsmann.de/welcome/ (accessed 28 Mar. 2018).

the(ir) insurers. Second, the insurance ombudsman association deals with claims against insurance agents, brokers, and/or consultants.

1. Claims Against Insurers

74. The proceedings are governed by the rules of procedure of the insurance ombudsman association for the out-of-court settlement of claims against insurers) (*Verfahrensordnung des Versicherungsombudsmanns*, hereafter 'VomVO').[88]

a. Complainants

75. According to § 2 paragraph 1 sentence 1 VomVO the ombudsman procedure is in principle only made available where the complainant is a consumer in terms of § 13 BGB.[89] § 13 BGB defines a consumer 'as natural person who enters into a legal transaction for purposes that predominantly are outside his trade, business or profession'.[90]

76. It is important to note, however, that according to § 2 paragraph 1 sentence 2 VomVO the insurance ombudsman association may hear complaints brought by individuals who find themselves in the same situation as a consumer (*verbraucheraehnliche Lage*). Whether or not such a situation is given depends according to § 2 paragraph 1 sentence 3 VomVO in particular on the nature and the size of the business activity, the insurance contract and the claim made against the insurer. Smaller business policyholders, and in particular sole traders and micro businesses, may petition the insurance ombudsman association since they are likely to face many of the same problems as consumers when they get involved in a coverage dispute with their insurers. The use of the verb 'may' in § 2 paragraph 1 sentence 2 VomVO, however, implies that the insurance ombudsman association has some sort of discretion (not) to hear the complaints by smaller business policyholders.[91]

88. The German text of the VomVO as of 23 Nov. 2016 is available at https://www.versicherungsombudsmann.de/das-schlichtungsverfahren/verfahrensordnungen/vomvo).
89. *See* Gal, The German Insurance Ombudsman System. pp. 22 et seq., https://www.versicherungsombudsmann.de/wp-content/uploads/2016/10/The_German_Insurance_Ombudsman_System.pdf.
90. The German text of the BGB is available at www.gesetze-im-internet.de/englisch_bgb/englisch_bgb.html.
91. *See* Gal, The German Insurance Ombudsman System. pp. 22 et seq., https://www.versicherungsombudsmann.de/wp-content/uploads/2016/10/The_German_Insurance_Ombudsman_System.pdf.

77. Due to the reference to § 13 BGB not only individuals but also a partnership in terms § 705 BGB can file a complaint if its partners are natural persons and the purpose of the partnership for concluding the insurance contract is outside its trade, business or profession.[92]

78. The VomVO does not limit its scope of application to policyholders. Therefore, co-insureds, beneficiaries or legal successors are in principal admitted to file a complaint against the insurer provided that they are entitled vis-a-vis the policyholder and the insurer to exercise the rights under the insurance contract (for limitations with regard to co-insureds *see* paragraph 313).[93] It is important to note that these persons are only eligible to file a claim if the policyholder would be entitled to do so since their rights are derived from the contractual relationship between the policyholder and the insurer. If the policyholder does not qualify as a consumer (or a small business), as is the case with D&O-insurance policyholders, the co-insured directors and officers have no right to file a complaint.

b. Limits on the Insurance Ombudsman's Powers

79. There are some exclusions from the jurisdiction of the insurance ombudsman association contained in § 2 paragraph 4 VomVO. First, any complaint exceeding the amount of EUR 100,000 is inadmissible. Second, disputes concerning health and long-term care insurance contract are excluded since the PKV has established its own ombudsman procedure. Third, the ombudsman will not hear the complaint if the same subject matter has already been decided by or is still pending before another consumer conciliation board or a state court. Fourth, the ombudsman will dismiss the claim if the claim is manifestly without any prospect of success because e.g., the claim against the insurer is time- barred. Moreover, the ombudsman may decline jurisdiction if the factual or legal background is too complex that it unduly overburdens the capacities of the insurance ombudsman association or where the controversy relates to a legal issue of fundamental importance (§ 9 paragraph 1 VomVO).

c. Nature of the Insurance Ombudsman's Decision

80. If the amount in dispute does not exceed EUR 10,000 the decisions of the insurance ombudsman association are binding for the insurers in light of the statutes of the association by which the member submit themselves to the decision of the ombudsman rendered in accordance with the VomVO (*see* § 5 of the by-laws and § 10 paragraph 3 sentence 2, § 11 paragraph 1 VomVO).[94] Where the amount in dispute exceeds EUR 10,000 (up to EUR 100,000), the ombudsman renders a

92. For the application of § 13 BGB to partnerships, *see* BGH, 23 Oct. 2001 – XI ZR 63/91, BGHZ 149, pp. 80, 84 – NJW 2002, p. 368.
93. *See* Gal, The German Insurance Ombudsman System, p. 23, https://www.versicherungsombudsmann.de/wp-content/uploads/2016/10/The_German_Insurance_Ombudsman_System.pdf.
94. For the German text of the by-laws, *see* www.versicherungsombudsmann.de/wp-content/uploads/2017/05/SATZUNG.pdf.

non-binding recommendation. In practice, however, insurers usually also follow the ombudsman's recommendation. It is to be emphasized that the decisions of the ombudsman never bind the complainant who is not bound by the association's by-laws and free to bring the case before the courts if he/she is not satisfied with the ombudsman's decision (§ 11 paragraph 2 VomVO). His/her claims against the insurer do not expire during the proceedings before the insurance ombudsman association (§ 12 paragraph 1 sentence 1 VomVO).

2. Claims Against Insurance Intermediaries

81. Proceedings against insurance intermediaries before the insurance ombudsman association are governed by different set of rules (*Verfahrensordnung fuer Beschwerden im Zusammenhang mit der Vermittlung von Versicherungsvertraegen*, hereafter 'VermVO').[95] The claims must be related to and arise out of the conclusion and the procurement of insurance policies. The complainant is policyholder, and the complaint must be directed against an insurance agent, broker, or adviser. The procedure is available not only where the claimant is a consumer but also where the claimant is a businessperson or a legal person. Since insurance intermediaries are not members of the insurance ombudsman association they do not have to adhere to the decision of the ombudsman. Unlike the VomVO the VermVO does not have a clause according to which the claims against the intermediaries do not expire during the proceedings before the insurance ombudsman association. Claims against intermediaries, however, are time-barred by virtue of § 204 paragraph 1 no. 4 lit. a) BGB, which transposes Article 12 paragraph 1 of the Directive 2013/11/EU into German law.[96]

B. PKV-Ombudsman

82. The PKV-Ombudsman was founded in 2001 by the PKV and has its office in Berlin. The PKV-Ombudsman deals with complaints against health and long-time care insurers only. Unlike the insurance ombudsman association, it is not organized independently from the private health insurers as a registered association but is part of the PKV. The rules of proceedings differ significantly from those concerning the insurance ombudsman association in that the PKV-Ombudsman does not have the power to render decisions binding on the insurers. It only makes recommendations (§ 10 PKV-Statute).[97] Like the proceedings before the insurance ombudsman association the proceedings before the PKV-Ombudsman are free of

95. The German text of the 'Verfahrensordnung fuer Beschwerden im Zusammenhang mit der Vermittlung von Versicherungsvertraegen in terms of § 214 para. 1 no. 2 VVG', as of 23 Nov. 2016, is available at https://www.versicherungsombudsmann.de/wp-content/uploads/2017/05/VermVO.pdf.

96. Directive 2013/11/EU of the European Parliament and of the Council of 21 May 2013 on alternative dispute resolution for consumer disputes and amending Regulation (EC) No 2006/2004 and Directive 2009/22/EC (Directive on consumer ADR), O.J., 18 June 2013, L 165/63; *see also* Looschelders, in: Langheid/Wandt (eds), Kommentar zum VVG, 2nd ed., C.H. Beck 2017, § 214 n. 21.

97. For the German text of the PKV-Statute, *see* https://www.pkv-ombudsmann.de/statut/.

charge for policyholders (§ 6 paragraph 3 PKV-Statute) and their claims against insurers do not expire during the proceedings (§ 7 PKV-Statute).

II. Arbitration

83. Although it would be permitted to provide an arbitration clause, even in an insurance policy with a consumer (*see* § 1031 paragraph 5 ZPO), it is not seen very often in primary insurance (even if large risks are concerned). It is reported that arbitration clauses sometimes appear in D&O and other financial lines of business policies. By contrast, arbitration clauses are commonly used in marine insurance and reinsurance contracts. Arbitration clauses in marine insurance contracts may refer any dispute to an arbitration institution such as the *German Maritime Arbitration Association*[98] or ad hoc tribunals without any specific procedural rules.

84. Most reinsurance arbitration clauses provide for ad hoc arbitration. Such clauses often contain requirements for the arbitrators as regards their experience in the field of (re-)insurance and/or that they must have served on the board of directors of a (re-)insurance company for a certain period of time.[99]

§5. Consumer Protection

I. In General

85. General consumer protection legislation is applicable to insurance contracts whenever the policyholder is a consumer in terms of § 13 BGB (*see* paragraph 75). For example, the provisions on standard business terms (§§ 305 to 310 BGB), on the general obligations and principles applying to consumer contracts (§ 312a BGB), on off-premises contracts and on distance contracts (§§ 312b to 312h BGB) does apply to insurance contracts where the insured is a consumer. Except for the law on standard business terms and off-premises contracts, all afore-mentioned provisions are the result of the transposition of EU-directives. The unfair contract terms act ('AGB-Gesetz', later replaced by §§ 305–310 BGB) had already been enacted in 1976, and the doorstep cancellation act (*Haustuerwiderrufsgesetz*) had been adopted almost simultaneously with Directive 85/577/EEC on the protection of the consumer in respect of contracts negotiated away from business premises.[100]

86. On the procedural side, the act on injunction relieve (*Gesetz ueber Unterlassungsklagen bei Verbraucherrechts- und anderen Verstoeßen*, hereafter

98. For further information on the GMAA, *see* https://gmaa.de/start/index_en.html.
99. For details, *see* Echarti/Labes, in: Bruck/Moeller, Großkommentar zum VVG, 9th ed., vol. 11, DeGruyter 2013, § 209 VVG n. 180; Hubertus Labes, Rueckversicherungs-Schiedsgerichtsbarkeit, VersR 1996, p. 1463.
100. O.J., 31 December 1985, L 372/31.

'UKlaG'), which transposed the Directive 98/27/EC on injunctions for the protection of consumers' interests into German law,[101] is the most effective tool for enforcing consumer rights. This act grants, *inter alia*, authorised consumer protection agencies the right to seek injunctive relief e.g., against the use, or attempted use of unfair terms and conditions in insurance contracts (*see* §§ 1, 3 UklaG). The UKlaG does not provide for compensation of damages. There is yet no general collective redress mechanism in the German legal system.[102]

II. With Regard to Insurance

87. The VVG is focused on policyholder protection no matter whether the policyholder is a consumer or a businessperson or a legal person. In the eyes of the legislator, businesses are no more sophisticated than consumers when buying insurance.[103] This explains why the VVG does not distinguish between consumer and commercial insurance contracts but rather between contracts covering mass risks and contracts covering large risks (*see* paragraph 29), open policies and whether or not a broker acts for the insured. The VVG uses the term consumer only in context with the extra-judicial settlement of disputes in § 214 paragraph 1 no. 1 (*see* paragraph 72).

88. Where the policyholder is represented by a broker, the insurer is not obliged to provide advice to the policyholder prior to the conclusion of the contract and during the contract term (§ 6 paragraph 6 alternative 2 VVG) (for exception *see* paragraph 297). The same is true if the policyholder has mandated an insurance adviser (*see* paragraph 759)[104] In case the insurance contract covers a large risk, the insurer, too, does not owe any advice to the policyholder (§ 6 paragraph 6 alternative 1 VVG). Moreover, in large risk cases the insurer does not have to provide information about the terms of the contract in good time before the conclusion of the contract (§ 7 paragraph 5 VVG), and the insurer is entitled to deviate from the (semi-)mandatory provisions of the VVG aimed to protect the policyholder (§ 210 paragraph 1 VVG). Finally, the policyholder has no right to revoke the contract pursuant to § 8 paragraph 3 no. 4 VVG.[105]

89. It is important to note, however, that even under a large risk policy or an open cover policy any deviation from the VVG by means of standard business terms in the meaning of § 305 paragraph 1 sentence 1 BGB (*see* paragraph 160) is subject to content control on the basis of fairness and reasonableness of a clause (§ 307

101. O.J., 11 June 1998, L 166/51; repealed and replaced by Directive 2009/22/EC of 23 April 2009 on injunctions for the protection of consumers' interests, O.J., 1 May 2009, L 110/30.
102. For recent developments, *see* Herbert Woopen, Kollektiver Rechtsschutz – Ziele und Wege, NJW 2018 pp. 133 et seq.
103. *See* BT-Drucks. 16/3945, pp. 59 et seq.
104. *See* OLG Hamm, 8 May 2017 – 6 U 62/16, VersR 2017, pp. 1385, 1386 (stating that § 6 para. 6 alternative 2 VVG must be applied by means of analogy).
105. For further information on large risks, *see* Reinhard Renger, in: Bruck/Moeller, Großkommentar zum VVG, 9th ed., vol. 11, DeGruyter 2013, § 210 VVG n. 18 et seq.

BGB) (*see* paragraph 185). Where the policyholder is a consumer, any contract term pre-formulated by the insurer (even if it is for single use) is subject to the content control (§ 310 paragraph 3 no. 2 BGB) (*see* paragraph 176).

§6. COMPULSORY INSURANCE

90. The term 'compulsory insurance' is first and foremost associated with liability insurance, most notably with motor vehicle liability insurance. There are, however, other classes of compulsory insurance, namely the private comprehensive health insurance (*see* paragraph 694) and the private long-term care insurance. Everyone in Germany, who is not insured by statutory health insurance and statutory long-term care insurance, is required to take out these insurances with an insurance company. The health insurers and long-term care insurers, in return, are obligated to contract (*see* § 193 paragraph 5 sentence 1 VVG, § 110 paragraph 1 no. 1 SGB XI) (*Kontrahierungszwang*). Health insurers (but not the long-term care insurers[106]), however, may according to § 193 paragraph 5 sentence 4 VVG reject an application if the applicant was already insured by the insurer and the insurer has contested the contract of insurance because of threat or fraudulent misrepresentation, or has rescinded the contract of insurance because of an intentional breach of the obligation to provide information prior to conclusion of contract.

---

106. *See* Erich Koch, in: Kasseler Kommentar Sozialversicherungsrecht, 97. EL Dezember C.H. Beck 2017, SGB XI § 110 n. 6.

Part I. The Insurance Company

Chapter 1. The Insurance Company: Its Form

§1. Mutual Insurance, Premium Insurance, Other

91. German insurers must be legally organised in the form of stock corporations (*Aktiengesellschaft*, hereafter 'AG') including European companies (*Societas Europaea*, hereafter 'SE'), mutual insurance associations (*Versicherungsverein auf Gegenseitigkeit*, hereafter 'VVaG') or public sector insurers (*oeffentlich-rechtliche Versicherungsunternehmen*) (§ 8 paragraph 2 VAG).

§2. Public or Private Nature

92. While stock corporations and mutual insurance associations have a private law status, public sector insurers are organized under the public law applicable in the different Laender (*see* paragraph 17). Public sector insurers were founded as non-profit organizations with the purpose to serve a certain region and were equipped with monopoly authorization i.e. there was an obligation for building owners to take out buildings insurance with these companies. In the course of the deregulation of the German insurance industry in 1994, the monopoly authorization as well as the restriction for public insurers to do regional business was abolished. In response to the legislative changes, the Laender sold the public sector insurers to municipal savings banks (*Sparkassen*). The vast majority of Sparkassen are institutions under municipal trusteeship with public law status.[107]

§3. Factual data

93. The following data are taken from the Annual Report 2016 of BaFin published on 9 May 2017.[108]

107. Further information on the history and development of the public law insurance enterprises are available in Germany at homepage of the association of public sector insurers, https://www.voev.de (accessed 28 Mar. 2018).

108. For further details, *see* BaFin's Annual Report 2016 dated 9 May 2017 (hereafter 'BaFin report'), https://www.bafin.de/SharedDocs/Downloads/EN/Jahresbericht/dl_jb_2016_en.html (accessed 28 Mar. 2018).

I. Life Insurance

94. The direct life insurance business in 2016 remained at the same level as in the previous year with approximately 5.0 million new policies. At the same time, the total value of new policies underwritten rose by 4.7% to around EUR 264.2 billion compared with EUR 252.2 billion in 2015. There were a total of approximately 84.5 million direct life insurance contracts at the close of 2016, representing a 2.0% decrease compared with 2015. By contrast, the sum insured increased by 2.1% to EUR 3,014 billion. Term insurance policies recorded a decrease in the number of contracts from 13.4 million to around 13.0 million, although the sum insured rose from EUR 739.3 billion to EUR 781.4 billion. Gross premiums written in the direct insurance business of the German life insurers amounted to EUR 84.5 billion in the year under review (previous year: EUR 86.6 billion). This represented a 2.4% decline.[109]

II. Health Insurance

95. The private health insurers generated premium income totalling around EUR 37.1 billion in 2016. This is equivalent to an increase of approximately 1.2% compared with 2015. Comprehensive health insurance, with around 8.8 million persons insured and premium income of EUR 26 billion and thus 71% of the total premium income, is the most important business line by far for the private health insurers in 2016. Together with the other types of insurance, such as long-term care insurance, daily benefits insurance and other partial health insurance types, the private health insurers insure approximately 40.6 million people.[110]

III. Property and Casualty Insurance

96. Property and casualty insurers recorded a 2.7% year-on-year increase in gross premiums written in the direct insurance business in 2016 to EUR 71.0 billion (2015: EUR 69.2 billion). Gross expenditures for claims declined by 2.0% to EUR 23.1 billion (2015: EUR 23.6 billion). Gross expenditures for claims relating to prior years rose by 6.5% to EUR 17.9 billion. Provisions recognised for individual claims amounted to EUR 19.1 billion, compared with EUR 18.4 billion in the previous year; provisions recognised for individual claims relating to prior years amounted in total to EUR 58.3 billion, compared with EUR 56.3 billion in the previous year.[111]

---

109. BaFin Report, pp. 155-156.
110. *Ibid.*, p. 151.
111. *Ibid.*, pp. 155 and 156.

A. *Motor Vehicle Insurance*

97. With gross premiums written amounting to EUR 25.4 billion, motor vehicle insurance was by far the largest insurance class. This represented growth of 3.0% over the previous year. As in the previous years, the increase is attributable both to a rise in the number of policies and to higher average premiums. Gross expenditures for claims relating to the year under review increased by 3.7% year on year, while gross expenditures for claims relating to previous years were up 3.1%. Overall, gross provisions recognised for individual claims relating to the year under review were higher by 3.0% year on year, while they increased by 3.5% for outstanding claims relating to 2015.[112]

B. *General Liability Insurance*

98. Property and casualty insurers collected premiums of EUR 9.4 billion (+1.8%) for general liability insurance. Claims relating to the year under review declined by 1.7% in comparison with the previous year to EUR 960 million. Property and casualty insurers paid out EUR 3.2 billion for claims relating to earlier years (previous year: EUR 2.9 billion). Gross provisions for individual claims, which are particularly important in this insurance class, rose by 1.0% to EUR 2.9 billion for outstanding claims relating to the year under review. Gross provisions for outstanding individual claims relating to the previous year rose by 3.5% to EUR 18.6 billion.[113]

C. *Fire Insurance/Comprehensive Residential Buildings Insurance and Comprehensive Contents Insurance Contracts*

99. Insurers recorded gross fire insurance premiums written of EUR 2.2 billion (+2.0%). Gross expenditures for claims relating to the year under review fell sharply by 16.9% to EUR 571.4 million. Insurers collected premiums for comprehensive residential buildings insurance and comprehensive contents insurance contracts of EUR 9.5 billion (+5.8%). Expenditures for claims relating to the year under review declined by 7.7% year on year. By contrast, provisions for individual claims rose by 8.7%. Expenditures for claims relating to prior years were almost unchanged compared with the previous year, recording a marginal decline of 0.3%. Provisions for claims relating to previous years increased slightly by 2.0%.[114]

---

112. *Ibid.*, pp. 158 and 159.
113. *Ibid.*, p. 159.
114. *Ibid.*

D. Accident Insurance

100. Premium income for general accident insurance contracts rose by 2.0% year on year to EUR 6.5 billion. Gross expenditures for claims relating to the year under review amounted to EUR 412.2 million. EUR 2.3 billion was reserved for outstanding claims relating to the year under review (+0.4%), almost the same amount as in the prior year.[115]

115. *Ibid.*

Chapter 2. Access to Business

Authorization: Requirements and Procedures

101. The requirements and procedures to conduct business in Germany depend on whether the undertaking has its registered office in Germany, in an EU or EEA Member State in or in a third country.

§1. Domestic Insurers

I. Re-/Insurance Business in Germany

102. Any undertaking wishing to conduct re-/insurance business in Germany requires written authorization from BaFin (§ 8 paragraph 1 VAG). Authorisation will be only granted to undertakings organised as AG, SE, VVaG or corporate body or institution under public law (§ 8 paragraph 2 VAG). The re-/insurers may engage only in insurance business or such other business as is directly related with re-/insurance business (§ 15 paragraph 1 and 2 VAG). Furthermore, the authorisation to carry on life insurance business and the authorisation to carry on other classes of insurance are mutually exclusive. The same applies for the authorisation to carry on health insurance business and an authorisation to operate in other classes of insurance (§ 8 paragraph 4 VAG).

103. It is important to note that the non-authorisation of an undertaking or the non-compliance of an authorized insurer with the VAG has no effect on the validity of the insurance contract.[116] For example, where a company offers insurance without having obtained the prior approval by the BaFin, the insurance contract remains valid.[117]

---

116. *See* e.g., OLG Hamm, 10 Dec. 2009 – 2 U 111/09 VersR 2010, pp. 609, 610 (regarding non-compliance with § 15 para. 1 VAG).
117. *See* e.g., BGH, 12 Mar. 1964 – II ZR 226/62, VersR 1964, pp. 497, 498; BGH, 7 Jul. 1955 – II ZR 341/53, VersR 1955, pp. 481, 483; RG, 1 Jun. 1937 – VII 15/37, RGZ 155, pp. 138, 144; Armbruester, in: Proelss/Martin, VVG, 30 ed., C.H. Beck 2018, § 1 VVG n. 113.

A. Property and Casualty Insurance Business[118]

1. Business Plan (§ 9 paragraphs 1, 2 and 3 VAG)

104. Together with the application form the undertaking has to submit a business plan. The details can be found in § 9 paragraph 1, 2 and 3 VAG. The plan must contain the articles of incorporation, details of the organizational structure of the undertaking (e.g., in the form of an organizational chart), its registered office and its branches as well as details of the location of the insured risks (*see* § 57 paragraph 3 sentence 2 VAG). If risks located outside Germany are also to be insured, an explanation should be provided as to whether and, if so, in which states branches are to be established (on the term 'branch', *see* § 57 paragraph 2 VAG) and in which states this is not envisaged (on the term 'cross-border provision of services' *see* § 57 paragraph 1 sentence 1 VAG). The articles of formation of the undertaking insofar as they do not relate to general insurance policy conditions must be attached to the application. Details must be given of the classes of insurance which are to be provided and information about the risks that are to be covered within an insurance class, indicating the type of insurance cover and its purpose (i.e., what is to be insured, and against what, e.g., household against fire and natural forces). The basic features of reinsurance and the retrocession must be presented.[119]

105. The primary insurance undertaking must already, as of its authorisation, have eligible own funds of not less than the solvency capital requirement (SCR, *see* paragraph 131) on the basis of the expected overall volume of business. The basic own funds pursuant to § 89 paragraph 3 VAG in conjunction with § 95 VAG must at least be such that eligible basic own funds are available in the amount of the absolute floor of the minimum capital requirement (MCR, *see* paragraph 137). The MCR is defined in § 122 VAG. The absolute floor of the MCR is EUR 2.5 million, or EUR 3.7 million if one of the classes listed in nos 10–15 of Annex 1 to the VAG is to be provided (§ 1 paragraph 2 no. 1 and 2 of the Capital Resources Regulation (*Verordnung über die Kapitalausstattung von Versicherungsunternehmen*, hereafter 'KapAusstV')). The SCR is to be calculated on the basis of the balance sheet and profit and loss account estimates to be presented for the first three financial years in accordance with the provisions of the VAG (§§ 96 et seq. VAG). The amount of the minimum eligible own funds to be maintained is to be calculated on the basis of the MCR and the SCR requirement, whichever is greater.[120]

106. The undertaking must document the availability of the funds necessary for the establishment of the administration and the network of agents (organization fund) (§ 9 paragraph 2 no. 5 first half-sentence VAG). Additional information must

118. For more detailed information, *see* BaFin Guidance notice for the authorisation of insurance joint-stock companies for pursuit of property and casualty insurance business dated 15 Dec. 2016 (BaFin Guidance Notice), www.bafin.de/SharedDocs/Veroeffentlichungen/EN/Merkblatt/VA/mb_161215_zulassung_schaden_unfall_erstversicherer_va_en.html (accessed 28 Mar. 2018).
119. BaFin Guidance Notice, at II.2.
120. *Ibid.*, II.6.

be provided if the undertaking is subject to additional supervision due to its membership of an insurance group (§§ 245 et seq. VAG) or a financial conglomerate (within the meaning of the German financial conglomerates supervision act (*Finanzkonglomerate-Aufsichtsgesetz*, hereafter 'FKAG').[121]

107. Estimates of the balance sheet and the profit and loss account and, on this basis, estimates of the future SCR and MCR are to be presented for the first three financial years. The estimates for the profit and loss account must show the commission expenses and the other ongoing expenses for insurance business, the expected premium income, the expected expenses for claims incurred and the expected liquidity position. The reinsurers' shares are to be deducted from the expenses and income initially calculated on a gross basis. The calculation method serving as the basis for the estimates is to be indicated for the estimates of the SCR and the MCR.[122]

2. Details of the Nature and Scope of the Business Organization (§ 9 paragraph 4 no. 1 VAG)

108. In addition, details of the nature and scope of the business organization must be submitted which include information about the management board (senior management), other persons who effectively run the undertaking, supervisory board members, responsible actuary and additional persons who are responsible for other key tasks. The management board must consist of at least two members (§§ 33 paragraph 1, 188 paragraph 1 sentence 1 VAG) who must each be qualified in accordance with the requirements of § 24 paragraph 1 VAG ('fit and proper'). As well as the management board members, other persons who effectively run the undertaking (*see* § 24 paragraph 2 sentence 1 VAG), the members of the supervisory board, the responsible actuary (for accident insurance with premium refund; for the calculation of the premium reserve in relation to annuities under general liability insurance, motor vehicle liability insurance, motor vehicle accident insurance and general accident insurance without premium refund; for non-substitutive health insurance pursued on a similar technical basis to that of life insurance (SLT health)) as well as the additional persons who perform other key tasks must be fit and proper (§ 24 paragraph 1 and § 141 paragraph 1 sentence 2 to 4 VAG in conjunction with § 161 paragraph 1, § 162, § 156 paragraph 1 and § 147 VAG).[123]

109. The undertaking must provide information about enterprise agreements within the meaning of §§ 291, 292 AktG and about contracts regulating the outsourcing of important functions or activities.[124]

121. *Ibid.*, II.7.
122. *Ibid.*, II. 9.
123. *Ibid.*, III.1.a).
124. *Ibid.*, III.1.b).

3. Details of Qualifying Holdings (§ 9 paragraph 4 no. 2 VAG)

110. If qualifying holdings (§ 7 no. 3 VAG) are held in the insurance undertaking, their holders must be named. Holders of qualifying holdings are individuals or commercial partnerships that have a direct or indirect holding in an undertaking which represents 10% or more of the capital or of the voting rights or who have other options of exercising a significant influence over the management of that undertaking. Holders of qualifying holdings must also meet certain requirements in order to guarantee sound and prudent management of the undertaking.[125]

4. Close Links (§ 9 paragraph 4 no. 3 VAG)

111. Any close links within the meaning of § 7 no. 7 VAG with other natural persons or with undertakings must be indicated (§ 9 paragraph 4 no. 3 VAG).[126]

5. Compulsory Insurance Conditions (§ 9 paragraph 4 no. 4 VAG)

112. In the case that the undertaking wants to provide motor liability insurance, in addition to the compulsory insurance conditions, the applications for membership of 'Deutsches Buero Gruene Karte e.V.' and 'Verkehrsopferhilfe e.V.' must be presented or documentation of the applicable (fee) payment must be provided (*see* §§ 8 paragraph 1, 13 paragraph 1 sentence 5 PflVG).[127]

6. Small Insurance Undertakings

113. Specific requirements exist if the insurance undertaking is a so-called small insurance undertaking within the meaning of § 211 VAG, i.e., the undertakings annual gross written premium income, *inter alia*, does not exceed EUR 5 million and whose technical provisions, gross of the amounts recoverable from reinsurance contracts and special purpose vehicles, do not exceed EUR 25 million (§ 211 paragraph 1 no. 2 VAG in conjunction with Article 4 paragraph 1 lit. b) solvency II directive.[128]

114. For the documents to be submitted for the business plan within the meaning of § 9 paragraph 2 no. 4 VAG, pursuant to § 212 paragraph 3 no. 1 VAG details of those own-fund items pursuant to § 214 VAG which represent the absolute floor of the MCR are to be provided. SCR and MCR will be determined in accordance with the provisions of § 213 VAG and the regulation issued in accordance with section 217 paragraph 1 no. 1 VAG. The details of the nature and scope of the business

125. *Ibid.*, III.2.
126. *Ibid.*, III.3.
127. *Ibid.*, III.4.
128. EU Directive 2009/138/EC, O.J., 17 December 2009, L 335/1.

organization need only be provided in relation to the managing directors, the members of the supervisory board and, where applicable, the responsible actuary (§ 212 paragraph 3 no. 3 of the VAG).[129]

B. Health Insurance Business[130]

115. The MCR for undertakings pursuing health insurance is EUR 2.5 million (§ 1 paragraph 2 no. 1 KapAusstV)). Since health insurers are required by law to pay a minimum profit participation to policyholders, they must attach to their application a declaration of commitment which reads: 'The shareholder undertakes towards BaFin to make available the financial resources required to ensure that the allocation rates set out in § 150 and § 151 of the VAG in conjunction with the regulation issued in this respect comply with the stipulated minimum amount during the first five years by making allocations to the provision of premium refunds and to the provision for increasing age.'[131]

116. Independent trustees are to be involved in the case of premium adjustments in health insurance pursued on a similar technical basis to that of life insurance (§ 203 paragraph 2 VVG and § 155 paragraph 1 VAG) (*see* paragraph 702), of modifications to the general policy conditions (§ 203 paragraph 3 VVG) (*see* paragraph 706) and in the use of funds for the provision of premium refunds (§ 155 paragraph 2 VAG). Prior to the appointment of the trustees, their names must be submitted to BaFin, together with evidence of their qualification (§ 157 VAG).[132]

117. Health insurers must appoint a guarantee assets trustee and a deputy (§§ 128–130 VAG) who is responsible for safeguarding the guarantee assets of insurance undertakings. The compulsory insurance conditions (*see* § 193 paragraph 3 VVG and §§ 23, 119 SGB XI) have to be submitted. In addition, the principles used for the calculation of premiums and technical provisions within the meaning of §§ 341e-341h HGB including actuarial assumptions, mathematical formulae, arithmetical derivations and statistical evidence must be presented.

II. Re-/Insurance Business outside of Germany[133]

118. Where insurance undertakings domiciled in Germany intend to take up business operations in another EU/EEA Member State, the BaFin, upon receipt of

129. BaFin Guidance Notice, at IV.1.
130. *See* Bafin Guidance notice on the authorisation of insurance joint-stock companies for the pursuit of health insurance business dated 10 Mar. 2017, www.bafin.de/SharedDocs/Veroeffentlichungen/EN/Merkblatt/VA/mb_060402_krankenversicherung_ag_va_en.html (accessed 28 Mar. 2018) (BaFin Heath Insurance Business notice).
131. BaFin Heath Insurance Business notice, at II.7.
132. *Ibid.*, III.1.a)cc).
133. *See* Domestic insurers, www.bafin.de/EN/Aufsicht/VersichererPensionsfonds/Zulassung/InlaendischeVersicherer/inlaendische_versicherer_node_en.html (accessed 28 Mar. 2018).

the required documents, will assess the lawfulness of the intended business. If the requirements are met, BaFin sends to the supervisory authority of the country in which the undertaking intends to engage in insurance business the documents submitted by the insurer, a certificate of solvency and, in the case of cross-border provision of insurance services, a certificate specifying the classes of insurance the undertaking intends to operate and the risks it is permitted to cover. The supervisory authority of the host country communicates to the insurer the conditions under which, in the interest of the general good, the intended business must be pursued in the host Member State.

§2. EU/EEA Insurers[134]

119. If an EU/EEA Member State grants an insurer authorisation to carry on insurance business, the authorisation is valid in all other EU/EEA states. In order to be permitted to conduct insurance business in Germany, the insurer must undergo a notification procedure. To this end, the insurer must contact the home supervisor. After successfully passing the notification procedure, the insurer may carry on business in Germany via branches or through cross-border provision of services. This is referred to as 'European Passport' or 'Single-Licence-Principle'.

§3. Third-country Insurance Undertakings[135]

120. Primary insurers and reinsurers from third countries, i.e., countries that are not Member States of the EU/EEA, are subject to authorisation and must establish a German branch office if they wish to carry on primary insurance or reinsurance business in Germany. The requirements for the authorisation application and the branch office are based in particular on the provisions of §§ 68, 69 VAG.

121. § 67 paragraph 1 sentence 2 first half-sentence VAG provides an exception for primary insurance and reinsurance undertakings that wish to carry on solely reinsurance business in Germany. According to this exception, the requirement for authorisation and the establishment of a branch office does not apply if primary insurers or reinsurers from third countries carry on solely reinsurance business in Germany through provision of cross-border services and if the European Commission has decided in accordance with Article 172 paragraph 2 or 4 of the solvency II directive[136] that the solvency regimes for reinsurance activities carried out by undertakings in the relevant country are equivalent to the regime described in the solvency II directive.

134. *See* EU/EEA insurers, www.bafin.de/EN/Aufsicht/VersichererPensionsfonds/Zulassung/EU-EWR-Versicherer/eu_ewr_versicherer_node_en.html (accessed 28 Mar. 2018).

135. *See* Third-country insurance undertakings, https://www.bafin.de/EN/Aufsicht/Versicherer Pensionsfonds/Zulassung/DrittstaatenVersicherer/drittstaaten_versicherer_node_en.html (accessed 28 Mar. 2018).

136. EU Directive 2009/138/EC, O.J., 17 December 2009, L 335/1.

Chapter 3. Supervision

122. The BaFin supervises those private insurers operating in Germany, which are of material economic and financial significance, and public sector insurance undertakings engaging in open competition which operate across the borders of any of the Laender. The supervisory authorities of the Laender are mainly responsible for supervising public sector insurers whose activities are restricted to the particular Federal State in question and those private insurance undertakings which are of lesser economic and financial significance (*see* § 321 VAG).[137]

123. Insurers having their registered office in another EU Member State or in a state party to the Agreement on the EEA which conduct business in Germany under the freedom to provide service (Article 56 TFEU) are primarily subject to supervision by their home country. The BaFin does, however, consult the foreign supervisory authority if it identifies breaches of general German legal principles.[138]

§1. Solvency control

124. The term 'solvency' refers to an insurer's level of own funds, i.e., the assets of the undertaking, free of any foreseeable liabilities. Insurers must have own funds available to cover any unexpected losses they might incur. Own funds therefore ensure that policyholders' claims against the insurers are covered even under adverse circumstances.[139] There are two different solvency regimes the application of which depends on the size of the insurance undertaking.

I. Solvency I[140]

125. The supervisory regime solvency I which is based on the first, second and third life and non-life insurance directives on insurance (*see* paragraph 36) applies to undertakings to which solvency II does not apply i.e., small insurance undertakings, institutions for occupational retirement provision and death benefit funds. § 213 sentence 1 VAG stipulates that small insurance undertakings within the meaning of § 211 VAG must at all times have available own funds in an amount equivalent to the SCR specified by the KapAusstV (*see* paragraph 105).[141] The KapAusstV

137. *See* EU/EEA insurers, www.bafin.de/EN/Aufsicht/VersichererPensionsfonds/Zulassung/EU-EWR-Versicherer/eu_ewr_versicherer_node_en.html (accessed 28 Mar. 2018).
138. *See* Insurance companies, https://www.bafin.de/EN/Willkommen/Zulassung/Versicherer/Versicherungsunternehmen_node_en.html (accessed 28 Mar. 2018).
139. *See* Own funds and own funds requirements, https://www.bafin.de/EN/Aufsicht/VersichererPensionsfonds/Eigenmittelanforderungen/eigenmittelanforderungen_node_en.html (accessed 28 Mar. 2018).
140. *See* Solvency I – Own funds and own funds requirements, https://www.bafin.de/EN/Aufsicht/VersichererPensionsfonds/Eigenmittelanforderungen/SolvencyI/solvencyI_node_en.html (accessed 28 Mar. 2018).
141. BGBl. I 2016 p. 795.

also contains specific provisions for *Pensionskassen* (*see* paragraph 742) and death benefit funds. One-third of the SCR constitutes the MCR (§ 213 sentence 2 VAG). § 214 VAG lists own-fund items eligible for covering the SCR. The regulation on the supervision of pension funds (*Verordnung betreffend die Aufsicht ueber Pensionsfonds und ueber die Durchfuehrung reiner Beitragszusagen in der betrieblichen Altersversorgung*, hereafter 'PFAV') applies to pension funds (*see* paragraph 745).[142]

126. The SCR for all lines of business except life insurance is calculated on the basis of the higher of two indices: the premium index (annual premiums) or the claims index (average claims expenses incurred during the last three financial years). The SCR of life insurance business is primarily calculated based on the amount of the premium reserves and risk capital. On this basis, the SCR is calculated using a factor-based approach.[143]

II. Solvency II[144]

127. Under the solvency II regime own funds consist of basic own funds and ancillary own funds (§ 89 paragraph 2 VAG). Pursuant to § 89 paragraph 3 VAG basic own funds are composed of the excess of assets over liabilities and subordinated liabilities. § 89 paragraph 4 VAG states that ancillary own funds are own-fund items other than basic own funds which can be called up to absorb losses. Undertakings must apply for supervisory approval of ancillary own funds (§ 90 VAG).[145]

128. Own-fund items are classified in three tiers, depending on their value. The criteria for this classification are laid down in the VAG and defined more specifically in the delegated egulation 2015/35/EU (*Durchführungsverordnung*, hereafter 'DVO').[146] In the VAG, the requirements for Tiers 1–3 are laid down in §§ 91–93 VAG. In the delegated regulation, the requirements for Tier 1 are set out in Articles 69–71 DVO, for Tier 2 in Articles 72–75 DVO and the requirements for Tier 3 are

142. *Ibid.*, p. 842.
143. *See* Solvency I – Own funds and own funds requirements, https://www.bafin.de/EN/Aufsicht/VersichererPensionsfonds/Eigenmittelanforderungen/SolvencyI/solvencyI_node_en.html (accessed 28 Mar. 2018).
144. EU Directive 2009/138/EC, O.J., 17 December 2009, L 335/1; for further information on the legislation surrounding the implementation of Solvency II, *see* Solvency II, bases in law, guidelines and interpretative decisions of BaFin, https://www.bafin.de/EN/Aufsicht/VersichererPensionsfonds/Aufsichtsregime/RechtsgrundlagenLeitlinien/rechtsgrundlagen_node_en.html (accessed 28 Mar. 2018).
145. *See* Solvency II – Own funds and own funds requirements, https://www.bafin.de/EN/Aufsicht/VersichererPensionsfonds/Eigenmittelanforderungen/SolvencyII/solvencyII_node_en.html.
146. Commission Delegated Regulation (EU) 2015/35 of 10 October 2014 supplementing Directive 2009/138/EC of the European Parliament and of the Council on the taking-up and pursuit of the business of Insurance and Reinsurance (Solvency II), O.J., 17 January 2015, L 12/1.

defined in Articles 76–78 DVO.[147] In addition, the European Insurance and Occupational Pensions Authority (EIOPA) published guidelines on the classification of own funds (EIOPA-BoS-14/168).[148] BaFin requires all insurance undertakings subject to the solvency II directive to comply with these guidelines.

129. The Tiers are subject to quantitative limits. Therefore, not all of the own funds available to an issuer are necessarily eligible, i.e., not every own-fund item can be counted towards the SCR and the MCR. The requirements regarding the composition of eligible own funds are set out in §§ 94 and 95 VAG, which transpose Article 98 paragraphs 1 and 2 solvency II directive into German law. These requirements are specified in more detail at Level 2, in Article 82 DVO. The limits laid down in the delegated regulation are therefore applicable to all insurers subject to solvency II.

130. In case an undertaking intends to have its subordinated loans recognised as own-fund items, it does not have to apply for supervisory approval. There is thus no application procedure for this. If an undertaking submits a loan agreement to BaFin, requesting an assessment of whether this agreement can be recognised as an eligible own-fund item, it is to be expected that the dialogue with BaFin will take several months, depending on the complexity of the matter. Experience has shown that this process may even exceed a period of three months.[149]

A. *Solvency Capital Requirement*

131. Pursuant to § 89 paragraph 1 sentence 1 VAG, all insurers subject to solvency II must at all times have eligible own funds of at least the level of the SCR. The calculation of the SCR is governed by §§ 96 et seq. VAG. According to § 97 paragraph 2 VAG, the SCR corresponds to the Value at Risk (VAR) of the basic own funds subject to a confidence level of 99.5% over a one-year period. This means that insurers holding eligible own funds equivalent to the SCR will, with a probability of at least 99.5%, be able to cover any unexpected losses they might incur during the year to come.[150]

132. In the calculation of the SCR, all material quantifiable risks to which insurance or reinsurance undertakings are exposed are to be taken into account. Undertakings may use a standard formula or an internal model to calculate the SCR (§ 96 paragraph 1 VAG).

---

147. For details, *see* Diehl, in: Brand/Baroch Castellvi (eds), VAG, 1st ed., Verlag Nomos 2018, § 92 VAG ns 3 et seq.
148. *See* https://eiopa.europa.eu/Publications/Guidelines/COF_GLs_EN.pdf (accessed 28 Mar. 2018).
149. *See* Solvency II – Own funds and own funds requirements, https://www.bafin.de/EN/Aufsicht/VersichererPensionsfonds/Eigenmittelanforderungen/SolvencyII/solvencyII_node_en.html.
150. *Ibid.*

1. Standard Formula

133. If the SCR is calculated using the standard formula, it consists pursuant to § 99 VAG of the basic SCR in accordance with §§ 100–106 VAG, the capital requirement for operational risk in accordance with § 107 VAG and the adjustment for the loss-absorbing capacity of technical provisions and deferred taxes in accordance with § 108 VAG.

134. In order to calculate the basic SCR, appropriate provisions were stipulated defining which risks must be taken into account. The calculation comprises individual risk modules, which are subsequently aggregated. The basic SCR includes underwriting risks, market risks and credit risk, which are defined in § 7 no. 18, 20 and 32 VAG.

135. For individual underwriting risk modules, undertakings may adjust the parameters of the standard formula using their own parameters. However, these adjustments are subject to prior approval by the supervisory authority (undertaking-specific parameters, § 109 paragraph 2 VAG).[151]

2. Internal Model

136. Pursuant to §§ 111 et seq. VAG, undertakings may calculate the SCR using an internal model, which must be approved by the supervisory authority (§ 111 paragraph 3 VAG). If an internal model is not used to calculate the total SCR but only for individual risk modules or sub-modules of the basic SCR, for the operational risk pursuant to § 107 VAG or the adjustment for the loss-absorbing capacity of technical provisions and deferred taxes pursuant to § 108 VAG, it is called a partial internal model (§ 112 VAG). Insurers intending to use an internal model must fulfil extensive requirements in accordance with § 112 paragraph 2 and §§ 115–121 VAG).

B. Minimum Capital Requirement

137. Pursuant to § 89 paragraph 1 sentence 2 VAG insurers must at all times have eligible basic own funds of at least the level of the MCR. For this reason, only basic own funds classified as Tier 1 and Tier 2 are eligible for covering the MCR. Pursuant to § 122 paragraph 1 VAG, the MCR corresponds to an amount of eligible basic own funds, below which policyholders and beneficiaries would be exposed to an unacceptable level of risk were the insurer allowed to continue its operations. Therefore, authorisation of an insurer is withdrawn when the undertaking's amount of eligible basic own funds falls below the MCR and the undertaking is unable to re-establish the amount of eligible basic own funds at the level of the MCR within

151. *Ibid.*

a short period of time. The minimum amount of the MCR is governed by the KapAusstV. The calculation formula is laid down in Articles 248 et seq. Delegated Regulation 2015/35/EU.

III. Regulation on Reporting by Insurance Undertakings to the Federal Financial Supervisory Authority

138. The regulation on reporting by insurance undertakings to the BaFin (*Verordnung ueber die Berichterstattung von Versicherungsunternehmen gegenueber der Bundesanstalt fuer Finanzdienstleistungsaufsicht*, hereafter 'BerVersV') dated 19 July 2017,[152] requires all re-/insurers including small insurance undertakings, institutions for occupational retirement provision and death benefit funds to submit internal annual and quarterly interim reports to the BaFin. The internal annual report annually consists, *inter alia*, of balance sheets and profit and loss accounts (§§ 2–7 BerVersV), information in accordance with prescribed forms which are attached to BerVersV as annex 3 (§§ 9–14 BerVersV), and other accounting documents (§§ 16 or 17 BerVersV). The quarterly reports, depending on the different types of insurance undertakings, consist of data concerning, *inter alia*, the number of insurance contracts, expenses for claims incurred, expenses for premium refunds, and gross premiums written.

§2. Supervision of Tariffs and Insurance Conditions

I. Tariffs

139. In general, there are no restrictions on the premium tariffs in Germany. In the case of life insurance, § 138 VAG provides that the premiums must be calculated taking into account changes in actuarial assumptions. The premiums enable life insurers to meet all their commitments and, in particular, to establish sufficient benefit reserves for the individual life insurance contracts. Health insurers must calculate the premiums on the basis of sickness tables and other statistical data relevant to the Member State in which the risk is situated (in accordance with the mathematical methods used in insurance).[153]

140. There are restrictions as to the commission of the insurance intermediaries. According to § 50 paragraph 1 sentence 1 VAG the commission for the acquisition of a health insurance contract must not exceed 3% of the gross premium. The gross premium is defined in § 50 paragraph 1 sentence 2 VAG as the first premium

---

152. BGBl. I 2017 p. 2858.

153. For details, *see* Baroch Castellvi, in: Brand/Baroch Castellvi (eds), VAG, 1st ed., Verlag Nomos 2018, § 138 VAG n. 5.

extrapolated over 25 years. This cap corresponds to a nine monthly premiums as maximum commission (9 / (12 x 25) = 3 %).[154]

II. Insurance Policy Terms and Conditions

A. *Generals Remarks*

141. In accordance with Article 181 paragraph 1 solvency II directive, the VAG does not provide rules that policy terms and conditions need prior approval by the BaFin before use. For this reason, the undertaking is not required to submit policy terms and conditions for the various classes of insurance together with the application form. There are two exceptions with regard to the provision of compulsory insurance. Within the limits of Article 181 paragraph 2 of the solvency II directive, § 9 paragraph 4 no. 4 VAG requires as one of the preconditions for authorisation that the compulsory insurance policy terms and conditions are submitted to the BaFin before use (*see* paragraph 112). § 9 paragraph 4 no. 5 lit. b) VAG, in accordance with Article 206 paragraph 1 lit. b) of the solvency II directive, reiterates this requirement with regard to the compulsory health insurance.

B. *Compulsory Insurance*

142. It is to be noted that compulsory insurance can only meet its ends if first the coverage is prescribed with regard to the nature and extent of the risk to be insured, the minimum thresholds for the insured sum and the limits on exclusions from the insurance cover. Accordingly, private health insurance must cover at least all benefits of the basic tariff as defined in § 152 paragraph 1 VAG (*see* § 193 paragraph 5 VVG). The rules requiring the conclusion of a liability insurance policy for keepers of motor vehicles, lawyers, tax consultants, accountants and notaries specify, e.g., the minimum insurance sum and the maximum excess, contain a list of permissible exclusion clauses (*see* paragraph 589) and permissible duties to be observed by the policyholder (*see* paragraph 604).

154. *See* Laars/Both, in: Versicherungsaufsichtsgesetz, 4th online-edition, Nomos 2017, § 50 VAG n. 2; Boslak, in: Brand/Baroch Castellvi (eds), VAG, 1st ed., Verlag Nomos 2018, § 50 VAG n. 2.

Chapter 4. Technical Reserves and Investments

§1. Technical Reserves

143. Articles 76–86 solvency II directive have been to a great extent essentially verbatim adopted in §§ 75–88 VAG. Accordingly, (re-)insurance undertakings must establish technical reserves with respect to all of their insurance and reinsurance obligations towards policyholders and beneficiaries of insurance or reinsurance contracts (§ 75 paragraph 1 VAG). The value of technical reserves must correspond to the current amount insurance and reinsurance undertakings would have to pay if they were to transfer their insurance and reinsurance obligations immediately to another insurance or reinsurance undertaking (§ 75 paragraph 2 VAG). The calculation of technical reserves must be consistent with information provided by the financial markets and generally available data on underwriting risks (market consistency) (§ 75 paragraph 4 VAG). The value of technical reserve shall be equal to the sum of a best estimate and a risk margin (§ 76 VAG). The best estimate shall correspond to the probability-weighted average of future cash-flows, taking account of the time value of money (expected present value of future cash-flows), using the relevant risk-free interest rate term structure (§ 77 paragraph 1 VAG).[155] The risk margin must be such as to ensure that the value of the technical provisions is equivalent to the amount that insurance and reinsurance undertakings would be expected to require in order to take over and meet the insurance and reinsurance obligations (§ 78 paragraph 1 VAG).[156]

§2. Investments

144. In accordance with Article 132 paragraphs 1, 2 and 4 solvency II directive, § 124 paragraph 1 sentence 1 VAG provides that (re-)insurers must invest all their assets in accordance with the prudent person principle (*Grundsatz der unternehmerischen Vorsicht*). They are only allowed to invest in assets and instruments whose risks the undertaking concerned can properly identify, measure, monitor, manage, control and report, and appropriately take into account in the assessment of its overall solvency needs (§ 124 paragraph 1 sentence 2 no. 1 VAG).[157] All assets shall be invested in such a manner as to ensure the security, quality, liquidity and profitability of the portfolio as a whole.[158] In addition the localisation of those assets shall be such as to ensure their availability (§ 124 paragraph 1 sentence 2 no. 2

155. For details, *see* Axer, in: Brand/Baroch Castellvi (eds), VAG, 1st ed., Verlag Nomos 2018, § 77 VAG ns. 1 et seq.
156. For details concerning the calculation of the risk margin, *see* Axer, in: Brand/Baroch Castellvi (eds), VAG, 1st ed., Verlag Nomos 2018, § 78 VAG ns. 6 et seq.
157. For details, *see* Winter, in: Brand/Baroch Castellvi (eds), VAG, 1st ed., Verlag Nomos 2018, § 124 VAG ns. 12 et seq.
158. *See*, for details, the decision by BaFin on the interpretation of the 'prudent person principle', dated 1 Jan. 2016, available in German at https://www.bafin.de/SharedDocs/Downloads/DE/Auslegungsentscheidung/dl_ae_grundsatz_unternehmerischer_Vorsicht_va.pdf;jsessionid=AB392E7AF0014723088D13D904E23792.2_cid381?__blob=publicationFile&v=2 (accessed 28 Mar. 2018).

VAG). Assets held to cover the technical reserves must also be invested in a manner appropriate to the nature and duration of the insurance and reinsurance liabilities. Those assets shall be invested in the best interest of all policyholders and beneficiaries taking into account any disclosed policy objective (§ 124 paragraph 1 sentence 2 no. 3 VAG). In the case of a conflict of interest, insurance undertakings, or the entity which manages their asset portfolio, must ensure that the investment is made in the best interest of policyholders and beneficiaries (§ 124 paragraph 1 sentence 2 no. 4 VAG).

145. The use of derivative instruments is permitted insofar as they contribute to a reduction of risks or facilitate efficient portfolio management (§ 124 paragraph 1 sentence 2 no. 5 VAG). Investment and assets which are not admitted to trading on a regulated financial market must be kept to prudent levels (§ 124 paragraph 1 sentence 2 no. 6 VAG). Assets shall be properly diversified in such a way as to avoid excessive reliance on any particular asset, issuer or group of undertakings, or geographical area and excessive accumulation of risk in the portfolio as a whole (§ 124 paragraph 1 sentence 2 no. 7 VAG). Investments in assets issued by the same issuer, or by issuers belonging to the same group, must not expose the insurers to excessive risk concentration (§ 124 paragraph 1 sentence 2 no. 8 VAG).

146. In line with Article 132 paragraph 3 of the Solvency II Directive, § 124 paragraph 2 VAG restricts the type of assets for life insurers where the investment risk is borne by a policyholder who is a natural person to the assets listed in § 124 paragraph 1 nos 1–4 VAG.

Chapter 5. Accountancy

147. The accounting standards for insurers are laid down in §§ 341–341p HGB in conjunction with the regulation on the accounting of insurance undertakings (*Versicherungsunternehmens-Rechnungslegungsverordnung*, hereafter 'RechVersV'[159]), in §§ 74–87 VAG as well as in the regulation on the principles underlying the calculation of the premium reserve (*Deckungsrueckstellungsverordnung*, hereafter 'DeckRV'[160]). Special rules apply to small insurance undertakings in terms of § 211 VAG (§ 330 paragraph 4 sentence 2 HGB in conjunction with §§ 61, 62 RechVersV).

148. Insurance undertakings which have issued securities admitted to trading on a regulated market of an EU Member State within the meaning of Article 4 of the Regulation 1606/2002/EC of 19 July 2002[161] are obliged to prepare their consolidated accounts in conformity with the international accounting standards. By virtue of § 315e paragraph 3 HGB, insurance undertakings, which are obliged to prepare a consolidated financial statement, are allowed to prepare their consolidated accounts in conformity with international accounting standards even if they are not publicly traded in another EU Member State.

159. BGBl. I 1994 p. 3378; the English text of the RechVersV is available at https://www.bafin.de/SharedDocs/Veroeffentlichungen/EN/Aufsichtsrecht/Verordnung/RechVersV_va_en.html (accessed 28 Mar. 2018).
160. BGBl. I 2016 p. 767.
161. Regulation (EC) No. 1606/2002 of the European Parliament and of the Council of 19 July 2002 on the application of international accounting standards, O.J., 11 September 2002, L 243/1.

Chapter 6. Taxation of the (Re-)Insurance Company

§1. Corporate Tax

149. (Re-)Insurers providing (re-)insurance-related services are subject to the German Corporate Tax Act (*Koerperschaftsteuergesetz*, hereafter 'KStG') if they have their registered office or their management in Germany. Stock corporations (§ 1 paragraph 1 no. 1 KStG), mutual insurance associations (§ 1 paragraph 1 no. 3 KStG) as well as public sector insurance enterprises (§ 1 paragraph 1 no. 6 and § 4 KStG), as a general rule, have to pay 15% tax on all earnings (§ 23 KStG) plus a solidarity tax of 5.5% thereon (§ 4 solidarity tax act) (*Solidaritaetszuschlagsgesetz*, hereafter 'SolZG')). There are, however, some special rules for insurance undertakings. For example, small mutual insurance associations, whose operations are limited to a certain range of business, territory or group of persons (§ 210 VAG), under certain circumstances, are exempted from tax under § 5 paragraph 1 no. 4 KStG in conjunction with § 4 of the ordinance on the corporate tax implementation (*Koerperschaftsteuer-Durchfuehrungsverordnung 1994*, hereafter 'KStDV 1994').[162]

150. § 20 KStG allows insurers to set up equalization reserves and loss reserves in the tax balance sheet. Equalization reserves must be established and calculated if significant fluctuations in the annual requirement may be expected and these fluctuations are neither offset by premiums nor covered by reinsurance. Loss reserves must be established and calculated for claims that have occurred but not yet been reported by the balance sheet date. It is important to note that reserves for anticipated losses shall not be taken into account for the purposes of calculating taxable profits (§ 5 paragraph 4a income tax act (*Einkommensteuergesetz*, hereafter 'EStG')).

151. § 21 KStG contains rules for the fiscal treatment of premium refunds. Premium refunds are deductible to a certain extent. § 21a KStG sets special requirements for the evaluation and discounting of actuarial reserves.

§2. Trade Tax

152. Insurance undertakings, like other enterprises doing business in Germany are also subject to a trade tax (*Gewerbesteuer*). Trade tax is a local tax and is levied on an annual basis. The basis for taxation is the profit according to the EStG or the KStG.

162. For further details, *see* vom Twickel, in: Bluemich, EStG, KStG, GewStG, 139. ed., C.H. Beck 2018, § 5 KStG ns 61–64.

153. The basic municipal trade tax rate is 3.5% (§ 11 paragraph 2 of trade tax act (*Gewerbesteuergesetz*, hereafter 'GewStG'). It is supplemented by the application of a multiplier fixed by the respective municipality which varies from a minimum rate of 200% (§ 16 paragraph 4 sentence 2 GewStG), up to around 490% in the large cities. The effective trade tax rate ranges from 7% to around 17.5%. Small mutual insurance associations are exempted from municipal trade tax (§ 12a ordinance on the trade tax implementation (*Gewerbesteuer-Durchfuehrungsverordnung*, hereafter 'GewStDV'[163])).[164] Special rules apply to life insurers and health insurers (§ 9 Nr. 2a S. 5, Nr. 7 S. 8 GewStG).

§3. Value Added Tax

154. Services generated in Germany by a business enterprise are subject to value-added tax (VAT). Unlike income tax, value-added tax is a tax on transactions. The tax debtor is the final consumer. The tax payment debtor is entrepreneur who passes the value-added tax on to the customer by including it in the sales price. The standard tax rate is 19%. Insurance benefits to policyholders, however, are exempted from VAT (§ 4 no. 10 value-added tax act (*Umsatzsteuergesetz*, hereafter 'UStG')).[165]

§4. Insurance Tax

155. *See* taxation of insurance contracts *see* paragraph 804.

---

163. BGBl. I 2002 p. 4180.

164. For further details, *see* the information of the Federal Fiscal Authority ('Bundeszentralamt fuer Steuern'), http://www.steuerliches-info-center.de/EN/SteuerrechtFuerInvestoren/Unternehmen_Inland/Gewerbesteuer/gewerbesteuer_node.html (accessed 28 Mar. 2018).

165. *Ibid.*

Part II. The Insurance Contract: General

Chapter 1. Generalities (Characteristics, Interpretation, Categories, General Principles)

§1. Definition of Insurance

156. There is no statutory definition of what is a contract of insurance, neither under the VAG nor under the VVG.[166] § 1 VVG primarily defines the obligations of the parties to a contract of insurance in that the insurer undertakes to cover a certain risk of the policyholder or a third party by paying a benefit upon occurrence of the insured event, and the policyholder is obligated to pay the insurance premium to the insurer. From the definition of the obligations of the insurer and the policyholder, however, it is possible to conclude that the contract of insurance must have the following characteristics: (1) a promise of one party, the insurer, (2) to provide cover to another party, the policyholder, (3) against a specified risk on the occurrence of a future uncertain event (non-life contracts) or a certain event, the date of which is uncertain (life insurance), (4) in exchange for a premium. The BGH[167] and the BVerwG,[168] in numerous decisions, held that there must be, too, (5) a number of persons who are subject of the same risk and (6) that the provision of coverage by the insurer has to be based on calculations following the law of large numbers. In other words, there is only a contract of insurance when the terms of the insurance contract including the premiums are the result of actuarial calculations. If there are no such calculations, there can be no insurance, but only a bet or a financial transaction governed by rules other than the rules governing insurance.[169]

157. It is to be noted that the insured interest of the policyholder (*see* paragraph 209) is only an essential element for the validity of the contract of insurance. It is not a requirement for the classification of a transaction as a contract of insurance. The reason for this is that the existence of an insured interest is irrelevant for the

166. Cf. BT-Drucks. 16/3945, p. 56.
167. *See* e.g., BGH, 23 Nov. 2016 – IV ZR 50/16, NJW 2017, pp. 393, 394 (with further references).
168. *See* e.g., BVerwG, 29 Sept. 1992 – 1 A 26/91, NJW-RR 1993, p. 289 (with further references).
169. For the relatedness of insurance, betting and gambling, *see* Looschelders, in: Langheid/Wandt (eds), Kommentar zum VVG, 2nd ed., C.H. Beck 2017, § 1 n. 100.

authorisation to conclude insurance contracts under the VAG. The BaFin only examines whether or not the business for which the undertaking is seeking authorisation qualifies as insurance business and the formal requirements for authorisation are met.

§2. Rules on Interpretation of Insurance Contracts

158. There are different interpretation standards depending on whether a clause qualifies as standard term as opposed to an individually negotiated term.

I. Individually Negotiated Terms

159. If a term in the insurance contract is the result of individual negotiations between the policyholder (his/her broker) and the insurer, according to §§ 133, 157 BGB for the interpretation it is necessary to ascertain the true intention of the parties rather than to rely to the literal meaning of the clause, taking good faith and practice into consideration.[170]

II. Standard Contract Terms

A. *General Remarks*

1. Definition of Standard Contract Terms

160. § 305 paragraph 1 sentence 1 BGB defines standard clauses as 'contractual terms pre-formulated for a multiplicity of contracts, which one party to the contract (the user) presents to the other party upon the entering into of the contract'.[171] The user is the party on whose initiative the standard clause was included into the contract.[172] It is to be noted that it is not required that the user has drafted the clause.[173] The BGH has considered multiplicity as sufficient if standard terms are intended to be used at least three times.[174] Furthermore, the clause has to be dictated by the user. This requirement is met if the user makes an offer to incorporate the clause on a 'take it or leave it' basis, i.e., the other party must not have any real opportunity to alter them, but must be required to accept them as presented. It is to be noted that, by virtue of § 310 paragraph 3 no. 2 BGB, the rules on interpretation of standard

---

170. *See* e.g., BGH, 31 Mar. 2016 – III ZR 70/15, NJW 2016, p. 2656, para. 26; BGH, 27 Jan. 2010 – VIII ZR 58/09, NJW 2010, p. 2422, para. 33.
171. Translation provided by the German Federal Minister of Justice, http://www.gesetze-im-internet.de/englisch_bgb/index.html (accessed 28 Mar. 2018).
172. *See* BGH, 22 Jul. 2008 – IV ZR 74/08, RuS 2010, p. 100, para. 3.
173. BGH, 20 Jan. 2016 – VIII ZR 26/15, NJW 2016, p. 1230 para. 24.
174. *See* BGH, 11 Dec. 2003 – VII ZR 31/03, NJW 2004, p. 1454; BGH, 27 Sept. 2001 – VII ZR 388/00, NJW 2002, pp. 138, 139.

clauses apply to pre-formulated terms by the insurer when the policyholder is a consumer even if the term is intended only for single use, and to the extent that the consumer, by reason of the preformulation, had no influence on their contents.

161. Should the clauses have been subject to negotiations between the broker (on behalf of the policyholder) and the insurer, they do not qualify as standard clauses and the general rules on interpretation are to be applied (*see* paragraph 159). The same is true if the clauses are introduced into the contract by the policyholder's broker.[175] In that case the insurers would not be regarded as user in terms of § 305 paragraph 1 sentence 1 BGB. Whether the policyholder must be regarded as a user if the clause is introduced by his/her/its broker is questionable. It seems that the insurer has in fact almost always the opportunity to influence the content of a given clause. For this reason clauses introduced by brokers only in very exceptionable cases qualify as standard terms, and such clauses are subject of the rules on interpretation of individually negotiated terms.[176]

2. The Concept of the Average Policyholder's Understanding

162. For the interpretation of standard insurance clauses, the general standard, as established by the BGH, is the reasonable understanding of an average policyholder of the type of insurance in question which does not have any specific insurance knowledge.[177] Where a third party is (co-)insured (insurance for the account of a third party, *see* paragraph 308), the reasonable understanding of an average third party to the type of insurance contract in question must be also taken into account.[178] However, if there is a (tacit) consensus between the insurer and the policyholder that a given clause should have a meaning different from the one of an average (co-) insured, their mutual understanding as to its meaning prevails. In this case, the mutual understanding is given the same effect as if the parties had individually agreed on the clause.[179] This in turn means that the interpretation becomes a question of fact that allows for extrinsic evidence.

163. It should be noted that the concept of the average policyholder is first and foremost a normative one, and that in case of a dispute it is thus up to the courts to determine what the reasonable understanding of an average policyholder is. As a consequence, standard clauses must be interpreted literally and objectively. The scope as well as the purpose/intention of the insurer is only of relevance if they are discernible to the average policyholder. Moreover, standard clauses that limit the

175. *See* BGH, 22 Jul. 2008 – IV ZR 74/08, RuS 2010, p. 100, para. 4.
176. Cf. Reiff, in: Langheid/Wandt (eds), Muenchner Kommentar zum VVG, 2nd ed., vol. 3, C.H. Beck 2017, Allgemeine Versicherungsbedingungen n. 8.
177. *See* e.g., BGH, 13 Sept. 2017 – IV ZR 302/16, ZIP 2017, p. 1961, para. 16; BGH, 6 Jul. 2016 – IV ZR 44/15, BGHZ 211, p. 51, para. 17.
178. *See* e.g., BGH, 16 Jul. 2014 – IV ZR 88/13, VersR 2014, p. 1118 para. 16; BGH, 11 Sept. 2013 – IV ZR 303/12, VersR 2013, p. 1397, para. 13; BGH, 8 May 2013 – IV ZR 233/11, VersR 2013, p. 853, para. 40.
179. *See* e.g., BGH, 11 Jul. 2012 – IV ZR 164/11, RuS 2013, p. 297, para. 47.

coverage, such as exclusions, must be interpreted in a narrow sense (so-called *Restriktionsprinzip*, *see also see* paragraph 165).[180]

3. Legal Terms

164. Where the clause contains legal terms with an established legal meaning, the courts, however, will attach the same legal meaning to these terms and interpret them in accordance with the rules concerning the interpretation of statutes provided that it was discernible to the average policyholder that the term in question is a legal term.[181] For example, where the insurance provides coverage against theft, as is the case in comprehensive motor vehicle insurance (*see* paragraph 622), the court will attach to the term 'theft' the same meaning as under the theft definition in § 242 of the German criminal code (*Strafgesetzbuch*, hereafter 'StGB'). It is important to note, however, that the legal meaning is irrelevant when the parties have agreed otherwise or it was evident for the policyholder that the insurer has a different understanding of the legal term.

4. Ambiguous Clauses

165. Under § 305c paragraph 2 BGB ambiguous clauses are to be interpreted against the user. There is no such *contra proferentem* rule as regards individually negotiated clauses.[182] It is important to note that a standard clause is not ambiguous simply because the wording permits more than one way of reading it. In such case, the court will first look at the scope and purpose of the clause. Only if the court finds that the scope and purpose are not discernible for the average policyholder or does not support one way of reading the clause, § 305c paragraph 2 BGB applies. Insofar as several interpretations can be given in the context to a clause, the interpretation most favourable to the policyholder is to be applied.[183]

B. B2B Contracts

166. The rules on interpretation of standard clauses are also applied in the case where the policyholder is a business enterprise (by *argumentum e contrario*, *see* § 310 paragraph 1 sentence 1 BGB[184]) irrespective of whether the policyholder is a

180. *See* e.g., BGH, 17 Dec. 2008 – IV ZR 9/08, RuS 2009, p. 243, para. 17.
181. *See* e.g., BGH, 14 Jun. 2017 – IV ZR 161/16, RuS 2017, 421, para. 16; BGH, 20 Jul. 2016 – IV ZR 245/15, RuS 2016, 462, para. 22; BGH, 8 May 2013 – VI ZR 174/12, RuS 2013, p. 334, para. 12; BGH, 25 May 2011 – IV ZR 17/10, RuS 2012, p. 23, para. 14.
182. *See* e.g., BGH, 19 Nov. 1970 – VII ZR 238/68, VersR 1971, p. 172.
183. Cf. BGH, 24 Oct. 2017 – VI ZR 504/16, NJW 2018, p. 455 para. 22; BGH, 20 Jul. 2017 – VII ZR 259/16, NJW 2017, p. 2762.
184. The English translation of § 310 para. 1 sent. 1 and 2 BGB reads as follows: '§ 305 (2) and (3) and §§ 308 and 309 do not apply to standard business terms which are used in contracts with an entrepreneur, a legal person under public law or a special fund under public law.'

small, medium or large enterprise or the risk insured can be classified as large risk in terms of § 210 paragraph 2 VVG (*see* paragraph 29). In this regard the German law on standard terms goes beyond the protection standard of the Directive 93/13/EEC of 5 April 1993 on unfair terms in consumer contracts that only protects consumers.[185]

III. Supplementary Contract Interpretation

167. In practice the concept of supplementary contract interpretation plays an important role in insurance contracts.[186] Whenever there is an unintended gap in the contract, which affects its execution, the concept of supplementary contract interpretation comes into play. It is of no relevance whether the gap has already existed at the time of the conclusion of the insurance contract or has occurred later,[187] whether the parties have overlooked the issue or whether they have considered the issue as irrelevant at the time of the conclusion of the contract which later turned out to be wrong. The concept is also applicable to gaps caused by the invalidity of an unreasonable standard insurance contract term (*see* paragraph 207). Whether or not, and with what content the gap in the contract should be filled depends on what parties acting in good faith and with due regard to common usage would reasonably (and presumably) have agreed on at the time of the conclusion of the contract had they foreseen the gap in question.[188]

168. It is important to note that the gap is to be filled not on an individual but on an objective basis. That means that is not relevant what the individual parties of the dispute in question would have agreed on but what parties to contracts of such kind in general would have agreed on had they foreseen the gap in question ('abstract and general' as opposed to a 'specific and individual' standard).[189]

§3. Categories of Insurance

169. There are different ways to categorize or classify insurance.

185. O.J., 21 April 1993, L 95/29.
186. Cf. BGH, 20 Apr. 2017 – VII ZR 194/13, NJW 2017, p. 2025, para. 25; BGH, 5 Mar. 2008- IV ZR 89/07, BGHZ 175, p. 374, para. 22; OLG Karlsruhe, 26 Oct. 2010 NJOZ 2011, p. 1694, paras 38 et seq.
187. BGH, 12 Oct. 2012 – V ZR 222/11, NJW-RR 2013, p. 494, para. 14; BGH, 14 Nov. 2003 – V ZR 346/02, NJW-RR 2004, p. 6; BGH, 2 Jul. 2004 – V ZR 209/03, NJW-RR 2005, pp. 205, 206.
188. Cf. BGH, 3 Dec. 2014 – VIII ZR 370/13, NJW 2015, p. 1167, para. 26 (with further references).
189. *See* BGH, 12 Oct. 2005 – IV ZR 162/03, NJW 2005, pp. 3559, 3565; cf. BGH, 6 Apr. 2016 – VIII ZR 79/15, NJW 2017, p. 320, para. 39.

I. Insurance Supervision Act

170. At the supervisory level, based on the first generation of insurance directives the annex 1 of the VAG provides for 25 different classes of insurance. This annex is important because the insurer in its application for authorisation has to refer to the classes listed there that it wants to carry on. Moreover, annex 1 is of relevance for the determination of a large risk in terms of § 210 paragraph 2 VVG (*see* paragraph 29).

II. Insurance Contract Act

A. *Personal Insurance and Non-Personal Insurance*

171. The VVG distinguishes between personal insurance and non-personal insurance. In personal insurance such as health insurance (*see* paragraph 684), life insurance (*see* paragraph 709), occupational disability insurance (*see* paragraph 644) or accident insurance (*see* paragraph 654) the policyholder's or a third person's life and/or health is at risk. Non-personal insurance, by contrast, covers risks associated with the insured's property, other assets or activities.

B. *Insurance of Fixed Sums and Indemnity Insurance*

172. Another distinction can be made between insurance of fixed sums and indemnity insurance. While the former provides coverage for the actual loss of the policyholder (or a third party beneficiary), the latter pays out the sum agreed irrespective of whether the policyholder or third party beneficiary has suffered any financial loss. While insurance of fixed sums is limited to personal insurance, some kinds of personal insurances are based on the indemnity principle such as the comprehensive health insurance that covers expenses for the medical treatment (*see* paragraph 689), or may be taken out as indemnity insurance (e.g., accident insurance[190]).

C. *Property and Liability Insurance*

173. Indemnity insurance can be divided into property insurance and liability insurance. In property insurance, the loss refers to an object which belongs to the policyholder's assets (*see* paragraph 213). For this reason property insurance is sometimes referred to as 'active insurance'. In liability insurance (*see* paragraph 367), the loss is the increase in the policyholder's liabilities or the creation of a

190. *See* BT-Drucks. 16/3945, p. 109.

liability. It is sometimes referred to as 'passive insurance'. Further examples of passive insurances are the legal expenses insurance (*see* paragraph 451) and the comprehensive health insurance (*see* paragraph 689) that covers expenses for the medical treatment. A further distinction is made between facultative and compulsory liability insurance.

§4. General principles

I. First Insurance

174. Except for the marine insurance sector, which is not governed by the VVG (*see* paragraph 30), and the customary law doctrines of *Repraesentantenhaftung* (*see* paragraph 58) and *gewohnheitsrechtliche Erfüllungshaftung* (*see* paragraph 55) all principles of primary insurance law that amounted to general principles have been codified in the VVG. In the absence of any case law, there is some debate among scholars whether the VVG also reflects general principles of marine insurance and is as such applicable to marine insurance contracts. The majority of legal writers answer this question in the negative on the grounds that the reform in 2008 was aimed at providing more protection to the policyholders. They take the view that not the general principles embodied in the VVG in its present form, but the general principles embodied in its previous version (VVG 1908) as well as the general principles embodied in the abolished provisions on marine insurance apply to marine insurance contracts.[191]

II. Reinsurance

175. In the reinsurance business the general principles such as follow-the fortunes, follow-the-settlement and the reinsurer's right to inspect the cedent's file apply to reinsurance contracts subject to German law.[192]

§5. Inclusion and Content Control of Standard Terms and Conditions of Insurance Contracts

176. Whenever a clause in an insurance contract qualifies as standard term in the sense of § 305 paragraph 1 sentence 1 BGB or as a pre-formulated term in the meaning of § 310 paragraph 3 no. 2 BGB (*see* paragraph 160) it is subject to an inclusion

191. R. Koch, in: Bruck/Moeller, Großkommentar zum VVG, 9th ed., vol. 11, DeGruyter 2013, § 209 VVG n. 208; Looschelders, in: Langheid/Wandt (eds), 2nd ed., C.H. Beck 2017, § 209 VVG n. 11; Klimke, in: Proelss/Martin, VVG, 30th ed., C.H. Beck 2018, § 209 VVG n. 18; Schleif, Die Seeversicherung nach altem und neuem VVG, VersR 2010, pp. 1281, 1288.
192. Charlotte Echarti/Hubertus Labe, in: Bruck/Moeller, Großkommentar zum VVG, 9th ed., vol. 11, DeGruyter 2013, § 209 VVG n. 49 et seq.

and content control in accordance with §§ 305 to 310 BGB. It needs to be emphasized that not only for the content control but also for the inclusion control (especially for the determination of the surprising character of a clause in the sense of § 305c paragraph 1 BGB) the content of any particular standard term has to be determined by means of interpretation as outlined before (*see* paragraph 160).

I. Inclusion of Standard Terms in the Contract

177. In general, there are two provisions of importance for the inclusion of standard terms in the insurance contract, namely § 305 paragraph 2 BGB and § 305c paragraph 1 BGB. While the scope of § 305 paragraph 2 BGB is limited to contracts with private costumers, § 305c paragraph 1 BGB, which deals with surprising clauses, also applies to contracts with businesses.

A. Consumer Contracts

178. According to § 305 paragraph 2 BGB standard terms only become a part of the contract if the user of the terms makes a reference in its offer to them and gives the other party the opportunity to take notice of their content. Furthermore, the other party must agree to their inclusion. It is important to note, however, that § 305 paragraph 2 BGB only applies when the other party is a consumer (*see* § 310 paragraph 1 sentence 1 BGB). Where the other party is a business, the mere reference in the user's offer is sufficient. If the business party accepts the offer without objection against the inclusion, the standard terms govern the contract.[193]

179. In the primary insurance practice, § 305 paragraph 2 BGB plays no significant role since § 7 paragraph 1 VVG requires the insurer to inform the policyholder in writing of the terms of the contract, including the standard terms and conditions of insurance in good time before the policyholder submits his contractual acceptance (*see* paragraph 299).

180. It is to be noted that when concluding a contract of provisional insurance, the parties may agree that the insurer shall only send the applicant the standard terms of contract upon request and (at the latest) with the insurance policy. Where the standard terms are not communicated to the applicant at the time of the conclusion of the contract of provisional cover, the standard terms habitually employed by the insurer, and in the absence of such terms, the standard terms of the main contract will apply even without an explicit note to that effect (*see* paragraph 219).

193. Cf. Grueneberg, in: Palandt, BGB, 77th ed., C.H. Beck 2018, § 305 BGB n. 49 et seq.

B. Surprising Clauses

181. Pursuant to § 305c paragraph 1 BGB standard terms that are so unusual, i.e., surprising, that the other party to the contract could not reasonably have expected such a term in the agreement (*ueberraschende Klausel*), do not form part of the agreement. The question of whether a standard clause qualifies as a surprising term depends on the circumstances of the individual case. A standard clause may be surprising by virtue of its content because, e.g., it is inconsistent with negotiations between the parties prior to the conclusion of the contract, it materially alters the character of the contract by being contrary to the purpose of the contract, or it imposes additional duties on the other party which are unusual in the type of contract.[194]

182. For example, a clause in a general commercial liability insurance that excludes a certain risk is surprising if the policyholder during the negotiations with the insurance agent had made it clear that he/she wanted this risk to be covered and the insurance agent did not object.[195] Where a foreign citizen domiciled in Germany concludes a travel health insurance for a trip to his/her native country, a standard term, which defines as foreign country all countries except the country of which he/she is a national, is (not only) surprising since it cannot be reasonably expected by him/her.[196]

183. The surprising character of a standard clause, moreover, may arise by virtue of its language or presentation because it is formulated as an (objective) exclusion even though it refers to an act or omission of the policyholder (*verhuellte Obliegenheit*) or it is placed under the heading 'exclusions' but is in fact a 'duty' (for the distinction between an exclusion of cover and duties of the policyholder and the consequences arising therefrom *see* paragraph 269).

184. It should be noted, that it is generally possible for the user of standard terms to eliminate the surprising effect of a given term. There is, however, no general answer as to whether the presentation of the term in bold letters or in any other way apt to attract the attention of the other party suffices.[197]

II. Content Control

185. The content control (§§ 307–310 BGB) is aimed at the protection of the other party against standard terms which are detrimental to the other party to an

194. *Ibid.*, n. 3.
195. *See* e.g., LG Dortmund, 22 Jul. 2009 – 2 O 322/08, RuS 2009, pp. 410, 411.
196. Cf. BGH, 22 Nov. 2000 – IV ZR 235/99, NJW 2001, p. 1132.
197. Cf. BGH, 24 Sept. 1980 – VIII ZR 273/79, NJW 1981, pp. 117, 119.

extent which is incompatible with the requirement of good faith (unfairness control). In addition, the unfairness of standard terms may be resulting from the use of terms which are not clear and comprehensible (transparency control, *see* paragraph 203).

A. *Scope of Unfairness Control*

186. § 307 paragraph 3 sentence 1 BGB states that all standard terms derogating from legal provisions or supplementing legal provisions are subject to an unfairness control. According to settled case law only such terms that are of the essence of the contract because without them the contract cannot subsist (*essentalia negotii*) are exempted from content control.[198] The BGH, in its judgment dated 26 March 2014, held that the definition of the insured event in a general commercial liability insurance policy belongs to the essence of the contract. The BGH argued that in light of the fact that there is no legal provision defining the insured event in liability insurance, the contract would be unenforceable if the definition of the insured event were void. [199] This judgment has faced much criticism, partly because the BGH one month later in a serious of legal expense insurance cases decided to the contrary even though there is, too, no statutory insured event definition. It remains to be seen whether the BGH will uphold its judgment.[200]

187. Like the rules on interpretation of standard clauses and § 305c paragraph 1 BGB the unfairness control also applies in the case where the policyholder is a business enterprise (by *argumentum e contrario*, *see* § 310 paragraph 1 sentence 2 BGB), and/or the insurance contract covers a large risk in the sense of § 210 paragraph 2 VVG (*see* paragraph 29). In this regard the legislator despite criticism from scholars[201] preserved the legal situation prior to the reform of the VVG in 2008.[202]

B. *List of Unfair Terms*

1. Consumer Contracts

188. If the clause is subject to unfairness control, provided the policyholder is a private costumer, the courts in the next step will examine whether the clause belongs to the indicative and non-exhaustive catalogue of the terms set forth in §§ 308, 309 BGB which are regarded as unfair. While the legislator distinguished between clauses which are void per se (listed in § 309 BGB) and clauses which the

198. BGH, 26 Mar. 2014 – IV ZR 422/12, VersR 2014, p. 625 (with further references).
199. *Ibid.*
200. BGH, 30 Mar. 2014 – IV ZR 47/13, VersR 2014, p. 742, para. 17; BGH, 30 Mar. 2014 –IVZR 61/13, BeckRS 2014, 09828, para. 17; BGH, 30 Mar. 2014 –IVZR 60/13, BeckRS 2014, 09827, para.17; BGH, 30 Mar. 2014 –IVZR 62/13, BeckRS 2014, 09829, para. 17.
201. Werber, Halbzwingende Vorschriften des neuen VVG und Inhaltskontrolle, VersR 2010, pp. 1253 et seq.
202. Cf. BT-Drucks. 16/3945, p. 115.

court may set aside if they cause an unreasonable disadvantage to the consumer (listed in § 308 BGB), this distinction is of hardly any practical importance because the courts do not make use of their power of assessment. Rather the courts almost always hold clauses void which do not comply with § 308 BGB.[203]

a. § 309 BGB

189. According to § 309 BGB the following terms are per se void:

- No. 1: Prohibition of short-term price increases;
- No. 2: Restriction or exclusion of the right to refuse performance;
- No. 3: Prohibition of set-off;
- No. 4: Release form the duty to remind or to set a period of time for curing defects;
- No. 5: Lump-sum claim for damages which do not reflect the damages actually incurred;
- No. 6: Prohibition of contractual penalties;
- No. 7: Prohibition of the exclusion of liability for injury to life, body or health and in case of gross fault;
- No. 8: Prohibition of other exclusions of liability for breaches of duty:
  lit. a): Exclusion of the right to free oneself from the contract;
  lit. b): Defective delivery (Exclusion and referral to third parties; Limitation to cure, Expenses for cure, Withholding cure, Cut-off period for notice of defects, Making limitation easier);
- No. 9: Prohibition of contracts with too long duration;
- No. 10: Prohibition of the change of contract partner;
- No. 11: Prohibition of imposing liability on an agent with power to enter into a contract;
- No. 12: Prohibition to alter of the burden of proof;
- No. 13: Prohibition of imposing certain form requirements for notices and declarations;
- No. 14: Limitations of the right to sue.

190. Except for § 309 no. 12 and 13 BGB none of the afore-listed prohibitions plays an important role in insurance contracts. § 309 no. 12 BGB applies to exclusion clauses and clauses establishing a duty for the policyholder whenever the insurer shifts the burden of proof, which rests on the insurer e.g., for the fulfilment of an exclusion or the violation of a duty, to the policyholder. § 309 no. 13 BGB is of importance for clauses imposing on the policyholder the duty to give notice to the insurer e.g., of the occurrence of the insured event. According to § 309 no. 13

203. Cf. Harry Schmidt, in: Ulmer/Brandner/Hensen, AGB-Recht, 12th ed., Otto Schmidt 2016, § 308 BGB n. 3.

lit. b) BGB any clause that requires the notice to be in written form in terms of § 126 BGB is void. The insurer may only require text form in the sense of § 126b BGB.[204]

b. § 308 BGB

191. According to § 308 BGB the following terms are presumably void:

- No. 1: Unreasonably long or insufficiently specific period of time for the user's acceptance and performance;
- No. 1a: Unreasonably long period of time for the user's obligation to pay;
- No. 1b: Unreasonably long period of time for the inspection and acceptance of the performance of the user's contractual partner;
- No. 2: Unreasonably long or insufficiently specific additional period of time for the user's performance;
- No. 3: User's reservation of the right to revoke without cause;
- No. 4: User's reservation of the right to modify;
- No. 5: Fictitious declarations;
- No. 6: Fictitious receipt of a declaration of the user;
- No. 7: User's right to demand unreasonably high remuneration or unreasonably high reimbursement of expenses;
- No. 8: Unavailability of performance.

192. There has been no reported insurance cases where the courts relied on § 308 BGB.[205]

2. B2B Contracts

193. §§ 308 and 309 BGB do not apply to standard terms which are used in contracts with a business. It is important to note, however, that pursuant to § 310 paragraph 1 sentence 2 BGB the prohibitions set out in §§ 308 und 309 BGB nevertheless apply to business-to-business transactions within the framework of § 307 BGB in that they exemplify cases describing a rebuttable presumption of unfairness. Practices and customs that apply in business dealings have to be taken into consideration. For example, the prohibition of short-term price increases (§ 309 no. 1 BGB) does not apply to business-to-business transactions when the practice of using current daily (stock-market) prices is a characteristic feature for the type of

204. § 126b BGB reads as follows: 'If text form is prescribed by statute, a readable declaration, in which the person making the declaration is named, must be made on a durable medium. A durable medium is any medium that 1. enables the recipient to retain or store a declaration included on the medium that is addressed to him personally such that it is accessible to him for a period of time adequate to its purpose, and 2. allows the unchanged reproduction of such declaration.'

205. Cf. Bruns, in: Langheid/Wandt (eds.), Muenchener Kommentar zum VVG, 2nd ed., C.H. Beck 2017, § 308 BGB n. 1.

business in question.[206] According to the prevailing view among scholars the prohibition of imposing certain form requirements for notices and declarations set forth in § 309 no. 13 BGB is, too, not applicable whenever the contractual partner of the user is a business.[207]

C. Presumably Unfair Terms

194. Where a term is not listed in §§ 308, 309 BGB, it may still be void pursuant to § 307 paragraph 2 no. 1 and 2 BGB in conjunction with § 307 paragraph 1 sentence 1 BGB. § 307 paragraph 1 sentence 1 BGB states that provisions in standard business terms are void if, contrary to the requirement of good faith, they unreasonably disadvantage the other party. § 307 paragraph 2 BGB exemplifies two cases describing a rebuttable presumption of unfairness. An unreasonable disadvantage is to be assumed to exist if a provision first, is not compatible with essential principles of the statutory provision from which it deviates (no. 1), or second, limits essential rights or duties inherent in the nature of the contract to such an extent that attainment of the purpose of the contract is jeopardized (no. 2).

1. Presumption of Unfairness

a. § 307 paragraph 2 no. 1 BGB

195. The assumption laid down in § 307 paragraph 2 no. 1 BGB applies when the legal provision from which the standard term deviates has a *Leitbildfunktion*. Obviously, not every provision has a *Leitbildfunktion* because otherwise any deviation from statutes would be legally impossible. Only provisions, by which the legislator strived to balance out the interest of parties in a just and reasonable way, have a 'Leitbildfunktion'. On the other hand, it can be presumed that any legal provision is somehow aimed at ensuring an appropriate balance of interests between the contractual parties. For this reason the courts distinguish between provisions which are based on considerations of practicability (*Zweckmaessigkeitserwaegungen*) and thus represent one out of several possible ways, and provisions which represent the one and only way to reach this aim. Only the latter provisions have a *Leitbildfunktion* and any derogation from them triggers the presumption of unfairness.[208]

196. For example, 'cost inclusive' clauses in D&O insurance policies deviate from § 101 paragraph 2 sentence 1 VVG according to which the insurer shall reimburse the costs incurred in a legal dispute carried on upon its instructions and the

---

206. *See* e.g., Harry Schmidt, in: Ulmer/Brandner/Hensen, AGB-Recht, 12th. ed., Otto Schmidt 2016, § 309 no. 1 BGB n. 45; Wurmnest, in: Muenchener Kommentar zur BGB, 7th ed., C.H. Beck 2016, § 309 no. 1 BGB n. 33.
207. *See* e.g., Matthias Habersack, in: Ulmer/Brandner/Hensen, AGB-Recht, 12th ed., Otto Schmidt 2016, § 309 no. 13 BGB n. 12; Wurmnest, in: Muenchener Kommentar zur BGB, 7th ed., C.H. Beck 2016, § 309 no. 13 BGB n. 6; for a somewhat different view *see* OLG Schleswig 8 Nov. 2000 – 9 U 104/99, NJW-RR 2001, pp. 818, 819.
208. Cf. BGH, 1 Dec. 2004 – IV ZR 291/03, VersR 2005, pp. 266, 268et seq.

costs of defence even insofar as they exceed, together with the other indemnity, the sum insured. The OLG Frankfurt/M., in its judgment of 9 June 2011, held that the defence cost exclusive rule laid down in § 101 paragraph 2 sentence 1 VVG has *Leitbildfunktion* and therefore 'cost inclusive' clauses in D&O insurance policies are void,[209] whereas many scholars take the different view.[210] The decision has not become *res iudicata.*

b. § 307 paragraph 2 no. 2 BGB

197. The purpose of § 307 paragraph 2 no. 2 BGB is to prevent contractually important right and duties from being undermined by standard terms. In the determination of what right and duty is important regard is to be had to the statutory type of contract and the reasonable expectations of the user's contractual partner. In the insurance sector § 307 paragraph 2 no. 2 BGB plays an important role in the control not only of exclusions clauses but also of clauses which define the risk insured. For example, the purpose of an outstanding debt and occupational disability insurance is to ensure that the commitments made by the policyholder continue to be honoured in the event that his/her state of health no longer allows him/her to carry on an activity which will provide him/her with the necessary income to meet his/her obligations towards the lending bank. A clause according to which the insured 'shall be regarded as being in a state of total incapacity for work if, after 90 consecutive days' interruption of activity following an accident or illness, he finds himself unable to take up any activity, paid or otherwise' could jeopardize the purpose of the insurance contract, since the policyholder who is recognised as being fit to carry on some form of employment, even if such employment is unpaid, will not receive the coverage he/she needs to repay the loan.[211]

2. Rebuttal of the Presumption of Unfairness

198. It needs to be emphasized that any violation of § 307 paragraph 2 no. 1 and/ or 2 BGB only create a rebuttable presumption of unfairness. The presumption is rebutted if the insurer is able to demonstrate and to prove that it has a legitimate interest in the clause which overrides the interest of the policyholder.[212] In this regard § 307 paragraph 2 BGB differs from §§ 308, 309 BGB where in business-to-consumer transactions any conflict automatically renders the clause void. Where the policyholder is a business, however, it follows from § 310 paragraph 1 sentence 2 BGB reference to § 307 BGB that there is only a presumption of unfairness in case of non-compliance with §§ 308 and 309 BGB (except for § 309 nos 12 and 13 BGB, *see* paragraph 190).

209. Cf. OLG Frankfurt/M., 9 Jun. 2011 – 7 U 127/09, RuS 2011, p. 509.

210. *See* e.g., R. Koch, Kostenanrechnungsklauseln in der Haftpflichtversicherung, VersR 2016, pp. 1405, p. 1407.

211. Cf.OLG Hamm, 7 Sept. 2012 – I-20 W 12/12 NJW-RR 2013, pp. 547, 548, OLG Koblenz, 18 Nov. 2011, NJW 2012, pp. 2126, 2127.

212. Cf. BGH, 17 Oct. 2017 – XI ZR 157/16, NJW 2018, p. 383, para. 33.

199. When it comes to exclusion clauses that endanger the purpose of the insurance contract legitimate interests of the insurer are difficult to imagine. Where there is a deviation from a provision which has *Leitbildfunktion* there might be exceptional cases where the insurer is able to demonstrate and prove that its interest in the deviation is not only legitimate but also overrides the interest of the policyholder in maintaining the statutory legal status quo. For example, if one follows the judgment of the OLG Frankfurt/M. (*see* paragraph 196), the D&O insurer would have to explain why its interest in the derogation from § 101 paragraph 2 sentence 1 VVG is legitimate and overrides the policyholder's as well as the co-insured directors' and officers' interests to adhere to the statute. It would be then up to the court to evaluate the conflicting interests.

200. It is important to note that like with the interpretation of standard terms (*see* paragraph 162) and filling gaps by means of supplementary contract interpretation (*see* paragraph 167), the assessment of the conflicting interests is to be made on an abstract and general level leaving aside the individual circumstances of the insurer and the policyholder. By contrast, when the policyholder is a consumer, § 310 paragraph 3 no. 3 BGB states that the allegedly unfair clause must be assessed in the light of the circumstances in which the contract was drawn up ('specific and individual' as opposed to 'abstract and general' standard).

D. Unfair Clauses Beyond the Scope of §§ 309, 308 and 307 paragraph 2 BGB

201. Where there is no conflict – neither with §§ 308, 309 BGB nor with § 307 paragraph 2 BGB – a clause nevertheless may be unfair in terms of § 307 paragraph 1 sentence 1 BGB. For example, if one does not follow the above mentioned ruling of the *OLG Frankfurt/M.* that the defence cost exclusive rule laid down in § 101 paragraph 2 sentence 1 VVG has 'Leitbildfunktion' a cost inclusive clause would be only subject to the content control according to § 307 paragraph 1 sentence 1 BGB.

202. According to settled case law there is an unreasonable disadvantage of the other party in terms of § 307 paragraph 1 sentence 1 BGB, if the user, in an abusive way, attempts to enforce only its own interest at the expense of the other party and does not give adequate consideration to the other party's interest.[213] Since there is no presumption of unfairness it is not necessary that the legitimate interest in the clause of the user overrides the interest of his contractual partner.

III. Intransparent Clauses (§ 307 paragraph 1 sentence 2 BGB)

203. § 307 paragraph 1 sentence 2 BGB states that the unreasonable disadvantage may also arise where a standard term is not clear and comprehensible for the

213. *See* e.g., BGH, 25 Apr. 2001 – VIII ZR 135/00, NJW 2001, p. 2331; BGH, 3 Nov. 1999 –VIII–ZR 269/98,–NJW 2000, pp. 1110, 1112; BGH, 4 Jul. 1997 –V–ZR 405/96, NJW 1997, p. 3022.

other party. It is to be emphasized that pursuant to § 307 paragraph 3 sentence 2 BGB all standard terms, i.e., also those which do not derogate from legal provisions or supplement legal provisions are subject to a transparency control.

204. As is the case with the interpretation of standard terms (*see* paragraph 162), the benchmark is the average, reasonably observant and circumspect policyholder of the type of insurance in question.[214] The insurer must put the policyholder in a position to evaluate the coverage offered, in particular to assess any legal and economic disadvantages of a given clause.[215] To meet that end, the wording must not be ambiguous or misleading. Insurance policies moreover must not include any hidden clause which placement or presentation may make it difficult for the policyholder to understand circumstances related to the coverage or can contribute to erroneous understanding of such circumstances.

205. For example, clauses containing limitations or exclusions from coverage or imposing duties on the policyholder must not be placed or presented in a manner which makes it difficult for the policyholder of becoming acquainted with them before the conclusion of the contract. In this regard there is some overlap with the inclusion requirements set forth in §§ 305 paragraph 2 and 305c paragraph 1 BGB since such clause already may not form part of the contract. As a general rule, a clause is intransparent if it is likely to deter the average policyholder from exercising its rights under the insurance policy.[216]

206. The BGH, in its afore-mentioned judgment dated 26 March 2014 (*see* paragraph 186), held that the definition of the insured event in a general commercial liability insurance policy is not subject to any transparency control. The court argued that in light of the fact that there is no legal provision defining the insured event in the liability insurance the contract would be unenforceable if the definition of the insured event were void due its incomprehensibility. This line of reasoning seems to be hardly compatible with the Article 4 paragraph 2 of the Directive 93/13/EEC according to which terms defining the main subject matter of the contract are not subject to any unfairness control 'insofar as these terms are in plain intelligible language'.

IV. Legal Consequences of the Use of Unfair and/or Intransparent Terms

207. To the extent that the terms have not become part of the contract or are void as a result of the inclusion and content control, § 306 paragraph 2 BGB states that the contents of the contract are determined by the statutory provisions. If there is no

214. Cf. BGH, 23 Feb. 2011 – XII ZR 101/09, NJW-RR 2011, p. 1144, para. 10.
215. *See* BGH, 4 Mar. 2015 – IV ZR 128/14, VersR 2015, p. 571, para. 14; BGH, 11 Sept. 2013 – IV ZR 303/12, RuS 2013, p. 561, paras 14 et seq.; BGH, 24 May 2006 – IV ZR 263/03, RuS 2006, p. 366, para. 25.
216. Cf. BGH, 8 Oct. 2015 – I ZR 134/14, BeckRS 2016, 07030, para. 19; BGH, 20 Jul. 2005 – VIII ZR 121/04, BGHZ 164, pp. 11. 24.

statutory provision that fills the gap recourse to the principle of supplementary contract interpretation (*see* paragraph 167) is permitted if continuing the contract without filling the gap would represent unreasonable hardship for either party.[217] Where the gap cannot be filled by means of supplementary contract interpretation, the contract is void pursuant to § 306 paragraph 3 BGB. There are no reported insurance cases where a court hold an insurance contract void based on § 306 paragraph 3 BGB.[218]

217. Cf. BGH, 9 Feb. 2011 – VIII ZR 295/09, NJW 2011, p. 1342, para. 38; OLG Karlsruhe, 2 Feb. 2006 – 12 U 235/05, NJOZ 2006, pp. 1134, 1137.
218. Cf. Reiff, in: Langheid/Wandt (eds), Muenchener Kommentar zum VVG, 2nd ed., C.H. Beck 2017, vol. 3, Ch. 50, n. 115.

Chapter 2. Insurable Risk

§1. Insurable Risk

208. There are no express limits with regard to which risk is insurable. Under German law, the insurer is thus free to cover all possible risks unless the provision of coverage violates a statutory prohibition (§ 134 BGB) or is contrary to public order (§ 138 BGB). For example, if the provision of insurance to public entities of a foreign state violates an EU sanctions regulation the insurance contract will be void pursuant to § 134 BGB. The provision of coverage under a liability insurance policy for damages intentionally and unlawfully caused by the policyholder would be void according to § 138 BGB. The same is true if coverage would be provided against losses arising from criminal fines. From an economic (actuarial) point of view, the risk must be calculable, i.e., the risk must be quantifiable with regard to probability of occurrence and extent of damage.[219]

§2. Insured Interest

209. The insurability of a risk must be distinguished from the concept of the 'insured interest'. There is no statutory definition of the concept of insured interest. According to the BGH, this concept describes a financial loss that the parties to a contract of insurance consider as possible at the time of the conclusion of the contract and want to be compensated by the insurer in case the loss actually materializes.[220] The insured interest is of importance for all categories of indemnity insurances. It does not apply to insurances of fixed sums such as life insurance.[221]

210. According to § 80 paragraph 1 VVG the policyholder is released from his obligation to pay the premium, if no insured interest exists at the point in time when the insurance cover commences. The same is true if the interest does not arise in the case of an insurance taken out for a future enterprise or otherwise for a future interest. The insurer, however, may demand an appropriate administration fee.

211. In the case the insured interest ceases to exist during the term of contract, pursuant to § 80 paragraph 2 VVG the insurer shall be entitled to the premium to which he would have been entitled if the insurance had only been applied for up until the time when the insurer learned of the cessation of the interest. It follows from these consequences that the existence of an insured interest is a requirement for the validity of an indemnity insurance contract.[222]

---

219. Cf. Schradin, in: Langheid/Wandt (eds), Muenchener Kommentar zum VVG, 2nd ed., C.H. Beck 2017, vol. 3, Ch. 140, n. 10.
220. BGH, 20 Jan. 1988 – Iva ZR 165/86, NJW-RR 1988, p. 727.
221. Schnepp, in: Bruck/Moeller, Großkommentar zum VVG, 9th ed., vol. 3, DeGruyter 2010, § 80 VVG n. 11; Armbruester, in: Proelss/Martin, VVG, 30th ed., C.H. Beck 2018, § 80 VVG n. 4.
222. Schnepp, in: Bruck/Moeller, Großkommentar zum VVG, 9th ed., vol. 3, DeGruyter 2010, § 80 VVG nn. 58 and 74.

212. As the rules on insurance for the account of third party (*see* paragraph 308) indicate, it is of no relevance whose interest is insured. In many cases not only the interest of the policyholder but also of a third party with which the policyholder has a contractual or legal relationship is insured. For example, a commercial general liability policy insures by operation of law the interest of the policyholder and its employees to be discharged from liability towards injured parties.

213. In property insurance generally the owner's interest (*Sacherhaltungsinteresse*) is insured because any damage to his property causes him/her a loss. If the policyholder is not the owner but the lessee of a car, not only his/her interest to be discharged from any liability towards the lessor is insured (*Sachersatzinteresse*) but also the lessor's interest to get compensated (*Sacherhaltungsinteresse*).[223]

223. BGH, 8 Oct. 2014 – IV ZR 16/13, RuS 2014, p. 596, para. 13 (with further references).

Chapter 3. Formation of the Insurance Contract

§1. Actual Formation of the Contract

I. General Remarks

214. The formation of the contract of insurance follows the rules of general contract law. There must be an offer and acceptance (*see* §§ 145 et seq. BGB). In practise, the offer is made by the insurance applicant by filling out an application form. The offer will be forwarded to the insurer either by its insurance agent or an insurance broker acting on behalf of the insurance applicant. Another option may be to file the application online with the insurance company through its website. While there is no written form requirement, upon acceptance the insurer according to § 3 paragraph 1 VVG the insurer must issue and send the insurance certificate (*Versicherungsschein*) to the policyholder in text form (§ 126b BGB), i.e., by email, and upon his request as a written document. Making the certificate available for download is insufficient.[224]

II. Deviating Insurance Policy

215. If the certificate deviates from the application made by the policyholder, according to § 5 VVG the deviation shall be deemed to be approved by the policyholder provided that the insurer has expressly informed him/her of the deviation and has advised him/her that the deviations shall be deemed to have been approved if he/she does not object in writing within one month of receipt of the insurance policy. If the insurer fails to inform the policyholder of the deviation and/or his/her right to object, the contract shall be deemed to have been concluded as per the content of the policyholder's application. That is the case even where the deviation is in the policyholder's favour.[225]

III. Policyholders' Right of Revocation for No Cause

216. The policyholder may revoke his/her contractual agreement for any cause or for no cause at any time within two weeks (§ 8 paragraph 1 VVG); in the case of life insurance within 30 days (§ 152 VVG). The cooling-off period only commences once the policyholder has received full contractual documentation from the insurer (*see* § 8 paragraph 2 sentence 1 no. 1 VVG). Moreover, the policyholder must have been appropriately instructed on his right of revocation in text form (§ 126b BGB) (*see* § 8 paragraph 2 sentence 1 no. 2 VVG). The burden of proof that the policyholder has received the prescribed information lies with the insurer (§ 8

224. Rudy, in: Proelss/Martin, VVG, 30th ed., C.H. Beck 2018, § 3 VVG n. 3; Armbruester, in: Langheid/Wandt (eds), Muenchener Kommentar zum VVG, 2nd ed., C.H. Beck 2016, vol. 1, § 3 VVG n. 25.

225. BGH, 22 Jun. 2016 – IV ZR 431/14, RuS 2016, p. 554, para. 12.

paragraph 2 sentence 2 VVG). In case of incomplete information, the policyholder has an unlimited right to revoke. Only in exceptional cases he/she may have forfeited this right.[226]

217. The right of revocation is excluded where an insurance contract:

- is for less than one month's duration (§ 8 paragraph 3 sentence 1 no. 1 VVG);
- is for provisional cover, with the exception of distance selling policies (§ 8 paragraph 3 sentence 1 no. 2 VVG);
- is for pension funds which are based on provisions of employment agreements, with the exception of distance selling policies (§ 8 paragraph 3 sentence 1 no. 3 VVG);
- covers large risks (§ 8 paragraph 3 sentence 1 no. 4 VVG);
- has been satisfied – at the express request of the policyholder – in full by both parties (§ 8 paragraph 3 sentence 2 VVG).

218. If cover commences prior to the end of the revocation period, the insurer is only required to refund the premium pro rata for the remaining insurance period following the receipt of the notice of revocation (§ 9 paragraph 1 sentence 1 VVG). Where the insurer has not duly informed and instructed the policyholder about his revocation right, the insurer also must refund the premiums paid for the first year of cover, unless the policyholder has already made a claim under the policy (§ 9 paragraph 1 sentence 2 VVG).

§2. Provisional Cover

219. There are special rules dealing with provisional cover set forth in §§ 49–52 VVG. § 49 paragraph 1 VVG allows the parties to agree that the insurer shall only send the policyholder the terms of contract and the information in accordance with § 7 VVG and the VVG-InfoV upon request and at the latest with the insurance policy. Where no standard insurance terms are communicated to the applicant at the time of conclusion of the provisional cover agreement that cover is subject to the terms habitually employed by the insurer (*see* § 49 paragraph 2 VVG).

220. Pursuant to § 52 paragraph 1 sentence 1 VVG the provisional insurance contract ceases no later than at the time when cover under a further preliminary contract or the main insurance contract commences. If the holder of the provisional cover note subsequently concludes the main insurance contract with a different insurer he/she must inform the insurer providing provisional cover (*see* § 52 paragraph 2 VVG). If the main insurance contract made with the insurer issuing the

226. *See* e.g., OLG Koeln, 19 Sept. 2014 – 20 U 69/14, BeckRS 2016, 19746 (revocation 19 ears after the conclusion of the life endowment insurance contract); OLG Celle, 2 Feb. 2012 – 8 U 125/11, BeckRS 2012, 04142 (revocation two years after the termination of the life endowment insurance contract; KG, 21 Jun. 2002 – 6 U 7713/00, RuS 2003, pp. 98, 99 (revocation seven years after the conclusion of the home contents insurance contract).

cover note fails to operate because of a revocation or an objection by the holder of the cover note, the provisional insurance contract ceases at the latest when the insurer receives the revocation or objection (§ 52 paragraph 3 VVG). Where the provisional insurance contract was entered into for an indefinite period, either party may terminate the contract without notice. The insurer´s termination, however, only becomes effective two weeks after receipt (*see* § 52 paragraph 4 VVG).

§3. Validity Requirements

221. The validity of an insurance contract does not depend on any particular form. The obligation of the insurer to provide the policyholder with an insurance certificate in text form (*see* paragraph 214), and upon the policyholder's request as written document (*see* § 3 VVG), is required merely for reasons of evidence and not for validity.[227] The agreement can be oral or in writing (by post, fax or email). The existence of the contract may be proved through other means such as witnesses. As already indicated, there is no valid contract of insurance if there is no insured interest (*see* paragraph 211), and it is irrelevant of the insurer has received authorisation by the BaFin (*see* paragraph 103).

§4. Insurance Certificate

I. Contents

222. The insurance certificate is a rather short document that contains little more than the identification of the parties, of the insurance contract, the insured risks, and the coverage. The certificate together with the insurance standard terms constitutes the insurance policy (the insurance certificate is often inaccurately referred to as policy, e.g., in the English translation of the VVG).

223. When the insurance certificate is issued as a document in the name of the bearer the insurer is released from obligation by performance to the bearer of the document (§ 4 paragraph 1 VVG in conjunction with § 808 BGB). In life insurance practice, the insurer is only obliged to make payment to the policyholder (or any beneficiary) upon return of the insurance certificate (*see* § 4 paragraph 2 VVG).

II. Compulsory Liability Insurance

224. The insurance certificate as proof for the existence of cover is of particular importance in the area of compulsory liability insurance where there is a supervisory system, which exercises control over the concluding and maintenance of compulsory insurance. For example, according to § 6a BNotO, without proof of the conclusion of a liability insurance contract in accordance with § 19a BNotO an

227. *See* BT-Drucks. 16/3945, p. 57.

appointment as a notary is not possible. Similar rules can be found for lawyers (§ 12 paragraph 2 sentence 2 federal lawyers' act (*Bundesrechtsanwaltsordnung*, hereafter 'BRAO')), tax consultants (§ 14 paragraph 2 tax advisers act (*Steuerberatungsgesetz*, hereafter 'StBerG')), auditors (§ 16 paragraph 1 no. 3 law regulating the profession of auditors (*Wirtschaftsprueferordnung*, hereafter 'WPO')), and patent attorneys (§ 18 paragraph 2 patent attorneys act (*Patentanwaltsordnung*, hereafter 'PatAnwO')). Concerning the use of cars, the law requires that, prior to the registration of the car, the keeper must prove the conclusion of a motor liability insurance contract (§ 7 no. 4 PflVG in conjunction with § 3 FZV). A similar rule exists for the keeper of an aircraft (§ 8 paragraph 2 no. 3 air traffic licensing ordinance (*Luftverkehrszulassungsordnung*, hereafter 'LuftVZO'[228]). Air carriers will be granted a license to operate only on production of proof that the required liability insurance has been concluded (§ 20 paragraph 1 air traffic act (*Luftverkehrsgesetz*, hereafter 'LuftVG') in conjunction with § 62 paragraph 1 no. 8 LuftVZO).

III. Insurance for the Account of a Third Party

225. Whenever the policyholder makes the contract of insurance not only for his own account but also for account of a third party, only the policyholder is entitled to exercise the rights of the co-insured persons, as provided for in §§ 44 paragraph 1 sentence 2, 45 paragraphs 1 and 2 VVG. Furthermore § 45 paragraph 2 VVG states that the policyholder is authorised to receive benefits from the insurer and to assign the rights of the insured person without the agreement of the insured person if he is in possession of the insurance certificate. By contrast, pursuant § 44 paragraph 2 VVG the co-insured is entitled to the benefits if he/she in possession of the insurance certificate.

§5. Commencement of Cover

I. General Rule

226. The formation of the contract (*formeller Versicherungsbeginn*) must be distinguished from the commencement of cover, i.e., the point in time from which the insurer is obliged to provide coverage (*materieller Versicherungsbeginn*). According to § 10 VVG, unless otherwise agreed, the insurance cover shall commence at the start of the day on which the contract is concluded, i.e., 0 hrs 00 min. In practice, no contract is concluded at that time. Hence, the insurer always provides up to almost 24 hours retroactive insurance in terms of § 2 VVG (*see* paragraph 228).

228. BGBl. I 2008 I p. 1229.

II. Exceptions

A. *Waiting Periods*

227. Typically in health insurance (*see* paragraph 698), life insurance (*see* paragraph 736), occupational disability insurance (*see* paragraph 646), long-term care insurance and legal expenses insurance (*see* paragraph 486) the cover is limited by the exclusion of certain risks for a so-called waiting period (*Wartezeit*). For example, in life insurance there is no cover for suicide within three years after the conclusion of the contract (§ 161 paragraph 1 VVG). In health insurance contracts, § 197 paragraph 1 VVG limits the length of the waiting periods. They shall not exceed three months as general waiting periods in respect of comprehensive health insurance, daily hospital allowance insurance and daily sickness allowance insurance, and eight months as special qualifying periods in respect of childbirth, psychotherapy, dental treatment, dental prostheses and orthodontics (*see* paragraph 698). In the case of long-term care insurance, the waiting period may not exceed three years.

B. *Retroactive Insurance*

228. According to § 2 paragraph 1 VVG the parties may agree on insurance cover for a period of time prior to the conclusion of the contract. If the insurer knows when submitting its acceptance that the occurrence of the insured event is impossible, it is not entitled to an insurance premium. If the policyholder knows when submitting his/her offer that an insured event has already occurred, the insurer is not obligated to effect payment.

Chapter 4. Obligations of the Policyholder

229. There are two types of obligations of the policyholder under German insurance law. On the one hand there are *Obliegenheiten* (hereafter referred to as 'duty/duties'), on the other hand there are *Rechtspflichten* (hereafter referred to as 'obligation/s'). The main difference between these two concepts is that duties of the insured are unenforceable and their violation does not entitle the insurer to damages but may exempt the insurer from its obligation to provide coverage (for details *see* paragraph 241). Obligations are enforceable and their violation entitles the insurer to damages. In cases of an insurance for the account of a third party, the co-insured has only to observe duties (*see* paragraph 315).

§1. Payment of the Premium

230. There is basically only one obligation for the policyholder, i.e., to pay the premium. There are different types of premium. A single premium is one which the policyholder must pay on conclusion of the insurance contract and then no further premiums are due. For policies with regular premiums a distinction is to be made between the premium that has to be paid for the first insurance period (first premium) and the premiums that must be paid upon the beginning of a new insurance period (renewal premiums). According to § 12 VVG the period of insurance shall be one year unless otherwise agreed by the parties.

I. Premium Due Dates

231. Pursuant to § 33 paragraph 1 VVG the policyholder must pay a single premium or the first premium without delay 14 days after receipt of the insurance policy. The due date of the renewal premium depends on the period insured and special agreements between the parties (e.g., payment within 4 weeks of the commencement of the new insurance period or only after the receipt of an invoice). If the policyholder does not pay the single, first or renewal premium on the due date the insurer may sue the policyholder for the premium, plus interest and fees.

II. Non-payment or Late Premium Payment

232. There are two different regimes concerning the consequences following from the non-payment or late premium payment of the first/single premium and the renewal premium.

A. Non-payment or Late Payment of the Single or the First Premium

1. Right of Withdrawal

233. The delayed payment of the single or the first premium entitles the insurer to withdraw from the contract as long as the payment has not been made, unless the policyholder is not responsible for the non-payment (§ 37 paragraph 1 VVG). In other words the insurer's right of withdrawal expires at the latest with the payment of the first premium.

2. Release from Obligation to Perform

234. In case an insured event occurs before the payment has been made, the insurer is free from its obligation to perform, unless the policyholder is not responsible for the non-payment (§ 37 paragraph 2 sentence 1 VVG). It is important to note that the insurer is only released from its obligation if he had informed the policyholder of the legal consequences of non-payment of the premium in text form in a special notice or by means of a conspicuous note in the certificate of insurance (§ 37 paragraph 2 sentence 2 VVG).

B. Non-payment or Late Payment of a Renewal Premium

235. The delayed payment of a renewal premium alone does not entitle the insurer to immediately terminate the contract, nor is the insurer free from its obligation to perform. Only after the expiration of a deadline for payment of at least two weeks set by the insurer in text form (§ 126b BGB), the insurer is entitled to terminate the contract and is not obliged to perform in case of an insured event (§ 38 paragraph 1 sentence 1, paragraph 2 VVG). Where there a more than one policyholder the insurer must set a deadline in separate written notifications even if they have the same address.[229]

236. It is important to note that the setting of the deadline is only effective if the insurer indicates the individual amounts of the premium which are in arrears, the interest and costs as well as the legal consequences following from the expiration of the deadline (§ 38 paragraph 1 sentence 2 VVG). Where there are several insurances grouped in a single certificate of insurance (e.g., comprehensive health insurance, daily hospital allowance insurance and daily sickness allowance insurance), the amounts in arrears must be indicated for each kind of insurance.[230]

237. The termination shall become void if the policyholder makes the payment within one month after the contract has been terminated or, if the termination has

229. BGH, 8 Jan. 2014 – IV ZR 206/13, NJW 2014, p. 1010, para. 13.
230. OLG Duesseldorf, 17 Aug. 2010 – 4 U 2/10, VersR 2010, p. 1439 .

been linked to the setting of a deadline, within one month after the deadline expires. The subsequent payment does not affect the obligation of the insurer if the insured event takes place during the one month period i.e., the insurer remains released from its obligation to perform (§ 38 paragraph 3 sentence 3 VVG).

§2. Duties of the Policyholder

238. The duties of the insured (policyholder and co-insured persons) can be categorized in duties prior to the conclusion of the contract and during the contract period. The duties during the contract period can be sub-divided in duties to be observed prior to or after the occurrence of the insured event. A further distinction may be made between statutory duties set forth in the VVG and contractual duties. It is to be noted that due to the semi-mandatory regime of the statutory duties (*see* §§ 32, 87, 104 VVG) the insurers include verbatim terms in their standard terms and conditions. All of these duties shall enable the insurer to calculate an adequate premium and to make sure that there will be an equilibrium between the premium and the risk insured during the insurance period.[231]

I. Pre-contractual Duty of Disclosure

239. The rules dealing with the duty of disclosure prior to the conclusion of the contract and the consequences following from non-compliance with this duty can be found in §§ 19–22 VVG.

A. Scope and Limits of the Policyholder's Duty to Disclose Information

240. According to § 19 paragraph 1 sentence 1 VVG the policyholder must, at the time of the making of the contract, provide notice of only those circumstances known to him which are material for the insurer's decision to conclude the contract and about which the insurer has queried in text form. The policyholder is under no duty to volunteer information. Nor is he obliged to provide answers to oral questions. The questions must be specific enough, clear and concise (non-ambiguous) so that there is only one right answer. Moreover, the question must refer to present or past facts, not to future ones since there can be no certainty, only presumption.[232]

231. Cf. Langheid, in: Langheid/Wandt (eds), Muenchener Kommentar zum VVG, 2nd ed., vol. 1, C.H. Beck 2016, § 19 VVG n. 1.

232. For further details *see* Rolfs, in: Bruck/Moeller, Großkommentar zum VVG, 9th ed., vol. 1, DeGruyter 2008, § 19 VVG n. 28 et seq.

B. Consequences of the Breach of the Duty to Disclose Information

1. Termination or Modification of the Contract or Premium Increase

241. Where the policyholder deliberately or with gross negligence has made incorrect statements the insurer may withdraw from the contract (§ 19 paragraph 2 and 3 sentence 1 VVG). If the policyholder acted without fault or violated the duty with simple negligence, the insurer may terminate the contract with a one month's notice period (§ 19 paragraph 3 sentence 2 VVG). If the insurer terminates the contract, in accordance with § 39 paragraph 1 sentence 1 VVG it is entitled to that share of the premium for that period of insurance which corresponds to the period in which the insurance cover existed. In the case of withdrawal the insurer can demand the pro rata premium which it is entitled to until the withdrawal announcement is effective (§ 39 paragraph 1 sentence 2 VVG).

242. The insurer's right of withdrawal or termination is excluded, if, having known of the undisclosed circumstances, he would have concluded the contract, albeit on different terms and conditions (unless the policyholder acted deliberately) (§ 19 paragraph 4 sentence 1 VVG). In that case the insurer is entitled to modify the policy accordingly. The new conditions will upon request of the insurer take effect retroactively, and in the case the policyholder is at no fault, from the current insurance period (§ 19 paragraph 4 sentence 2 VVG). For example, if the policyholder forgot to declare a chronically asthmatic condition, although the insurer had asked about such conditions, the insurer is not permitted to withdraw from the contract, when it usually insures asthma sufferers with an extra premium. If the modifications led to an increase in the premiums payable by more than 10% or the insurer excludes the originally undisclosed risk from coverage, the policyholder may terminate the contract (§ 19 paragraph 6 VVG). Private health insurers' rights to terminate or modify policies are limited in that they have to demonstrate at least negligence on the part of policyholders (§ 194 paragraph 1 sentence 3 VVG).

243. The insurer must prove that the policyholder breached his duty of disclosure. If the insurer can prove it, the policyholder is under an onus of disproving the assumption of intent and gross negligence (*see* § 19 paragraph 3 sentence 1 VVG).

244. Insurers will only be entitled to the rights of withdrawal, termination or amendment of the policy if they have informed policyholders separately in text form (§ 126b BGB) of the consequences of the violation of the disclosure duty. There is no need, however, to inform the policyholder about the consequences of fraudulent non-compliance with this duty.[233] The insurer's right will be excluded if he or his agent (§ 70 VVG) is aware of the relevant circumstances at the time of contract conclusion (§ 19 paragraph 5 VVG). The same applies when the health insurer instructed a doctor to examine the policyholder.[234]

---

233. BGH, 12 Mar. 2014 – IV ZR 306/13, NJW 2014, p. 1452, para. 15.
234. Cf. BGH, 10 May 2017 – IV ZR 30/16, RuS 2017, p. 408, para. 13.

245. Moreover, the insurer must make use of his rights within one month after he received knowledge of the violation of the disclosure duty (§ 21 paragraph 1 sentence 1 VVG), and no later than five years from the conclusion of the contract (or three years for private health insurance policies) (§ 21 paragraph 3 VVG). In the case of intentional or fraudulent behaviour this period will be extended to ten years (§ 21 paragraph 3 VVG). The insurer must give reasons (i.e., circumstances) when asserting his rights (§ 21 paragraph 1 sentence 3 VVG). It is not prevented from subsequently specifying the reasons or relying on other grounds as long as the one-month period has not expired.[235]

2. Consequences in the Case of an Insured Event

246. If an insured event occurs prior to the insurer having exercised his right to withdraw from the contract, the insurer will be released from his obligation unless the grossly negligent or deliberate violation of the disclosure duty was neither causal for the occurrence nor for the ascertainment of the event insured or for the scope of the insurer's obligation to provide cover (§ 21 paragraph 2 sentence 1 VVG). In cases where the policyholder acted with fraudulent intent (*Arglist*), the insurer is released from his duty to perform under the policy even if there is no causal link between the loss and the non-disclosure (§ 21 paragraph 2 sentence 2 VVG). It does not follow from the plain language of the new rules but from the lack of the causal link requirement in cases of fraud that, where the (non-fraudulent) non-disclosure was not causal for the occurrence of the insured event but only for greater costs, the insurer is only released from his obligation to perform with regard to these costs.[236] Thus a distinction between deliberate and fraudulent non-disclosure needs to be drawn.

247. For example, where the holder of a health insurance policy ignored the question when asked by the insurer prior to the conclusion of the contract if he/she were taking drugs and grossly negligent or deliberately failed to disclose that he/she was on anticoagulant medication that thins the blood, the insurer would be released from his obligation to pay if the policyholder needed to be hospitalized because he/she had taken a drug overdose. The insurer, however, would be required to pay if the policyholder suffered a traumatic injury in a car accident except for the greater cost attributed to the non-disclosed medication (e.g., for extra-transfusions due to greater loss of blood volumes). If the policyholder acted fraudulently the insurer, however, would have the right to reject his/her claim in full. The loss of coverage for loss not connected to the fraudulently non-disclosed circumstances is based on the presumption that such harsh consequence would have a general preventive effect on policyholders.[237]

---

235. For further details, *see* Armbruester, in: Proelss/Martin, VVG, 30th ed., C.H. Beck 2018, § 21 VVG n. 13 et seq.
236. For a somewhat different view, *see* Rolfs, in: Bruck/Moeller, VVG, 9th ed., DeGruyter 2008, § 21 VVG n. 40.
237. Cf. BT-Drucks. 16/3945, p. 66.

3. Avoidance of the Contract on the Ground of Fraud

248. It is important to note that the right of the insurer to avoid the contract for fraudulent deception by the policyholder under § 123 BGB remains in force (§ 22 VVG). This situation triggers the question if the insurer can avoid a contract for deceit on the grounds that the policyholder, without having been asked a specific question by the insurer, did not disclose facts that he/she knew or should have known would have influenced the insurer's decision whether or not to take on the risk. In order to avoid overlap the courts have only found for fraud if, first, the conduct of the policyholder has been contrary to the insurer interests, and second, the policyholder is aware of the fact that his/her conduct possibly has an impact on the claim settlement.[238]

II. Duties During the contract

A. Duties to Be Observed Prior to the Occurrence of the Insured Event

1. Statutory Duty Not to Increase the Risk

249. The rules dealing with the increase of risk and the consequences following therefrom can be found in §§ 23–27 VVG, which are according to § 32 sentence 1 VVG semi-mandatory. These rules do not apply to apply to health insurance (§ 194 paragraph 1 sentence 2 VVG).

a. Forms of Risk Increase

250. § 23 VVG distinguishes between three different settings.

i. Conscious Increase of Risk by the Policyholder

251. § 23 paragraph 1 VVG deals with the situation where the policyholder consciously aggravate the risk insured or permit its aggravation by a third party without the consent of the insurer. This is the case when the homeowner and holder of a homeowners' comprehensive insurance covering damage from, *inter alia*, fire changes after the conclusion of the insurance contract the use of commercial building into a brothel.[239] § 23 paragraph 1 VVG does not apply to transport insurance (*see* paragraph 357).

---

238. Cf. BGH, 21 Dec. 2012 – IV ZR 97/11, VersR 2013, p. 175, para. 29; BGH, 4 May 2009, VersR 2009, p. 968, para. 9.
239. *See* BGH, 22 Jun. 2012 – IV ZR 150/11, RuS 2012, p. 489, para. 11.

ii. Unconscious Increase of Risk by the Policyholder

252. § 23 paragraph 2 VVG covers the case where the policyholder only subsequently realises that he/she has aggravated the risk insured or the he/she has permitted its aggravation by a third party. This is the case when the owner of a production site and holder of environmental liability insurance realises only after commissioning of the production facility that harmful vapours are released from the site.

iii. Increase of Risk Not Caused by the Policyholder

253. Finally, § 23 paragraph 3 VVG deals with the situation where the risk increased independently of the policyholder's will, e.g., if the owner of a car and holder of a comprehensive car insurance covering, *inter alia*, the risk of theft loses the key of the car.

b. Requirements for Risk Increase

254. While it follows from § 27 VVG that the aggravation of the risk insured is only of relevance if it is material, the VVG does not provide an definition of what circumstances amount to an increase of risk. According to settled case law, there is an increase of risk in the meaning of § 23 VVG if after the conclusion of the contract the circumstances which were the basis for the calculation of the premium have changed to the effect that the probability of the occurrence of an insured event, an increase of damage, or an unjustified insurance claim has increased to such an extent that the insurer would have not concluded the contract at all or for a higher insurance premium only.[240]

255. It is important to note that the increase must be of certain duration. A short-term or temporary increase does not amount to an increase of risk in the sense of § 23 VVG. The single use of car under the influence of alcohol therefore cannot be regarded as an increase of risk.[241] In life insurance (§ 158 paragraph 1 VVG), occupational disability insurance (§ 176 VVG) and accident insurance (§ 181 paragraph 1 VVG) only such changes of the circumstances of the risk, as by express agreement in text form (§ 126b BGB) are to be regarded as increase of risk, constitute an increase of risk.

c. Consequences of the Breach of the Duty Not to Increase the Risk or the Duty to Notify the Insurer of Increase of Risk

256. While the conscious aggravation of the risk insured in itself constitutes a violation of the policyholder's duty not to increase the risk without consent of the insurer, in situations where the policyholder only later realises that he/she has increased the risk or where the risk was increased independently of his/her will, the

240. BGH, 16 Jun. 2010 – IV ZR 229/09, RuS 2010, p. 331, para. 16; BGH, 5 Jun. 2004 – IV ZR 183/03, RuS 2004, p. 328 (with further references).
241. Cf. BGH, 18 Oct. 1952 -II ZR 72/52, VersR 1952, pp. 387, 388.

failure to inform the insurer about the risk increase without undue delay in accordance with § 23 paragraph 2 and 3 VVG constitutes the violation of a duty. The consequences of the breach of one of the afore-mentioned duties are set forth in §§ 24–26 VVG.

i. Termination or Modification of the Contract or Premium Increase

257. In case of the policyholder has consciously aggravated the risk insured, the insurer is entitled to terminate the contract without prior notice. If the policyholder has acted neither intentionally nor with gross negligence, the insurer may terminate the contract subject to a notice period of one month (§ 24 paragraph 1 VVG). Irrespective of the degree of fault, the one month notice period also applies if the policyholder unconsciously increased the risk or did not cause the increase of risk (§ 24 paragraph 2 VVG). In the alternative, the insurer may demand an insurance premium commensurate with the increase of the risk, or may exclude insurance cover for the increased risk (§ 25 paragraph 1 VVG). In the absence of any case law, the majority of legal writers take the view that such an exclusion has no retroactive but prospective effect.[242]

258. The right of termination or to increase the premium or to exclude the cover must be exercised within one month after the insurer learns of the increase of the risk or if the situation existing prior to the increase is restored (§§ 24 paragraph 1, 25 paragraph 1 sentence 2 VVG). If the insurance premium increases by more than 10% or the insurer excludes insurance cover for the increased risk, the policyholder, in turn, is entitled to terminate the contract without prior notice within one month of receipt of the communication from the insurer (§ 25 paragraph 2 sentence 1 VVG).

ii. Consequences in the Case of an Insured Event

259. Depending on the degree of fault and the extent to which the increase of the risk had an influence on the insured event and the insurer's obligation to perform, the insurer may be released from its obligation to provide cover. The details can be found in § 26 VVG. If the breach of the duty not to increase the risk or of the duty to notify the insurer of any risk increase is based only on the policyholder's ordinary negligence, the insurer must provide full insurance cover.

260. Where the policyholder intentionally breached one of his duties the insurer is released from performance if the increase of the risk led to the insured event (§ 26 paragraph 1 sentence 1 VVG). If the increase of risk did not cause the insured event but led to a greater loss, the insurer is released to the extent the loss has become bigger (§ 26 paragraph 3 no. 1 VVG).

---

242. Karczewski, in: Rueffer/Halbach/Schimikowski (eds), VVG, 3rd ed., Nomos 2015, § 25 n. 2; Wrabetz/Reusch, in: Langheid/Rixecker (eds), VVG, 5th ed., C.H. Beck 2016, § 25 VVG n. 9, 16;; Looschelders, in: Looschelders/Pohlmann (eds), VVG, 3rd ed., Carl Heymanns 2016, § 25 VVG n. 6; Armbruester, in: Proelss/Martin, VVG, 30th ed., C.H. Beck 2018, § 25 VVG n. 8.

261. There is some discussion among scholars on the question as to whether a causal connection is required in the case of fraud on the side of the policyholder. Some authors take the view the insurer is free from its obligation to perform even if the increased risk has not led to the insured event or has not caused a greater loss, where the policyholder fraudulently breached his/her duties.[243] They rely on §§ 21 paragraph 2 S. 2, 28 paragraph 2 sentence 2 and 82 paragraph 4 sentence 1 VVG. According to these provisions, which deal with the statutory duties to disclose information prior to the conclusion of the contract and to avert and minimize loss upon the occurrence of the insured event and with contractual duties, no causal link is required in the case of a fraudulent breach by the policyholder. In the authors' view these provisions reflect a general principle and thus must be applied by means of analogy to the breach of duties set forth in § 23 VVG. There is no case law on that issue.

262. In the event of a grossly negligent breach, the insurer is only entitled to reduce the insurance cover in proportion to the severity of gross negligence within a band of 0% to 100% (principle of proportionality) (§ 26 paragraph 1 sentence 2 VVG). Like in the case of a wilful breach, there must be a causal link between the breach of the duty and the insured event or the loss for which the policyholder claims performance.

263. With regard to the burden of proof it is to be noted that the insurer must prove that the policyholder breached one of his duties under § 23 VVG. If the insurer provides evidence, § 26 paragraph 1 sentence 2 VVG states the burden of proof that there was no gross negligence is on the policyholder, i.e., there is an assumption that the policyholder acted grossly negligently. It is on the insurer to prove that the policyholder breached his/her duty not to increase the risk intentionally. On the other hand, it is up to the policyholder to prove that he acted only with ordinary negligence. Moreover, the policyholder must prove that his/her breach did not cause the insured event, nor did it led to a greater loss.

264. There is some dispute of whether there is not only an assumption of gross negligence but also of intent when the policyholder breaches the duty to notify the insurer of the increase of the risk.[244] The KG, in its judgment dated 17 July 2016, held that there is an assumption of intent, i.e., the policyholder must prove that he

---

243. Loacker, in: Schwintowski/Broemmelmeyer (eds), VVG, 3d ed., ZAP VERLAG 2017, § 26 VVG n. 17; Looschelders, in: Looschelders/Pohlmann (eds), VVG, 3rd ed., Carl Heymanns 2016, § 26 VVG n. 19; Langheid, in: Langheid/Rixecker (eds), VVG, 5th ed., C.H. Beck 2016, § 26 VVG n. 9.

244. *See* Wandt, Versicherungsrecht, 6th ed., Vahlen 2016 n. 867; Looschelders, in: Looschelders/Pohlmann (eds), VVG, 3rd ed., Carl Heymanns 2016, § 26 VVG n. 15; for a different view Felsch, Neuregelung von Obliegenheiten und Gefahrerhoehung, RuS 2007, pp. 485, 488; Karczewski, in: Rueffer/Halbach/Schimikowski (eds), VVG, 3rd ed., Nomos 2015, § 26 n. 18.

was not acting wilfully.[245] It remains to be seen how the BGH will deal with this issue (there is an appeal against the decision of the KG pending before the BGH).[246]

2. Contractual Duties

265. Beside the statutory duties not to increase the risk and to notify the insurer of an increase of risk, the parties to a contract of insurance always agree on precautionary duties in the sense of § 28 paragraph 1 VVG for the purpose of reducing the risk or for the purpose of preventing an increase of risk. For example, in cyber risk policies the parties commonly agree that the policyholder must regularly update his/her antivirus and anti-malware software. The consequences arising from the breach of a precautionary duty are laid down in § 28 paragraph 2 and 3 VVG. They are very similar to those under §§ 24–26 VVG. § 28 VVG is according to § 32 sentence 1 VVG a semi-mandatory rule.

a. Termination of the Contract

266. In case the policyholder's breach of a precautionary duty was intentional or grossly negligent the insurer is entitled to terminate the contract. The policyholder is under an onus of disproving the assumption of intent and gross negligence (§ 28 paragraph 1 VVG).

b. Consequences in the Case of an Insured Event

267. The insurer is released from providing coverage if it proves that the policyholder intentionally breached its contractual obligation (§ 28 paragraph 2 sentence 1 VVG). In cases of a grossly negligent breach of a contractual duty, the insurer is entitled to reduce the cover under the contract in proportion to the severity of gross negligence (§ 28 paragraph 2 sentence 2 VVG). If the policyholder breached a contractual duty fraudulently, the insurer is free from its obligation to provide cover (§ 28 paragraph 3 sentence 3 VVG).

268. In respect of coverage (as opposed to the insurer's right of termination) the policyholder is only under an onus of disproving the assumption of gross negligence (§ 28 paragraph 2 sentence 2 VVG). While the insurer must provide evidence that the policyholder acted with intent or fraudulently, it is up to the policyholder to prove that the breach had no influence on the occurrence or determination of the insured event, or on the determination or the extent of the insurer's obligation to pay indemnity (§ 28 paragraph 3 sentence 1 VVG).

---

245. KG, 15 Jul. 2016 – 6 U 24/16, RuS 2017, p. 582.
246. The file number is IV ZR 207/16.

c. Distinction Between Contractual Duties and Exclusions

269. Contractual duties need to be distinguished from exclusions. Whenever a clause makes the coverage dependent on a certain conduct of the insured it qualifies as a duty, whereas clauses qualify as exclusions if they limit the coverage to a certain risk irrespective of whether or not the insured can influence the risk. According to settled case law for the distinction between duties and exclusions neither the wording nor is the heading of relevance under which the clauses are set out in the policy. Following the rules of interpretation (*see* paragraph 162) what matters is the understanding of an average policyholder. If from his/her viewpoint a certain conduct is expected the clause qualifies as a duty.[247]

270. On that basis, the BGH, it its judgment dated 18 May 2011 held that the exclusion of liability for ships under § 132 VVG 1908, which is almost identical with § 138 VVG, is in fact a duty.[248] According to § 132 VVG 1908 the insurer is not liable for a loss resulting from the ship's sailing in unseaworthy condition or improperly equipped or manned. The BGH argued that it is up to the policyholder to make sure that the ship is seaworthy, and for that reason the provision requires policyholders to take precautionary measures. As a consequence the BGH qualified the legal provision as hidden duty (*verhuellte Obliegenheit*) the violation of which releases the insurer from coverage only if the policyholder was at fault. Even though the judgment deals with the qualification of legal provisions, the rationale can be transferred one-to-one to standard terms that included § 132 VVG 1908 verbatim in their standard terms and conditions.

271. In light of the semi-mandatory regime of § 28 VVG the distinction between duties and exclusions is very important for insurers. A clause in an insurance policy which is entitled as exclusion or placed under the heading 'exclusions' but in fact imposes a duty on the policyholder is intransparent in terms of § 307 paragraph 1 sentence 2 BGB, since the placement of such clause in a wrong context is likely to deter the innocent policyholder from exercising its rights under the insurance contract (*see* paragraph 205).[249]

B. Duties to Be Observed after the Occurrence of the Insured Event

1. Statutory Duties

272. The statutory duties to be observed after the occurrence of the insured event are aimed at enabling the insurer to investigate the claim before the evidence disappears (also with regard to possible recourse claims against third parties who caused the damage), to mitigate the extent of damages, and to avoid anything that could result in costs increasing.

247. BGH, 18 May 2011 – IV ZR 16/09, RuS 2012, p. 130, para. 29.
248. *Ibid.*, para. 30.
249. Cf. R. Koch, Abschied von der Rechtsfigur der verhuellten Obliegenheit, VersR 2014, pp. 283, 291; Felsch, Verhuellte Obliegenheiten – ein Nachruf, RuS 2015, pp. 53, 59.

a. Duty to Notify of the Occurrence of the Insured Event and to Provide Information

273. According to §§ 30 and 31 VVG the policyholder must immediately provide notice of the insured event and, upon the insurer's request, provide detailed information that puts the insurer in the position to ascertain the insured event and the extent of its obligation to perform. These provisions, however, do not contain sanctions in case of non-observance of these duties. For that reason the insurers always incorporate the statutory duties to give notice and information in their standard terms and further include a clause stating that in the event of a violation of these duties, the consequences of § 28 paragraph 2 and 3 VVG apply. According to § 28 paragraph 4 VVG, however, the insurer can only claim (partial) release from the obligation to perform if it has previously pointed out to the policyholder in text form (§ 126b BGB) the consequences of a breach of the duties to notify and to notify. There is no need to inform the policyholder about the consequences of fraudulent non-compliance with these duties.[250]

b. Duty to Avert and Mitigate Losses

274. The duty to avert and mitigate losses is set forth in § 82 paragraph 1 VVG. This provision is supplemented by § 82 paragraph 2 sentence 1 VVG which states that the policyholder must seek instructions from the insurer if the circumstances permit, and to follow the instructions of the insurer, where reasonable. If the policyholder fails to comply with these duties the consequences set forth in § 82 paragraph 3 and 4 VVG are identical with those under § 28 paragraphs 2 and 3 VVG (*see* paragraph 267). The standard of care is that of an uninsured person in similar circumstances.[251]

275. It is important to note that the insurer is obliged to reimburse the policyholder for the expenses incurred under § 82 paragraph 1 VVG to the extent that the policyholder could deem them necessary under the circumstances (§ 83 paragraph 1 sentence 1 VVG). Limited to property insurance, [252] pursuant to § 90 VVG the policyholder may even claim expenses incurred to prevent an imminent insured event from happening or to minimize its impacts. These rules also apply when the policyholder's attempts to avert or mitigate the losses were unsuccessful. The reimbursement is limited to the sum insured unless the expenses result from the policyholder's following the insurer's instructions (§ 83 paragraph 3 VVG).

c. Duty to Safeguard Recourse Against Third Parties

276. If the policyholder has a claim against a third party (wrongdoer) for indemnification of his/her loss, the insurer is subrogated to the claim to the extent that it indemnifies the policyholder for the loss (§ 86 paragraph 1 sentence 1 VVG). § 86

250. BGH, 12 Mar. 2014 – IV ZR 306/13, NJW 2014, p. 1452, para. 16.
251. Cf. BGH, 23.6.2004 – IV ZR 219/03, RuS 2004, pp. 376, 379 (with regard to exclusion pursuant to § 61 VVG 1908, which has been replaced without chance by § 81 VVG).
252. BT-Drucks. 16/3945, p. 82.

paragraph 2 sentence 1 VVG requires from the policyholder to safeguard his claim for damages in accordance with the applicable form and time requirements, and to assist the insurer wherever necessary in asserting the claim. If the policyholder fails to comply with these duties the consequences set forth in § 86 paragraph 2 sentence 1 VVG are identical with those under § 28 paragraph 2 VVG, i.e., the insurer can claim (partial) release from its obligation to perform.

277. It is important to note that the scope of § 86 paragraph 1 and 2 VVG is limited to indemnity insurance. The concept of subrogation is aimed at preventing unjust enrichment of the insured by virtue of recovery from both the insurer and the wrongdoer. There is no subrogation where the policyholder makes no double recovery (so-called *Kongruenzprinzip*). For example, comprehensive motor vehicle insurance covers damage to the insured's car caused by a third party but not for the extra costs for renting a car while the policyholder's car is being repaired. Thus only the policyholder's claim against the wrongdoer for the costs of repair is subrogated to the insurer upon compensation.

278. It follows from § 86 paragraph 1 sentence 2 VVG according to which the subrogation of the claim may not be to the detriment of the policyholder, that the latter's claim against the wrongdoer for compensation of the extra costs not covered takes precedence over the insurer's subrogated claim (*Quotenvorrecht*) where the wrongdoer has not the means to satisfy both claims.[253]

279. Under § 86 paragraph 3 VVG whenever the wrongdoer is a person with whom the policyholder is sharing a common household when the loss occurs, there is no subrogation unless that person intentionally caused the loss.

2. Contractual Duties

280. Beside the statutory duties, the parties to a contract of insurance, in practice, agree on further duties which largely specify the existing and sometimes supplement statutory duties such as to provide a list of the stolen property or to report the theft to the police. Failure to observe such duties may (partially) release the insurer from its obligation to perform in accordance with § 28 paragraph 2 and 3 VVG.

253. *See* BGH, 25 Nov. 2009 – XII ZR 211/08, RuS 2010, p. 105, para. 14.

Chapter 5. Obligations of the Insurer

281. The obligations of the insurer can be categorized in main and ancillary obligations.

§1. Main Obligations

I. Paying out the Fixed Sum or Indemnifying the Policyholder

282. As described earlier (*see* paragraph 172), depending on whether there is an insurance of fixed sums or an indemnity insurance the main obligation of the insurer is to pay out the fixed sum (e.g., life insurance, occupational disablement insurance and accident insurance) or to indemnify the policyholder when a loss is suffered (e.g., property insurance, liability insurance, transport insurance, comprehensive health insurance). In general, the insurance indemnity will be made by the payment of money unless the parties have agreed on restitution in kind (i.e., repair). Moreover, in indemnity insurance the insurer is obliged to reimburse the policyholder's expenses for averting and mitigating the loss (§ 83 VVG) and the expenses caused by the investigation and ascertainment of the loss for which the insurer is liable and to the extent that they were necessary under the circumstances (§ 85 VVG).

II. Limitations

283. In the case of indemnity insurance, there are two principles which can limit the obligation of the insurer. The insurer is generally not obliged first to pay more than the amount necessary to indemnify the losses suffered by the policyholder, and second to pay more than the maximum stated in the policy (sum insured).

A. Determination of the Loss

284. In liability insurance the loss of the policyholder is determined by the amount of the policyholder's liability. In property insurance the calculation of the loss depends on whether or not the parties have agreed on the market value of the goods at the time the insured event occurred (*Zeitwertversicherung*). In that case, § 88 VVG states that the loss shall be deemed to be the amount which the policyholder must spend upon occurrence of the insured event to replace or to restore the insured property less the amount resulting from the difference between old and new. In most property insurances the parties, however, have agreed that there will be no reduction in value resulting from the depreciation. In that case the insurer is going to pay the actual costs of replacing insured property with new objects of the same kind and quality ('new for old' policies) (*Neuwertversicherung*). Mainly in the area of transport insurance the parties may fix the insured value by agreement at a certain amount (*taxe*) which is regarded as the value of the insured interest at the time of the occurrence of the insured event (§ 76 VVG).

B. Under- and Over-Insurance

285. If the sum insured is considerably less than – either the market or the new for old – value of the goods at the time when the insured event occurred (under-insurance), the insurer shall only be liable in the proportion that the sum insured bears to this value (§ 75 VVG). Whenever the sum insured considerably exceeds the value of the goods (over-insurance), each contracting party may request that the sum insured be reduced with immediate effect in order to eliminate the over-insurance, thereby also reducing the premium proportionally (§ 74 VVG).

286. The provisions on under- and over-insurance as well as on the taxe do not apply to liability insurance contracts since the determination of the insured value is not possible. Liability insurers limit their obligation to indemnify the policyholder by means of claims series clauses (*see* paragraph 382) and aggregation clauses (*see* paragraph 381).

C. Multiple Insurance

287. Multiple insurance does not increase the insurer's liability. Whenever an interest is insured against the same risk with more than one insurer and the sums insured exceed the insured value (property insurance), or if for other reasons the sum of damages which would have to be paid by the insurer in the absence of the other insurance exceeds the total loss (liability insurance), according to § 78 paragraph 1 VVG the insurers are jointly and severally liable in that each insurer must pay the sum in accordance with its contract, but the policyholder cannot demand more than the total amount of the loss.

§2. Ancillary Obligations

288. The ancillary obligations of the insurer can be divided in the obligation to provide advice prior to the conclusion of the contract and during the term of the policy (§§ 6, 6a, 7c, 7d VVG) and in the obligation to provide information about the contents of the insurance contract (§ 7, 7a, 7b, 7d VVG). Pursuant to § 1a VVG, which transposes Article 17 IDD into German law (*see* paragraph 37), insurers must carry out direct distribution honestly, fairly and professionally in accordance with the best interests of their customers.

I. Obligation of the Insurer to Provide Advice and Documentation

A. *Obligation of the Insurer to Provide Advice and Documentation Prior to the Conclusion of the Contract*

1. Material Scope of the Obligation

289. According to § 6 paragraph 1 sentence 1 VVG, the insurer is required to give advice to the policyholder before the conclusion of an insurance contract if there is a reason to do so, taking into account all relevant circumstances of the case including the demands and needs of the policyholder, the nature and complexity of the envisaged insurance contract and the amount of the premium to be paid. The advice must be provided in a clear and comprehensible manner (§ 6 paragraph 2 sentence 1 VVG) and documented in text form (§ 6 paragraph 1 sentence 2 VVG in conjunction with § 126b BGB). The documentation requirement is intended to facilitate the production of evidence for the policyholder, e.g., if he/she claims for damages for inappropriate advice.

290. There is some debate among scholars on how much consideration should be given to the amount of the premium in determining the obligation to provide advice.[254] Does it mean that insurers offering private general liability insurance for a premium of no more than EUR 70 per anno owe no or very little advice even though the liability insurance is of existential importance and difficult to understand for the customer due to its complex nature? There is no clear answer to that question. Since it is to be expected that the insurer will consider the cost of advice as a further determinant for insurance premium pricing, it is ultimately up to the policyholder to pay for the advice. For that reason, the premium – as little as it may be – should be of no relevance when it comes to the question of whether or not the advice was reasonable.

291. Upon the implementation of the IDD, the obligations of the insurer towards the customer are specified in greater details in §§ 6a, 7c VVVG (insured based investment products) and § 7d VVG (group insurance). These provisions apply whenever the insurer is directly involved in the insurance distribution activities.

2. Waiver of the Right to Receive Advice and/or Documentation

292. Policyholders may waive their right to receive advice and/or documentation by issuing a separate written declaration to this effect (§ 6 paragraph 3 VVG). Such waiver, however, is only valid if the insurer refers in the same document to the disadvantageous effects of the waiver (e.g., the above-mentioned evidentiary problems). In this way, policyholders are protected from hasty waivers.

254. Pohlmann, Viel Laerm um nichts - Beratungspflichten nach § 6 VVG und das Verhaeltnis zwischen Beratungsaufwand und Praemie, VersR 2009, pp. 327 et seq.

293. There is disagreement among scholars over whether a waiver by means of a standard clause drafted by the insurer is permitted or the waiver must be made as a result of individual negotiations. Those who believe that no individually negotiated waiver is required argue that otherwise the option to waive would be superfluous since such waiver would always qualify as standard clause as defined under the German law of general conditions of business.[255] However, if it is the policyholder who tells the insurer that he does not need advice it seems questionable whether a pre-formulated waiver signed by the policyholder indeed qualifies as standard clause. On the other hand, if the insurer realizes that the policyholder's request for a waiver is based on his misconceptions, e.g., about the extent of coverage, there can be no doubt that the insurer must advise him accordingly. As the latter example shows, the reasonableness of the advice depends on the circumstances of the specific case. A waiver by means of standard clause without having interviewed the policyholder therefore does not comply with essential basic principles of the advisory obligation rule. Such a waiver places the policyholder at an unreasonable disadvantage und is therefore invalid.[256]

B. Obligation of the Insurer to Provide Advice and Documentation During the Term of the Policy

294. According to § 6 paragraph 4 VVG the obligation of the insurer to provide advice continue for the entire term of the insurance agreement whenever the insurer realises that the policyholder requires information and advice because e.g., it became evident he/she has a wrong perception about the insurance coverage. [257] That means that the insurer does not have a general obligation to question and counsel, but only one that arises from a specific situation. There must be indications from which the insurer can draw further conclusions. In the view of the LG Wuppertal the issuance of new standard terms, which provide better coverage than the standard terms included into the original insurance contract, do not give a reason for the insurer to provide advice to the policyholder.[258] If it becomes apparent to the insurer that the policyholder is possibly or actually underinsured the insurer has to advice

255. Muenkel, in: Rueffer/Halbach/Schimikowski (eds), VVG, 3d ed., Nomos 2015, § 6 VVG n. 31; Gaul, Zum Abschluss des Versicherungsvertrags, VersR 2007, pp. 21, 23; Funck, Ausgewaehlte Fragen aus dem Allgemeinen Teil zum neuen VVG aus der Sicht einer Rechtsabteilung, VersR 2008, pp. 163, 166; Blankenburg, Verzicht auf Beratung und Informationsrechte nach dem neuen VVG, VersR 2008, p. 1146; Armbruester in: Langheid/Wandt (eds), VVG, vol. 1, 2nd ed., C.H. Beck 2016, § 6 n. 170.

256. *See* Schimikowski, VVG-Reform: Die vorvertraglichen Informationspflichten des Versicherers und das Rechtzeitigkeitserfordernis, RuS 2007, pp. 133, 136 et seq. (regarding § 7 VVG); Franz, Das Versicherungsvertragsrecht im neuen Gewand, VersR 2008, pp. 298, 300.

257. Cf. OLG Karlsruhe, 15 Jan. 2013 – 12 U 121/12, VersR 2013, pp. 885, 886; OLG Saarbruecken, 19 October 2011 – 5 U 71/11, VersR 2012, p. 1029; LG Hamm, 12 Aug. 2015 – 20 U 149/15, zfs 2016 p. 449.

258. OLG Karlsruhe, 15. Jan. 2013 – 12 U 121/12, VersR 2013, pp. 885, 886.

the policyholder.[259] The policyholder may in individual cases, i.e., not by means of a standard term, waive the right to advice by written declaration.

C. *Consequences in Cases of Breach of the Obligation to Provide Advice and Documentation*

295. If the insurer breaches its obligation to provide advice and documentation, it is liable to indemnify the policyholder for any loss or damage resulting therefrom (§ 6 paragraph 5 sentence 1 VVG). Would the policyholder not have concluded the contract if he/she had been advised properly by the insurer, the policyholder may demand cancellation of the contract, repayment of premiums and/or lost profits. Where the principles of the 'Gewohnheitsrechtliche Erfuellungshaftung' (*see* paragraph 55) apply, the policyholder may demand performance from the insurer.

296. In the case the insurer uses insurance agents to fulfil its duties, any bad advice of the insurance agent, which according to § 278 BGB acts as a vicarious agent of the insurer, is imputed to the insurer. Since the agent according to § 61 VVG also owes pre-contractual advice and documentation towards the policyholder (but no advice during the term of the policy, *see* paragraph 776), the insurer and its agent are joint debtors[260] and general contract law applies (§§ 421 et seq. BGB). If the agent fulfils his own advisory obligations he also satisfies the insurer's advisory obligations (§ 422 BGB).

D. *Personal Scope of the Obligation to Provide Advice and Documentation*

297. Insurers' advisory and documentation obligations towards policyholders are not restricted to private costumers but also apply towards businesses. If the contract is concluded via a broker on behalf of the policyholder, the insurer is, however, released from its obligations (§ 6 paragraph 6 VVG). Furthermore, insurers' obligations to provide advice to the policyholder and to document such advice do not apply to distance contracts within the meaning of § 312b paragraphs 1 and 2 BGB and policies covering large risks within the meaning of § 210 paragraph 2 VVG (*see* paragraph 29). Whenever the insurer realises that the policyholder is misled, the insurer is according to the principle of good faith (§ 242 BGB) nevertheless obliged to correct the misconception.[261]

---

259. Rudy, in: Proelss/Martin, VVG, 30th ed., 2018, § 6 n. 70; Armbruester, in: Langheid/Wandt (eds), VVG, vol. 1, 2nd ed., C.H. Beck 2016, § 6 VVG n. 351.
260. Werber, § 6 VVG und die Haftung des Versicherers fuer Fehlberatung durch Vermittler, VersR 2008, p. 285.
261. Armbruester in: Langheid/Wandt (eds), VVG, vol. 1, 2nd ed., C.H. Beck 2016, § 6 VVG n. 352; Rixecker, in: Langheid/Rixecker (eds), VVG, 5th ed., C.H. Beck 2016, § 6 VVG n. 37).

298. Was the insurance contract negotiated by an insurance broker, and during the term of the insurance cover the contract between the policyholder and the broker ceases to exist, the insurer must comply with § 6 paragraph 4 VVG.[262] Such a situation becomes relevant upon the opening of insolvency proceedings against the assets of the policyholder because in that case the brokerage contract comes to an end (§§ 115, 116 insolvency act (*Insolvenzordnung*, hereafter 'InsO')) whereas the contract of insurance continues.[263]

II. Insurer's Obligation to Provide Information

299. The insurer must inform the policyholder about the contents of the insurance contract which includes first and foremost the provision of the insurance certificate and the standard terms and conditions of insurance (§ 7 paragraph 1 VVG). The insurer further has to provide information as set out in the VVG-InfoV (*see* paragraph 300). Additional information on cross-selling (§ 7a VVG) and group insurance (§ 7d VVG) must be provided.

A. *Material Scope of the Obligation to Provide Information*

1. Ordinance on the Obligation to Supply Information Pertaining to Insurance Contracts

300. The VVG-InfoV requirements on the provision of information go beyond what is required under the insurance directives[264] and the distance selling directives.[265] The VVG-InfoV provides for information duties:

- for the entire insurance sector (§ 1 VVG-InfoV);
- in connection with life insurance, occupational disablement insurance, accident insurance and with health insurance policies (§§ 2, 3 VVG-InfoV);
- for communication over telephone (§ 5 VVG-InfoV); and
- during the term of the policy (§ 6 VVG-InfoV).

262. Armbruester in: Langheid/Wandt (eds), VVG, vol. 1, 2nd ed., C.H. Beck 2016, § 6 VVG n. 351.
263. Huber in: Gottwald (ed.), Insolvenzrechts-Handbuch, 5th ed., C.H. Beck 2015, § 36 n. 42 et seq.; Neuhaus, Berufsunfaehigkeitsversicherung, 3rd ed., C.H. Beck 2014, Ch. V n. 46.
264. Directive 92/49/EEC of 18 June 1992 on the coordination of laws, regulations and administrative provisions relating to direct insurance other than life assurance and amending Directives 73/239/EEC and 88/357/EEC (Third Non-life Insurance Directive) (O.J., 11 August 1992, L 228/1) and Directive 2002/83/EC of 5 November 2002 concerning life assurance (O.J., 19 December 2002, L 345/1).
265. Directive 2002/65/EC of 23 September 2002 concerning the distance marketing of consumer financial services and amending Directive 90/619/EEC and Directives 97/7/EC and 98/27/EC (O.J., 9 October 2002, L 271/16).

301. Moreover, the VVG-InfoV requires from the insurer to provide a brief product information sheet (*Produktinformationsblatt*) with the key details of the insurance cover (§ 4 VVG-InfoV).

2. Time of the Provision of Information

302. The information must be given to the policyholder 'in good time' (*rechtzeitig*) prior to their making an offer of a contract. In determining what is 'in good time' the insurer need to consider the importance and the complexity of the information to the policyholder in helping him to decide whether the contract meets his needs. The policyholder must have sufficient time to examine the information before finally giving his formal acceptance. Some authors, however, take the view that it is only necessary to hand out the statutorily prescribed information prior to making an offer. They argue that it is up to the policyholder to decide whether he feels sufficiently informed and makes an offer or not. That does not seem to be the right approach to the legislative intent behind the new rule which is first and foremost aimed at policyholder self-protection.[266]

303. The 'in good time' requirement brings an end to the pre-reform practice of sending the policyholder all contracting documents only along with the insurance policy. Under this so-called policy model, the policyholder applied for the policy without having received the general conditions of insurance and further prescribed information. The insurer then accepted the application and sent his general conditions as well as all other contractual documents to the policyholder.

3. Waiver of the Right to Receive Information

304. The policyholder may waive the right to be informed prior to the conclusion of the contract in cases where he/she needs to receive insurance coverage as soon as possible and has no need for extensive information, e.g., because he/she finds the desired policy easy to understand or because he/she has already informed herself/himself thoroughly (§ 7 paragraph 1 sentence 3 VVG). Any such waiver must be expressly made in writing as a separate declaration and, like in the case of advice, be individually negotiated (*see* paragraph 293). A standard form waiver is thus invalid.[267] Whether this provision, as far it allows individually negotiated waivers, is applicable to distance selling policies is questionable since Article 12 paragraph 1 of the financial services distance selling directive provides that 'consumers may not waive the rights conferred on them by this directive'.[268]

---

266. *See* BT-Drucks. 16/3945, pp. 47 et seq.
267. *Ibid.*, pp. 60 et seq.
268. Cf. Doerner/Staudinger, Kritische Bemerkungen zum Referentenentwurf eines Gesetzes zur Reform des Versicherungsvertragsrechts, WM 2006, pp. 1710, 1712; Schimikowski, VVG-Reform

305. If a waiver is given or a policy is concluded via telephone or by another means which does not allow for written information to be provided, the information must be given immediately following the conclusion of the policy. Moreover, policyholders must be informed during the term of the policy of any changes to the information provided.

B. Consequences in Cases of Breach of the Obligation to Provide Information

306. Any failure of the insurer to provide the necessary information has no effect on the validity of the contract, but the policyholder has a right of revocation for an unlimited period. The revocation period pursuant to § 8 VVG does not commence. Where the policyholder suffers any loss from the insurer's failure he is entitled to damages under general contract law (§§ 280 paragraph 1, 241 paragraph 2, 311 paragraph 2 BGB). Unlike with the obligation to provide advice and documentation, the insurer's obligation to give information prior to contract applies only to the insurer itself, but not to the insurance agent as well.

C. Personal Scope of the Obligation to Provide Information

307. The information obligations are not limited to consumers. Policies covering large risks, however, are exempt from these requirements. Is the holder of such policy a natural person, pursuant to § 7 paragraph 5 VVG the applicable law and the competent supervisory authority need to be disclosed.

- Die vorvertraglichen Informationspflichten des Versicherers und das Rechtzeitigkeitserfordernis, RuS 2007, pp. 133, 136 et seq.; Ebers, in: Schwintowski/Broemmelmeyer (eds), 3rd ed., ZAP VERLAG 2017, § 7 VVG note 42.

Chapter 6. Insurance and Third Parties

§1. Insurance for the Account of a Third Party

308. All types of insurance can be concluded for the account of a third party (co-insured person). In fact, all liability insurance contracts provide not only coverage for the policyholder, i.e., the person making the contract, but also for numerous other persons. Generally, the co-insured's are not named but only classified on the basis of their characteristics in the policy. For example, the personal liability insurance includes spouses, registered civil partners, and family members living in the policyholder's household (*see* paragraph 397).

309. The motor liability insurance includes not only the keeper and the actual driver of the car, but also the:

- owner of the car;
- co-driver, who in the scope of his work relationship with the policyholder or the keeper of the car regularly accompanies the driver as replacement driver or to provide assistance with loading or other jobs;
- employer or official superior, if the car is used for official purposes with the policyholder's agreement; and
- bus conductor whose work is within in the scope of his work relationship with the policyholder or the keeper of the car (*see* paragraph 587).

310. The general commercial liability insurance provides coverage for all employees of the policyholder (*see* paragraph 401). The D&O-insurance provides coverage for the policyholder's co-insured directors and officers against claims of the policyholder (i.e., the company which has concluded the contract) and claims of third parties (*see* paragraph 427). The private health insurance extends coverage to spouses, registered civil partners and children.

311. In property insurance where the insurance has not been taken out by the owner but by the possessor the car, the owner is co-insured. For example, when the leasing agreement requires the lessee of a car to take out comprehensive motor vehicle insurance the lessor is co-insured.

312. In life insurance, accident insurance and occupational insurance only in exceptional cases third persons are included in the coverage. It is more favourable for the policyholder to appoint a third person as beneficiary (*Bezugsberechtiger*) because he/she does not need the insurer's consent for the appointment and any later replacement of the designated beneficiary by another one (§§ 159, 176 and 185 VVG).

§2. Relationship Between the Co-insured and the Insurer

313. The legal framework for the insurance for the account of a third party can be found in §§ 43–48 VVG. The most significant feature is that the co-insured is entitled to the benefits under the contract of insurance (§ 44 paragraph 1 VVG) while the policyholder has the right to dispose in his own name of the rights arising for the insured under the insurance contract, i.e., only the policyholder may demand payment or bring an action against the insurer if there is a dispute over the coverage (§ 45 paragraph 1 VVG). The rationale behind this division of material and formal 'ownership' is that the insurer ought to deal with the party with whom it contracted but not with co-insureds whose names it does not know.

314. In motor liability insurance (*see* paragraph 588) and in the D&O-insurance (*see* paragraph 423), however, the policies regularly provide that the co-insureds have not only material, but also formal 'ownership'. In all other types of insurance, however, only under exceptional circumstances the co-insured are authorized to demand payment and/or to sue the insurer, e.g., where (1) the policyholder agrees that the co-insured pursues his claims (§ 45 paragraph 2 VVG), (2) the co-insured is in the possession of the insurance certificate (§ 44 paragraph 2 VVG) or (3) the insurer denies coverage and the policyholder takes no legal action against the insurer.[269]

315. Pursuant to § 47 paragraph 1 VVG, whenever knowledge and conduct of the policyholder are of relevance under the VVG, the knowledge and conduct of the co-insured are also relevant. That means that all exclusions and duties linked to the conduct of the policyholder apply to the co-insured. It is important to note, however, that the co-insured's non-compliance with duties to be observed prior or after the insured event occurred, in general, affect only his/her right to the benefits under the contract. The same is true when the insurer is not liable because the co-insured intentionally inflicted damage to the policyholder's property or on another person (§ 103 VVG). For example, where an employee of the company, in the course of his/her activities for the company, wilfully cause damage to another person's property, the insurer is still obliged to release the company from the claim of the injured party (unless the employee is a 'Repraesentant' of the company (*see* paragraph 59)). By contrast, damage caused by the policyholder with intent adversely affects the

269. Cf. BGH, 27 May 1998 – IV ZR 166/97, NJW 1998, pp. 2537, 2538; BGH, 29 Apr. 1998 – IV ZR 21/97, NJW 1998, pp. 2449, 2450, with further references.

co-insured's coverage.[270] The same is true according to case law[271] and the prevailing view among scholars[272] in the case that there is a legitimate interest of the insurer to make coverage for co-insured dependent on the policyholder's compliance with his/her/its contractual duties.

§3. Relationship Between the Policyholder and the Co-insured

316. The BGH has described the relationship between the policyholder and the co-insured – i.e., division between material and formal 'ownership' – as a fiduciary relationship (*Treuhandverhaeltnis*) once the insured event has occurred.[273] Where due to the policyholder's non-compliance with duties to be observed after the insured event occurred the co-insured's right to the benefit is negatively affected, the co-insured is entitled to claim damages from the policyholder for the breach of the fiduciary relationship (§§ 241 paragraph 2, 280 BGB).

317. Where the policyholder and the co-insured have agreed on the provision of insurance cover e.g., in the employment contract, the co-insured may in addition base his/her damage claim on the breach of the agreement if there was limited or no cover as a result the policyholder's non-compliance with duties to be observed prior or after the insured event.[274]

270. Cf. BGH, 8 Feb. 1965 – II ZR 171/62, VersR 1965, pp. 425, 428.
271. Cf. BGH, 14 Dec. 1967 – II ZR 169/65, NJW 1968, pp. 447, 449; for a some what different view *see* BGH, 15 Nov. 1978 – IV ZR 183/77, VersR 1979, pp. 176, 177.
272. Cf. R. Koch, in: Looschelders/Pohlmann (eds), VVG, 3rd ed., Carl Heymanns 2017, § 47 VVG n. 17; Brand, in: Bruck/Moeller, VVG, 9. ed., vol. 4, DeGruyter 2010, § 47 VVG n. 11; for somewhat different view *see* Huebsch, in Schwintowski/Broemmelmeyer (eds), VVG, 3rd ed., ZAP VERLAG 2017, § 47 VVG n. 10.
273. BGH, 10 Oct. 1985 – I ZR 124/83, VersR 1986, pp. 285, 286 with further references.
274. R. Koch, in: Looschelders/Pohlmann (eds), VVG, 3rd ed., Carl Heymanns 2017, § 46 VVG n. 8.

Chapter 7. Termination of the Insurance Contract

§1. Ordinary Termination

318. As with other contracts of continuing obligations, the parties (policyholder and insurer) are free to determine the term of the insurance agreement. Where it is concluded for an unlimited period, according to § 11 paragraph 2 VVG both parties may terminate the agreement to the end of the current period of insurance. They may agree to waive the right of termination for no more than two years. According to § 11 paragraph 4 VVG a policyholder may terminate a contract of insurance concluded for a period of more than three years to the end of the third or each successive year, subject to a notice period of three months.

319. Special rules apply to life insurance (§ 168 VVG) (*see* paragraph 733), occupational disability insurance (§ 176 VVG) (*see* paragraph 644) and health insurance. According to § 205 paragraph 6 VVG the policyholder may only terminate the comprehensive health insurance contract if he/she concludes a new contract with another insurer. The termination shall not become effective until the policyholder proves that he/she has taken out insurance with another insurer. The insurer is not allowed to terminate comprehensive health insurance contracts (§ 206 VVG) (*see* paragraph 699).

§2. Extraordinary Termination

I. Occurrence of an Insured Event

320. The VVG provides for extraordinary termination rights of the parties with or without notice. For example both parties may terminate the contract after the occurrence of an insured event pursuant to § 92 VVG (property insurance) and § 111 VVG (liability insurance).

II. Non-disclosure

321. Pursuant to § 19 paragraph 3 sentence 2 VVG the insurer has the right to terminate the contract by giving a notice of one month whenever the policyholder breached his duty of disclosure either without fault or by acting with negligence (*see* paragraph 241).

III. Increase of Risk

322. In case of an increase of risk the insurer may terminate the contract subject to a notice period of one month (§§ 24 paragraph 1 sentence 2, 24 paragraph 2 VVG). Where the policyholder has aggravated the risk intentionally or acting with gross negligence the insurer is entitled to terminate the contract with immediate effect (§ 24 paragraph 1 sentence 1 VVG) (*see* paragraph 257).

IV. Non-compliance with Contractual Duties

323. According to § 28 paragraph 1 VVG the insurer may terminate the contract without prior notice within one month after learning of the policyholder's non-compliance with a duty ('Obliegenheit') to be observed prior to the occurrence of an insured event, unless the non-compliance was not intentional or based on gross negligence (*see* paragraph 266).

V. Delayed Premium Payment

324. The insurer is entitled to rescind from the contract if the single premium or the first premium has not been paid in good time (§ 37 paragraph 1 VVG). In case of delayed payment of renewal premiums the insurer is entitled to terminate the contract without prior notice after the expiration of a payment deadline of no less than two weeks (§ 38 paragraph 1 VVG) (*see* paragraph 235).

325. Special rules apply to life insurance (§§ 168 VVG) (*see* paragraph 732), occupational disability insurance (§ 176 VVG) (*see* paragraph 643) and health insurance (§ 206 VVG) (*see* paragraph 698).

Part III. Property and Liability Insurance

Chapter 1. Fire insurance

§1. Legal Regime

326. Fire insurance is subject to the provisions applying to all classes of insurance (§§ 1–73 VVG), the provisions applying to indemnity insurance (§§ 74- 87 VVG) and the provisions applying to property insurance (§§ 88–99 VVG). Moreover, special rules exist for building fire insurance (§§ 142–149 VVG). The latter provisions are aimed at the protection of the mortgage creditor (i.e., a bank).[275] For example, the insurer must inform the mortgage creditor, who has reported his mortgage, if the policyholder has not paid the single or first premium in good time, or the policyholder is in delay with the payment of the renewal premium, or the insurer has terminated the contract due to the non-payment of the renewal premium (§ 142 paragraph 1 VVG). The mortgage creditor then may step in and effect payment to secure the insurance coverage.

327. The insurer must also inform the mortgage creditor of the occurrence of the insured event (§ 142 paragraph 2 VVG). Where the mortgage still exists, the consent of the mortgage creditor, as a rule, is required in order for the termination of the building fire insurance by the policyholder to be valid. This consent must be submitted to the insurer no later than one month before expiry of the insurance contract (§ 144 VVG). This provision does not apply if the contract is terminated by the policyholder after a claim (§ 92 paragraph 1 VVG) or, after the insured property is sold, by the purchaser (§ 96 paragraph 2 VVG).

328. If, under the terms of the insurance contract, the insurer is only obliged to indemnify the policyholder for the reconstruction of the building, a payment made without security that the money will be used for the reconstruction or repair is only effective vis-à-vis a mortgage creditor if the insurer or the policyholder has notified him that the payment is to be made without security and if one month has elapsed since receipt of the notice (§ 94 paragraph 1 VVG).

275. Staudinger, in: Langheid/Wandt (eds), VVG, 2nd ed., C.H. Beck 2017, § 143 VVG n. 1.

§2. Stand-Alone Fire Insurance Policies

I. Insured Perils

329. The standard fire insurance, which can be taken out by businesses, is based on the model terms and conditions issued by the GDV (*Allgemeine Bedingungen fuer die Feuerversicherung*, AFB 2010 as of 1 April 2014).[276] The policy includes damage caused by explosion, lightning and a crash or impact of an aircraft. The policy provides for definitions of these perils. Fire, e.g., is defined as a conflagration with flames which has occurred without an intended source or has left the source and is in a position to spread by its own means (A § 1 no. 2 AFB 2010). An explosion is a sudden manifestation of force based on the escape of gas or steam (*see* A § 1 no. 4 AFB 2010). The insurer provides indemnification for all insured items that have been either destroyed or damaged or lost.

330. There are a number of peril exclusions. For example, there is no coverage for damage due to a fire ignited for a purpose or due to heat needed for working, singeing (except as a result of a fire) or implosion (A § 1 no. 5 lit. b), c) and d) AFB 2010). Damage due to war, civil unrest, atomic energy or earthquake is always excluded (A § 1 no. 5 lit. a), A § 2 nos 1 to 3 AFB 2010).

II. Insured Items

331. Insured are buildings and other items on the site (without additional equipment), goods and chattels (if the policyholder is the owner or has acquired the items with reservation of title or he has assigned the items as a security) (A § 3 nos 1–4 AFB 2010).

III. Insured Expenses

332. In addition to compensation for the insured items, the policyholder's costs are reimbursed for expenses incurred in preventing or containing damage, even if unsuccessful. According to A § 5 nos 2–5 AFB 2010, which is in fact an expression of § 83 VVG (*see* paragraph 275), the following expenses will be reimbursed:

- cleaning up and demolition costs;
- moving and protection costs;
- reconstitution of files, data storage media, etc.; and
- costs of extinguishing the fire, fire brigade costs being excluded.

276. *See* https://www.gdv.de/resource/blob/6066/85284e0424e1d3a5cd4b50df1b2d88fc/01-allgemeine-bedingungen-fuer-die-feuerversicherung--afb-2010--data.pdf (accessed 28 Mar. 2018).

IV. Insured Location

333. The insurance covers only property and the rooms of buildings at the insured location named in the policy. If goods and chattels outside the insured location are to be insured, the policyholder must take out off-premises insurance. This restriction does not apply if items while they are being removed from the insured location due to an actual or impending threat e.g., of fire get damaged, destroyed or lost (A § 6 no. 1 lit. a) AFB 2010). Moreover, cash as well as other valuables are insured if they are kept in locked rooms or containers in a building that is designated as the insured location (A § 6 no. 3 AFB 2010).

V. Insured Value

334. Fire insurance is generally offered as a 'new for old' policy (*see* paragraph 284). In the case of buildings, e.g., this is the usual local cost of rebuilding, including all the expenses entailed (architects' fees, construction and planning costs) (A § 7 no. 1 lit. a) aa) AFB 2010).

VI. Extended Coverage

335. There are model terms and conditions issued by the GDV which provide extended coverage for the insurance of additional perils to fire insurance (*Allgemeine Bedingungen fuer die Versicherung zusaetzlicher Gefahren zur Feuerversicherung*, ECB 2010 as of 1 April 2014).[277] The ECB 2010 cover the following forms of perils:

- civil unrest, malicious damage, strike or lockout (§ 2 ECB 2010);
- motor collision, smoke, sonic boom (§ 3 ECB 2010);
- sprinkler-leakage (§ 4 ECB 2010);
- tap water (§ 5 ECB 2010);
- storm and hail (§ 6 ECB 2010);
- burglary, vandalism, robbery (§ 6 ECB 2010);
- flooding (§ 8 ECB 2010);
- earthquake (§ 9 ECB 2010);
- subsidence or landslip (§ 10 ECB 2010);
- snow pressure or avalanche (§ 11 ECB 2010); and
- volcanic eruption (§ 12 ECB 2010).

It needs to be pointed out that the insurance of these perils is subject of separate, legally independent contracts on insurance (A § 1 sentence 2 and 3 ECB 2010). As a result, contracts on the insurance against more than one of the afore-listed perils

277. *See* https://www.gdv.de/resource/blob/6018/097c98583f82273ee75b3ff4be3bf9b2/12-allgemeine-bedingungen-fuer-die-versicherung-zusaetzlicher-gefahren-zur-feuerversicherung--ecb-2010--data.pdf (accessed 28 Mar. 2018).

may have different dates of inception of cover, and the termination of the extended coverage for one specific peril has no effect on the coverage for other insured perils.

§3. Multi-Peril Policies

336. Property insurance policies often do not only provide coverage against fire, explosion, lightning, and a crash or impact of an aircraft but include coverage against other (named) perils. In that case, if not agreed otherwise, the special provisions on fire insurance (§§ 142–149 VVG) apply only for the damage caused by fire.

I. Building Insurance

337. The standard policy wording for building insurance issued by the GDV (*Allgemeine Wohngebaeude Versicherungsbedingungen*, VGB 2010 as of 1 March 2013),[278] e.g., includes in addition to basic fire cover and the other perils conventionally covered under a fire policy, damages caused by the escape of tap water, burst pipes, frost, storm and hail (A § 1 no. 1 VGB 2010). A buildings insurance policy also include elemental losses caused e.g., by flood, backwater, snow pressure, earthquakes, avalanches, volcano outbreaks, landslides (§ 4 VGB 2010). There is no standard coverage for damage due to war, civil unrest, atomic energy or earthquake are always excluded (A § 1 no. 2 lit. a)–c) VGB 2010).

II. Comprehensive Household Insurance

338. There are no special provisions under the VVG dealing with comprehensive household insurance. §§ 142–149 VVG are not applicable.

339. The householder's comprehensive insurance is based on the model terms and conditions issued by the GDV (*Allgemeine Hausrat Versicherungsbedingungen*, VHB 2016 as of 26 May 2017).[279] The standard cover includes damages caused to items in the policyholder's household for use or consumption (including cash and valuables), furniture, carpets, curtains, pictures (*see* A 8 VHB 2016) not only by fire, explosion, lightening, and a crash or impact of an aircraft, storm and hail but also by other perils such as implosion, tap water and vandalism after a break in. Like under the VGB 2010, there is no standard coverage for damage due to war, civil unrest, atomic energy or earthquake are always excluded (A 2 VHB 2016).

---

278. *See* https://www.gdv.de/resource/blob/6182/55b2a393d1c49dad829d50cb0de2fa26/01-allgemeine-wohngebaeude-versicherungsbedingungen--vgb-2010---wert-1914--data.pdf (accessed 28 Mar. 2018).

279. *See* https://www.gdv.de/resource/blob/6114/2d6b8855f1102c0006655438aa0f3a5d/01-allgemeine-hausrat-versicherungsbedingungen--vhb-2016---quadratmetermodell--data.pdf (accessed 28 Mar. 2018).

Chapter 2. Loss of Benefits Insurance

§1. Business Interruption Insurance

I. Types of Business Interruption Insurance

340. There are no special provisions under the VVG dealing with loss of benefits insurance e.g., for business interruption. The GDV has issued standard terms and conditions which are linked to the same perils as in a standard commercial property insurance policy, e.g., fire, explosion, storm, flood etc. (*Allgemeine Feuer-Betriebsunterbrechungs-Versicherungs-Bedingungen*, FBUB 2010 as of 1 April 2014),[280] or to damages to machinery (all-risks policy) (*Allgemeine Bedingungen fuer die Maschinen-Betriebsunterbrechungsversicherung*, AMBUB 2011 as of 1 January 2011).[281] There other types of interruption insurance such as electronic equipment business interruption insurance, assembly business interruption insurance, or insurance against damage caused by business interruptions as a result of a breakdown of public utilities (electricity, heat, gas or water).

A. *Fire Interruption Insurance*

341. In general, there is only cover if the interruption is the result of the direct physical loss, damage, or destruction to policyholder's property by an insured peril under fire business interruption policy (*see* A § 1 no. 1 FBUB 2010). Fire business interruption policies regularly exclude coverage for damage due to war, civil unrest and atomic energy (*see* A § 3 FBUB 2010). It should be noted that coverage will be provided if the business interruption is the result of direct physical loss due to wilful and malicious act or vandalism.

B. *Machinery Interruption Insurance*

342. The machinery interruption insurance is an all-risks policy. A § 3 no. 1 AMBUB 2011 only exemplifies perils which are insured such as:

- operating errors, clumsiness or the intention of a third person;
- construction or material defects or bad workmanship;
- short circuit, overcurrent or electrical surge;
- failure of measuring equipment, control gear or security devices;
- lack of water, oil or lubrication;

---

280. *See* https://www.gdv.de/resource/blob/6120/8d3b52913f8c4b26fb6ab434b594078d/01-allgemeine-feuer-betriebsunterbrechungs-versicherungs-bedingungen--fbub-2010--data.pdf (accessed 28 Mar. 2018).

281. *See* https://www.gdv.de/resource/blob/6084/35ac5155d0d0ca67d249de73f51e9e21/01-allgemeine-bedingungen-fuer-die-maschinen-betriebsunterbrechungsversicherung--ambub-2011--data.pdf (accessed 28 Mar. 2018).

- tearing because of centrifugal force;
- excess pressure or underpressure; and
- storm, frost or ice drift.

343. Pursuant to A § 3 no. 5 AMBUB excluded from coverage are losses caused by damage:

- due to intent of the policyholder or his 'Repraesentanten' (*see* paragraph 59);
- due to war, warlike events, civil war, revolution, rebellion, mutiny;
- due to civil unrest;
- due to atomic energy, nuclear radiation or radioactive substances;
- due earthquakes;
- due to flooding;
- due to defects already present on taking out the insurance policy and which must have been known by the policyholder or his 'Repraesentanten';
- due to usual work-related wear and tear or ageing, both normal and premature;
- due to the use of an item whose need for repair must have been known to the policyholder or his agent. Nevertheless, the insurer will provide indemnification if the damage was not caused by the need for repair or if the item at the time the damage occurred had at least been repaired in a makeshift manner with the insurer's consent; and
- for which a third party as supplier or contractor was responsible or which arose from a repair assignment.

II. Extent of Indemnification

344. The business interruption insurance covers the loss of earnings which includes the fixed costs such as continuing expenses for wages, interest, fees etc. and the profits that would have been earned had there been no interruption (*see* A § 1 no. 2 FBUB 2010/AMBUB 2011). In general, recovery is limited to the actual loss for the period of time it would take to repair or replace the building, in which the business is conducted, or the machinery. The policy will usually provide for as a sort of waiting period (time deductible), which begins 48–72 hours after the direct physical loss has suspended operation. In addition, there is a maximum period of coverage (*Haftzeit*) – frequently 12 months (*see* A § 1 no. 3 FBUB 2010/AMBUB 2011).

III. Duties of the Policyholder

345. The policyholder has the duty to provide prompt notice of how and where the damage occurred (*see* B § 8 no. 2 a) bb) FBUB 2010/AMBUB 2011), to take reasonable steps to protect the property from further damage (*see* B § 8 no. 2 a) aa) FBUB 2010/AMBUB 2011), and to allow the examination of physically damaged property by the insurer (*see* B § 8 no. 2 a) gg) FBUB 2010/AMBUB 2011). Moreover the policyholder has the duty to give the insurer access to financial books and records which includes information on profit and loss statements, production reports, inventory, invoices and purchase orders.

§2. EXTRA EXPENSE INSURANCE

346. Extra expense insurance (*Mehrkostenversicherung*) is designed to cover a business from expenses that it may incur while normal business operations are interrupted or disrupted. Extra expenses are defined as costs incurred during an agreed period of time to avoid or minimize business interruption or disruption after a material damage (*see* clause TK 4940 (11) AMBUB as of 1 January 2018).[282]

282. *See* https://www.gdv.de/resource/blob/5864/8bd1244ce0b5b727f6c569fa7f9c0d22/02-klauseln-zu-den-allgemeinen-bedingungen-fuer-die-maschinen-betriebsunterbrechungsversicherung--tk-ambub-2011--data.pdf (accessed 28 Mar. 2018).

Chapter 3. Transport Insurance

§1. Legal Regime

347. Transport insurance is subject to §§ 130–141 VVG. These provisions do not apply to air transport and sea waterway transport.[283] It is disputed among scholars whether they apply when the transport is to be made partly over sea and partly on inland waterways or over land.[284] Under § 147 VVG 1908 such forms of combined transport were covered by the then provisions on transport insurance. The legislator, however, removed this provision without any explanation, and for that reason it seems plausible to argue that §§ 130–141 VVG are not applicable to combined transport. There is no case law yet on this subject.

348. Transport insurance qualifies by definition as a large risk insurance (§ 210 paragraph 2 no. 1 VVG in conjunction with VAG Annex 1 nos 4, 6, 7 and 12). For that reason the provisions on transport insurance are not (semi-)mandatory. Any deviation in standard policy wordings, however, is subject to unfairness control (*see* paragraph 186).

§2. Scope of Coverage

349. The scope of cover of transport insurance is described in § 130 VVG.

I. Cargo Insurance

350. According to § 130 paragraph 1 VVG, transport insurance provides coverage against all risks to which goods are exposed during transportation over land or inland waterways (including storage in the ordinary course of transportation). The means of transport (e.g., rail, truck, car, or bike) and the mode of transport (e.g., road, railroad) are irrelevant for the classification as transport insurance.[285] The GDV has issued standard terms and conditions for all risks cargo insurance (DTV Cargo 2000/2011).[286]

283. Schwampe, in: Bruck/Moeller, Großkommentar zum VVG, 9 ed., vol. 6/1, DeGruyter 2016, § 130 VVG n. 13.
284. For the discussion, *see* Schwampe, in: Bruck/Moeller, Großkommentar zum VVG, 9 ed., vol. 6/1, DeGruyter 2016, § 130 VVG n. 14.
285. Cf. Schwampe, in: Bruck/Moeller, Großkommentar zum VVG, 9 ed., vol. 6/1, DeGruyter 2016, § 130 VVG n. 28.
286. DTV Cargo Insurance Conditions 2000/2011 ('All risks') as of August 2011, http://www.tis-gdv.de/tis_e/bedingungen/avb/ware/ware.html (accessed 28 Mar. 2018).

II. Hull of None Ocean-going Ship Insurance

351. Where the ship is covered against the risks of inland waterway transportation, pursuant to § 130 paragraph 2 sentence 1 VVG the insurer covers all risks to which the ship is exposed including contributions to gross average insofar as the average measure serves the avoidance of loss to be compensated by the insurer (§ 130 paragraph 3 VVG). It should be noted that the § 130 paragraph 2 sentence 1 VVG only applies to the insurance of (none ocean-going) ships. In practice, the insurers do not provide coverage against all risks but only named risks such as collision, fire, explosion, lightning, theft and vandalism (No. 3 AVB Flusskasko 2008/2013).[287]

III. Protection and Indemnity Insurance

352. The hull of none ocean-going ship insurance moreover provides cover against the loss incurred by the policyholder as a result of a collision with another ship or with fixed or floating objects for which he is liable towards a third party (§ 130 paragraph 2 sentence 2 VVG). It should be noted that the provisions on liability insurance (§§ 100–112 VVG) do not apply to the ship's P&I insurance.[288]

IV. Forwarder's Liability Insurance

353. The forwarder's liability insurance (*Verkehrshaftungsversicherung*) which covers claims arising from loss and/or damage to the transported goods against carriers, forwarding and warehousing companies does not qualify as transport insurance. It is subject to the rules on liability insurance.[289]

§3. Deviations from General Rules

354. Transport insurance is subject to the provisions applying to all classes of insurance (§§ 1–73 VVG), the provisions applying to indemnity insurance (§§ 74–87 VVG) and the provisions applying to property insurance (§§ 88–99 VVG). There are special rules under §§ 131–141 VVG which are tailored to the requirements of transport insurance (cargo, hull and P&I) and mostly contain deviations from the general rules applicable to all kinds of (indemnity) insurance.

---

287. *Allgemeine Bedingungen für die Versicherung von Flusskasko-Risiken 2008/2013*, AVB Flusskasko 2008/2013 as of August 2013, http://www.tis-gdv.de/tis/bedingungen/avb/fluss/fluss.html (accessed 28 Mar. 2018).

288. Abele, in: Bruck/Moeller, Großkommentar zum VVG, 9ed., vol. 6/1, DeGruyter 2016, DTV-VHV 2003/2011 Einleitung n. 3; Heiss/Trümper, in: Beckmann/Matusche-Beckmann (eds), Versicherungsrechts-Handbuch, 3rd ed., C.H. Beck 2015, § 38 n. 346.

289. *See* BT-Drucks. 16/3945 p. 92.

I. Duty of Disclosure

355. For example, departing from §§ 19 paragraph 2, 21 paragraph 1 VVG the insurer is according to § 131 paragraph 1 sentence 1 VVG entitled to refuse payment in case of the policyholder's breach of the duty of disclosure. Pursuant to § 131 paragraph 1 sentence 2 VVG the insurer remains liable insofar as the circumstance which was not disclosed or not disclosed correctly was not the cause of the occurrence of the insured event or of the extent of the liability. § 131 paragraph 1 sentence 1 VVG is silent on the issue of whether the policyholder must have acted with fault. Some scholars take the position that negligence is required.[290] No. 4.3 paragraph 2 DTV-Cargo 2000/2011 requires negligence.[291]

356. In contract practice, there are regularly clauses according to which the insured is obliged to disclose all material facts and circumstances, and to answer completely and truthfully all questions posed by the insurer prior to the inception of cover (*see* no. 4.1 DTV-Cargo 2000/2011). Such clauses deviate from § 19 paragraph 1 VVG since that provision obliges the policyholder to disclose only such facts the insurer has requested in writing. Although it is permitted in large risks insurance policies to deviate from (semi-)mandatory rules such as § 19 VVG (*see* § 32 VVG) it is recalled that any such deviation is subject to the unfairness control in accordance with § 307 BGB (*see* paragraph 186). Moreover, it is debatable whether or not policy provisions which form part of the insurance contract have legal effect prior to the conclusion of the contract.[292]

II. Increase of the Risk

357. Another deviation from the general rules can be found in §§ 132–134 VVG. According to § 132 paragraph 1 sentence 1 VVG the policyholder, notwithstanding § 23 paragraph 1 VVG, may increase the risk insured or change it in another manner and permit changes by a third party. The policyholder is under the duty to disclose the alteration to the insurer without undue delay (§ 132 paragraph 2 sentence VVG). Unlike under § 24 VVG (*see* paragraph 257), the insurer is not entitled to terminate the contract on account of an increase of the risk insured.

358. §§ 133 and 134 VVG exemplifies two cases of risk increase, i.e., change of transportation and unsuitable means of transport. Provided that the policyholder transports the goods by a means of transport other than that agreed or reloads them although direct transportation was agreed, the insurer is not obligated to effect payment (§ 133 paragraph 1 sentence 1 VVG). The same is true if only a specific means of transport or a specific transport route was agreed (§ 133 paragraph 1 sentence 2

290. For the discussion, *see* Schwampe, in: Bruck/Moeller, Großkommentar zum VVG, 9 ed., vol. 6/1, DeGruyter 2016, § 131 VVG n. 17 et seq.
291. DTV Cargo Insurance Conditions 2000/2011 ('All risks') as of August 2011, http://www.tis-gdv.de/tis_e/bedingungen/avb/ware/ware.html (accessed 28 Mar. 2018).
292. *See* e.g., Heiss/Trümper, in: Beckmann/Matusche-Beckmann (eds), Versicherungsrechts-Handbuch, 3rd ed., C.H. Beck 2015, § 38 n. 102.

VVG). The insurer, however, is obligated to effect payment if, after the commencement of the insurance, the transportation was changed or relinquished without the consent of the policyholder or as the result of an insured event (§ 133 paragraph 2 VVG).

359. The policyholder has the duty to use a means of transport which is suited to taking on board and transporting the goods (§ 134 paragraph 1 VVG). Any breach of this duty by intent or gross negligence releases the insurer from its obligation to pay unless the breach was not the cause of the occurrence of the insured event or the extent of the liability (§ 134 paragraph 2 VVG).

III. Reimbursement of Expenses

360. Unlike under § 83 VVG, the sum insured is not a limit for the expenses incurred by the policyholder in loss avoidance or minimisation. In contrast, § 135 paragraph 1 VVG provides that such expenses as well as the costs of the ascertainment and establishment of the loss, shall be reimbursed by the insurer even if they exceed the sum insured when added to the remaining compensation (§ 135 paragraph 1 VVG).

IV. Insured Value of the Goods

361. Not the market value of the goods at the time the insured event occurred as stated in § 88 VVG deemed to be the insured value but the ordinary market value, or in its absence, the ordinary value of the goods at the place of shipping at the commencement of the insurance, plus insurance costs, costs arising up until the time when the carrier takes receipt of the goods and the final amount of freightage paid (§ 136 paragraph 1 VVG).

V. Causation of the Insured Event

362. While § 81 paragraph 2 VVG entitles the insurer in cases where the policyholders gross negligently caused the insured event to only reduce the compensation depending on the policyholder's severity of gross negligence, § 137 paragraph 1 VVG provides that the transport insurer is not obligated to effect any payment.

VI. Unfitness of the Ship

363. § 138 VVG deals with non-fitness of ships in the case of insurance of a ship. § 138 VVG is phrased like an exclusion from coverage. It states that the insurer is not obligated to pay compensation for a loss resulting from the ship's sailing in unfit condition or improperly equipped or manned or if the loss is a consequence of the ship's worn-out condition. The BGH, however, has ruled that § 138

VVG is not an exclusion but a duty (not to increase the risk). As a consequence, the insurer is only released from liability only if the policyholder acted gross negligently (*see* paragraph 262).[293]

VII. Sale of the Insured Object or Goods

A. *Objects and Goods*

364. § 139 VVG contains deviations from §§ 95–97 VVG in the case of the sale of insured objects or goods for which an individual policy or a certificate of insurance has been issued. In this case the buyer shall, notwithstanding § 95 VVG, not be liable to pay the premium. The insurer moreover cannot claim exemption from obligation to indemnify the buyer on account of non-payment of premium unless the buyer knew or ought to have known the reason for this exemption. Deviating from §§ 96, 97 VVG the insurer is not entitled to terminate the contract on the grounds of the sale of the insured goods, and the policyholder is not obliged to notify the sale of the goods to the insurer.

B. *Ships*

365. In the case of the sale of an insured ship, § 140 VVG states that the insurance ends, notwithstanding § 95 VVG when the ship is turned over to the buyer. If the ship is *en route* the insurance ends when it is turned over to the buyer at the port of destination.

VIII. Abandonment by the Insurer

366. § 141 VVG states that the insurer is, in the event of an insured loss, entitled to discharge itself from all further liabilities by payment of the sum insured. The insurer, however, remains under the duty to indemnify the policyholder for costs of averting or minimising the loss or in repairing or replacing the insured good, incurred before he/she was notified of the insurer's intention to discharge itself from liability by payment of the sum insured. The insurer's right to discharge itself from liability by payment of the sum insured ceases if the policyholder fails to receive notification of this intent within one week of the insurer becoming aware of the loss event and its direct consequences.[294]

293. BGH, 18 May 2011 – IV ZR 16/09, RuS 2012, p. 130, para. 30.

294. For details, *see* Schwampe, in: Bruck/Moeller, Großkommentar zum VVG, 9 ed., vol. 6/1, DeGruyter 2016, § 141 VVG ns. 7 et seq.

Chapter 4. Liability Insurance

§1. Legal Regime

367. Liability insurance is subject to §§ 100–124 VVG. While §§ 100–112 VVG apply to all classes of liability insurance, §§ 113–124 VVG apply to compulsory liability insurance only. There are model terms and conditions issued by the GDV for almost all types of liability insurance (except for professional liability insurance), which provide cover for claims for damages resulting from bodily injury and damage to property, or financial loss in the course of the insured activities or businesses. It is to be noted that liability as such is regulated by law and defined by the legislator irrespective of any existing insurance coverage, e.g., in the BGB, the StVG, the product liability act (*Produkthaftungsgesetz*, hereafter 'ProdhaftG'), the environmental liability act (*Umwelthaftungsgesetz*, hereafter 'UmweltHG'), etc.

§2. Obligations of the Insurer

I. Indemnification and/or Defence

368. The obligations of the liability insurer are laid down in § 100 VVG. The insurer must indemnify the policyholder (and/or any co-insured person) from existing liability and hold the policyholder harmless where the latter's liability is asserted by a third party. The coverage includes the recovery of the costs of defending any claim against the policyholder or of reaching a settlement in respect of such claim. According to § 106 VVG the policyholder is not entitled to claim compensation from the insurer as long as his liability to the third party has not been ascertained by final judgment (or binding arbitration award), acknowledgement or settlement (with the insurer's consent). The insurer is obliged to pay the compensation within two weeks beginning at the time when the third party's claim is established with binding effect for the insurer.[295]

II. Scope of Defence Costs

369. Pursuant to § 101 paragraph 1 VVG the insurance includes the expenses incurred in court and out of court in the defence against the claim asserted by the third party. Further, the insurance covers costs of defence in criminal proceedings instituted for an act which could result in the policyholder becoming liable vis-à-vis the third party. At the policyholder's request the insurer shall advance the costs. § 101 paragraph 2 VVG states that the insurer must cover the costs for defence even if they exceed, together with the costs for indemnifying the policyholder, the sum insured ('costs in addition').

---

295. For further details, *see* R. Koch, in: Bruck/Moeller, Großkommentar zum VVG, 9 ed., vol. 4, DeGruyter 2013, § 106 VVG n. 12 et seq.

370. However, some types of liability insurance, such as D&O liability, are exclusively offered on a 'cost-inclusive' basis. The commercial general liability insurance equally provides coverage for claims in Common law jurisdiction only on a 'cost-inclusive' basis. Since 'cost-inclusive' clauses deviate from § 101 paragraph 2 VVG there is some discussion on their validity. The OLG Frankfurt/M., in its judgment of 9 June 2011, held that a 'cost inclusive' clause in a D&O policy is void because it places the policyholder and the co-insured persons at an unreasonable disadvantage in terms of § 307 paragraph 2 no. 1 BGB (*see* paragraph 195).[296] The insurer lodged an appeal against the judgment with the BGH and settled the claim before the oral hearing was scheduled. Scholars are divided on this issue, and it remains to be seen how the BGH will rule when it has the chance to do so.[297]

III. Exercising Full Control over Defence

371. The insurer's obligations in respect of defending the policyholder depend first and foremost upon the wording of the policy. In general, the insurer reserves its right to conduct all negotiations with third party claimants against the policyholder, to defend any proceedings which may be brought and to approve any settlement with the third party on the policyholder's behalf (*see* e.g., no. 5.2, 25 AHB[298]). As compensation, if a coverage question turns on the same facts or law at issue in the underlying dispute between the injured party and the policyholder, the insurer is bound by the results of any judicial finding of liability on the part of the policyholder.[299] The same is true when the insurer wrongfully denies coverage and refuses to conduct negotiations or to defend the policyholder.[300] It is therefore not necessary for the policyholder to require the insurer to be joined in the dispute in accordance with the §§ 64 et seq. ZPO.

§3. Scope of Coverage

372. The obligation to defend and/or to indemnify the policyholder only arises if the claim against the policyholder falls within the scope of coverage.

296. Cf. OLG Frankfurt/M., 9 Jun. 2011 – 7 U 127/09, RuS 2011, p. 509.
297. For the discussion, *see* R. Koch, Kostenanrechnungsklauseln in der Haftpflichtversicherung, VersR 2016, pp. 1405 et seq.; Terno, Wirksamkeit von Kostenanrechnungsklauseln, RuS 2013, pp. 577 et seq.
298. *Allgemeine Versicherungsbedingungen für die Haftpflichtversicherung*, AHB as of February 2016, https://www.gdv.de/resource/blob/6132/6a2283f21432edcdf9291a53e9967fd0/01-allgemeine-versicherungsbedingungen-fuer-die-haftpflichtversicherung--ahb--data.pdf (accessed 28 Mar. 2018).
299. BGH, 30 Sept. 1992-IV ZR 314/91, RuS 1992, pp. 406, 407; for further details *see* R. Koch, in: Bruck/Moeller, Großkommentar zum VVG, 9ed., vol. 4, DeGruyter 2013, § 106 VVG n. 19 et seq.
300. BGH, 7 Feb. 2007-IV ZR 149/03, VersR 2007, pp. 1116, 1117; for further details *see* R. Koch, in: Bruck/Moeller, Großkommentar zum VVG, 9 ed., vol. 4, DeGruyter 2013, § 106 VVG n. 12 et seq.

I. Risk Insured

373. The scope is, first, defined by the risk insured in that the policyholder's liability must arise from risks of everydai life (*see* paragraph 395), from his activities as specified in the insurance contract such as carrying on a particular business (*see* paragraph 398), the ownership of business premises, the management of companies (*see* paragraph 419), the shipment of goods, the manufacturing and sale of goods (*see* paragraph 402), the use of motor vehicles (*see* paragraph 583), providing professional activities (*see* paragraph 415), etc. (principle of speciality of the risk insured).

II. Liability Imposed by Law

374. The liability of the policyholder must follow from the (private and/or public) law which includes statutory liability provisions as well as judge-made law. Contractual liability based on an agreement or special consent is, in general, only covered if it does not go beyond liability imposed by law.

III. Heads of Damage Insured

375. The damages suffered by the injured party (personal injury, damage to private property, pecuniary loss) must be insured. Professional liability policies often provide coverage only for pecuniary loss and exclude claims for damages resulting from personal injury or damage to property (*see* paragraph 415).

IV. Insured Event

376. The insured event must take place within the policy period. Since the conduct of the policyholder that gives rise to liability will occur some time before the injured party claims for compensation, the point in time relevant for the determination of the insured event as trigger for the insurer's liability is of great importance.

A. Occurrence of the Damage

377. Policies covering liability for personal injury or damage to property (e.g., personal liability insurance, commercial general liability insurance, product liability insurance) are commonly written on an 'events' basis (*see* paragraphs 396, 400, 406). Under an events based policy the immediate bodily injury or property damage producing event (the defectively manufactured product leads to an accident causing bodily injuries) triggers the coverage not the act giving rise to the policyholder's liability (manufacturing of the defective product), nor the claim made by the injured party at a later date (once the injured party had found out that the product was defective).

B. Occurrence of the Act, Error or Omission

378. Professional liability coverage, also known as errors and omissions (E&O) insurance, is commonly written on an 'occurrence' basis (*see* paragraph 417). Coverage is provided for any injury or damage resulting from an act, error or omission of the policyholder during the policy period irrespective of whether the damage occurs during this period or on a later date i.e., after the termination of the contract.

C. Verifiable First Discovery

379. Where environmental damage is concerned 'the verifiable first discovery' of the personal injury, damage to property, or financial loss triggers the coverage (*see* paragraphs 410, 413).

D. Claims Made

380. Where coverage is provided on a 'claims made' basis, the insurer faces liability for any claim against the policyholder during the policy period arising out of an actual or alleged negligent act, error or omission occurred during the policy period. Claims-made policies typically extend coverage to wrongful acts occurred prior to the inception date of the policy, provided that the policyholder was not aware of the wrongful act at the time of the conclusion of the insurance contract. A further typical form of extension can be found in the form of an extended claim period, which is triggered where the policy is not renewed. In Germany, the claims-made form is commonly used in directors and officers (D&O) liability insurance policies (*see* paragraph 426).

V. Limit of Indemnity

381. Restrictions in coverage follow from the limit of indemnity, i.e., the maximum amount that the insurer will pay. The limit can operate either on an 'each and every' claim basis or on an 'aggregate' basis. In the first alternative, the full limit of indemnity under the policy applies separately to each claim which might arise during the period of insurance. In the second alternative, the limit of indemnity applies as a maximum total payment irrespective of the number of claims notified during the period of insurance (*see* e.g., no. 6.2 AHB).

382. The insurer's liability is further limited by 'series clauses'. Such clauses work on the basis of two fictions in that two or more claims arising from one specific cause, which is attributable, e.g., to the same event, condition, defect or hazard, or failure to warn, are treated as a single insured event that, depending on the definition of the insured event, deemed to have happened on the date of the first occurrence of the damage (e.g., no. 6.3 AHB), of the act, error or omission, of the first verifiable first discovery (e.g., no. 7.2 UmweltHM[301]) or of the earliest claim was first made (e.g., no. 4.5 AVB-AVG[302]).

VI. Exclusions

383. Exclusions from coverage play an important role in liability insurance. While the rationale behind statutory exclusions is public policy (e.g., no cover where the policyholder wilfully caused the damage, *see* § 103 VVG), contractual exclusions are aimed at preventing the policyholder from shifting business risks to the insurer (e.g., no claims due to loss or damage to work or objects manufactured by the policyholder), avoiding collusion among policyholders (e.g., claims of policyholder's family or between several policyholders under the same insurance policy), protecting the insurer from incalculable risks (e.g., losses due to the use of genetically modified organisms or claims for damage due to asbestos) or avoiding overlap between different kinds of liability insurance covers offered by the insurer (e.g., no cover for product recall or environmental damage under commercial general liability policies but under special recall and environmental liability policies).

384. No. 7 AHB contains the following exclusions, which are of relevance for all insurances covering liability for personal injury or damage to property:

(i) liability for intended damage (no. 7.1 AHB);
(ii) liability for defective products sold and services rendered with full knowledge of the defect (no. 7.2 AHB);
(iii) liability on the grounds of a contractual agreement or express warranty that extends liability imposed by law (no. 7.3 AHB);
(iv) liability claims made by the policyholder himself against co-insureds, or between two or more policyholders of one and the same insurance contract, or between two or more co-insureds (no. 7.4 AHB);
(v) liability claims made against the policyholder (no. 7.5 AHB):

301. *Besondere Bedingungen und Risikobeschreibungen für die Versicherung der Haftpflicht wegen Schäden durch Umwelteinwirkung (Umwelthaftpflicht-Modell)*, UmweltHM as of September 2009, https://www.gdv.de/resource/blob/6204/072c0c9a3b5a3be826f31508b7aa2d80/19-besondere-bedingungen-und-risikobeschreibungen-fuer-die-versicherung-der-haftpflicht-wegen-schaeden-durch-umwelteinwirkung--umwelthaftpflicht-modell--data.pdf (accessed 28 Mar. 2018).

302. *Allgemeine Versicherungsbedingungen für die Vermögensschaden-Haftpflichtversicherung von Aufsichtsräten, Vorständen und Geschäftsführern*, AVB-AVG as of August 2017, https://www.gdv.de/resource/blob/6044/658f74bf7d24e9afbc21a885e95dda25/05-allgemeine-versicherungsbedingungen-fuer-die-vermoegensschaden-haftpflichtversicherung-von-aufsichtsraeten--vorstaenden-und-geschaeftsfuehrern--avb-avg--data.pdf (accessed 28 Mar. 2018).

- based on incidents involving the relatives of the policyholder who are members of the latter's household or who are co-insured;
- by the legal representatives of the policyholder if the latter is legally incapacitated or of limited legal capacity;
- by the legal representatives of the policyholder if the latter is a legal entity under private or public law, or an association without legal status;
- by the partners of the policyholder if they are personally liable without limitation and the policyholder is a partnership;
- by the policyholder's liquidators and administrators;

(vi) liability for damage to property the policyholder has rented, leased or borrowed (no. 7.6 AHB);

(vii) liability for damage to objects occurred in the course of the policyholder's business or occupational activities (e.g., processing, repair, transportation, testing, etc.); in the case of immoveable effects, this exclusion only applies if the effects or parts thereof were directly affected by the activity (no. 7.7 paragraph 1 AHB);

(viii) liability for damage to objects used as tools, auxiliary agents, material storage area, etc. in the course of the policyholder's business or occupational activities; in the case of immoveable effects, this exclusion only applies if the effects or parts thereof were directly affected by the activity (no. 7.7 paragraph 2 AHB);

(ix) liability for damage to objects situated in the area directly exposed to the policyholder's business or occupational activities; this exclusion does not apply if the policyholder can prove that, at the time of the activity, all the necessary steps to prevent damage occurring had been taken (no. 7.7 paragraph 3 AHB);

(x) liability for damages to objects manufactured or supplied, or to work performed by the policyholder as a result of any cause inherent in the manufacture or supply (no. 7.8 AHB);

(xi) liability for damages occurred abroad (no. 7.9 AHB);

(xii) liability for environmental damage pursuant to the UmweltHG; this exclusion does not apply to the insurance of personal liability risks (no. 7.10 lit. a AHB);

(xiii) liability for damages caused by substances, vibrations, noises, pressure, radiation, gases, vapours, heat or other phenomena that have spread in the soil, air or water (environmental damage); this exclusion does not apply to the insurance of personal liability risks and damage caused by products (also waste products) produced or delivered by the policyholder, through work or other activities after implementation or after completion of the work (product liability) (no. 7.10 lit. b AHB);

(xiv) liability for damage due to asbestos, or substances or products containing asbestos (no. 7.11 AHB);

(xv) liability claims for damage directly or indirectly related to energy-rich ionising radiation (e.g., alpha, beta and gamma radiation emitted from radioactive substances, as well as radiation generated by x-rays) (no. 7.12 AHB);

(xvi) liability for damage due to (no. 7.13 AHB):
- genetic engineering;

- genetically modified organisms ('GMO');
- products which contain compounds of GMOs, or were made from or with the aid of GMOs;

(xvii) liability for property damage arising from (no. 7.14 AHB):
- waste water, unless this is domestic waste water;
- subsidence of sites, or landslides;
- flooding caused by standing or flowing water;

(xviii) liability for damages arising from the exchange, transmission or provision of electronic data due to (no. 7.15 AHB):
- the deletion, suppression, rendering unusable or modification of date;
- the failure to record or to save data;
- disturbance of access to electronic data exchange; or
- transmission of confidential data or information;

(xix) liability for damages arising from personality rights or rights to a name (no. 7.16 AHB);

(xx) liability for damages for hostility, mobbing, harassment, unfair treatment, and other forms of discrimination (no. 7.17 AHB);

(xxi) liability for damage for personal injury/harm resulting from the transmission of an illness of the policyholder, as well as material/property damage caused by animals belonging to, kept by or sold by the policyholder, unless the policyholder can prove that he/she has not acted in a malicious or grossly negligent manner (no. 7.18 AHB).

385. Some of the afore-listed claims for damages are re-included in the cover, e.g., in the special conditions for the insurance of personal liability (e.g., liability for damage to property the policyholder has rented[303]), commercial general liability (e.g., liability for damages occurred abroad[304]), product liability (e.g., liability on the grounds of a contractual agreement or express warranty that extends liability imposed by law[305]).

VII. Policyholder's Non-compliance with Duties

386. The liability insurer may be (partially) released from his obligation to indemnify the policyholder where the latter has not complied with contractual or statutory duties (e.g., duty not to increase the risks, duty to give notice and information about the insured event, duty to avert and minimise the loss) (*see* paragraphs 273–280).

303. For further details, *see* R. Koch, in: Bruck/Moeller, Großkommentar zum VVG, 9 ed., vol. 4, DeGruyter 2013, Ziff. 7 AHB 2012 n. 170 et seq.
304. *Ibid.,* n. 257 et seq.
305. For further details, *see* R. Koch, in: Bruck/Moeller, Großkommentar zum VVG, 9 ed., vol. 4, DeGruyter 2013, Ziff. 4.ProdHM 2008 n. 5 et seq.

§4. Protection of the Injured Party

I. No Direct Claim

387. The injured party has no direct claim against the insurer based on his own right in the case of voluntary liability insurance. The injured party only has a derived right of action where (1) the policyholder has assigned his right against the insurer to be released from liability to the injured party, (2) the injured party has obtained an order of attachment and transfer (§§ 829, 835, 836 ZPO) of the policyholder's right, or (3) the policyholder is insolvent (*see* paragraph 391).

II. Protection Against Disposition of the Claim for Indemnity

388. According to § 108 paragraph 1 VVG, the policyholder may not dispose over his claim against the insurer to be released from liability towards the injured party. Any disposition such as the alteration, transfer, encumbrance or forfeiture of the claim is ineffective vis-à-vis the injured party. It is permitted, however, to assign the claim against the insurer to the injured party.[306] In that case the claim of the policyholder against the insurer to be released from liability will be converted into a claim for compensation of the injured party against the insurer by operation of law.[307] Where the liability of the policyholder has been established and quantified, the insurer is released not only from its obligation towards the policyholder but also from its obligation towards the injured party by making payment to the latter.[308]

389. § 105 VVG also serve the protection of the injured party to a certain extent because it invalidates clauses in the insurance contract according to which the insurer must not effect payment if the policyholder satisfies the injured party or acknowledges the injured party's entitlement without the insurer's consent. § 108 paragraph 2 VVG further provides that the assignment of the policyholder's claim against the insurer to be released from liability to the injured party cannot be excluded by means of standard clauses in terms of § 305 paragraph 1 sentence 1 BGB or § 310 paragraph 3 no. 2 BGB, if the policyholder is a private costumer.

III. Periodic Payments und Several Injured Parties

390. § 107 paragraph 1 VVG ensures that the injured party receives a partial payment whenever the policyholder is obligated to pay the injured party a pension and the sum insured is not equal to the capital value of the pension. Is there more

306. Cf. R. Koch, in: Bruck/Moeller, Großkommentar zum VVG, 9 ed., vol. 4, DeGruyter 2013, § 108 VVG n. 13.
307. Cf. BGH, 20 Apr. 2016 – IV ZR 531/14, RuS 2016, p. 455, para. 17; for further details *see* R. Koch, in: Bruck/Moeller, Großkommentar zum VVG, 9 ed., vol. 4, DeGruyter 2013, § 100 VVG n. 111, 112.
308. For further details, *see* R. Koch, in: Bruck/Moeller, Großkommentar zum VVG, 9 ed., vol. 4, DeGruyter 2013, § 100 VVG n. 167 et seq.

than one injured party and if the claims from the event on which the policyholder's liability is based exceed the insured sum, the insurer according to § 109 paragraph 1 VVG must satisfy the claims in proportion to their amount.

IV. Insolvency of the Policyholder

391. In the event of insolvency proceedings being opened in respect of the assets of the policyholder, the injured party may request from the insurer separate satisfaction from the policyholder's right against the insurer to be released from liability (§ 110 VVG). Where the claim, prior to the opening of the insolvency proceedings, has been established with binding effect for the insurer by final judgment, acknowledgement or settlement (§ 106 sentence 1 VVG), the injured party is entitled to claim payment from the insurer (according to an analogous application of § 1282 BGB, i.e., no order of attachment and transfer of the policyholder's claim against the insurer is necessary).[309]

392. Where the claim has not been established prior to the opening of the insolvency proceedings and the insolvency administrator denies the liability of the policyholder, the injured party has two options to obtain the insurance payment. Like any other creditor, the injured party can bring a declaratory action for the determination of the liability claim against the insolvency administrator – § 179 InsO – and, if he is successful, demand payment from the insurer.[310] Alternatively, based on the injured party's right to separate satisfaction in accordance with § 110 VVG, he/she can bring an action for payment against the insolvency administrator, and demand payment from the insurer if the court finds for him/her. In both cases, no order of attachment must be obtained and no transfer of the policyholder's right against the insurer to be released is necessary.[311]

§5. Types of Liability Insurance

393. Except for the very few risks which, from an economic (actuarial) point of view, are incalculable (*see* paragraph 208), against almost all types of liability claims insurance is available. Insofar as the insurances provide cover for claims for damages resulting from personal injury or damage to property such as personal liability, commercial general liability, product liability, environmental liability and motor vehicle liability, the model terms and conditions of the GDV (*see* paragraph 367) form the basis of the policies in underwriting practice. The same is true for environmental damage insurance which has been introduced upon the transposition

309. Cf. R. Koch, in: Bruck/Moeller, Großkommentar zum VVG, 9 ed., vol. 4, DeGruyter 2013, § 110 VVG ns. 14, 15.
310. *Ibid.,* n. 16.
311. *Ibid.,* n. 17.

of the Directive 2004/35/EC on environmental liability with regard to the prevention and remedying of environmental damage into German law.[312] There are no model terms and conditions for professional liability insurance. The model terms and conditions for D&O insurance (*see* paragraph 421) are not very favourable for businesses. For that reason, and due to the competitive environment with the associated downward pressure on prices, neither insurers nor brokers rely on them.

394. Naturally, this country report cannot deal in detail with the coverage of all types of liability insurance. In the following overview, the most widespread types of liability insurance are briefly described, with an emphasis on the insured risks and damages, the insured event and the personal scope of coverage.

I. Personal Liability Insurance

A. *Insured Risks and Damages*

395. There are no specific rules on personal liability insurance. Personal liability insurance policies provide cover resulting from liability of the insured imposed by law for personal injury (death, wounding or other bodily injury) and property damages arising from the policyholder's risks of everyday life (*Gefahren des taeglichen Lebens*), except for business, occupational or professional activities (A1-1 AVB PHV[313]).The coverage for financial loss that is not a result of bodily injury or property damage (pure financial loss) is basically limited to claims for damages due to alleged infringement of data protection laws (A1-6.15 AVB PHV).

B. *Insured Event*

396. The insured event is the event which resulted directly in the loss to the third party. The time of occurrence of the cause which led to the insured event is immaterial (A1-3.1 AVB PHV) (*see see* paragraph 376).

C. *Personal Scope of Coverage*

397. The insurance extends to the liability of the policyholder's spouse, unmarried children, family members living together in the same household as the policyholder, such as a mother, father, grandmother, grandfather, grandchild, sibling, niece or nephew (A1-2.1 AVB PHV). Insurance cover does not extend to liability claims brought by the policyholder against other persons insured under the policy, brought

312. O.J., 30 April 2004, L 143/56.

313. *Allgemeine Versicherungsbedingungen für die Privathaftpflichtversicherung*, AVB PHV as of April 2016, https://www.gdv.de/resource/blob/6242/730997c7b9a47a870be42ce584343bb2/09-avb-fuer-dieprivathaftpflichtversicherung-avb-phv-gdv-2016-data.pdf (accessed 28 Mar. 2018).

by other persons insured under the policy against the policyholder, and brought by other persons insured under the policy among themselves (A1-7.3 AVB PHV).

II. Commercial General Liability Insurance

A. Insured Risks and Damages

1. Business Activities Described in the Certificate of Insurance

398. Except for § 102 paragraph 1 VVG there are no specific rules on commercial general liability insurance. Commercial general liability policies cover the liability for damages to a third party or their property arising out of the policyholder business activities described in the insurance certificate (and any endorsements) (A.1-1 AVB BHV[314]). Claims for contract performance or damages in lieu of performance against the policyholder are not covered) (A.1-3.2 AVB BHV). Like in the personal liability insurance the coverage for pure financial loss is limited to claims for damages due to alleged infringement of data protection laws (A1-6.12.3 AVB BHV).

2. New Risks

399. There is automatic extension of cover, subject to a sublimit, for activities arising after conclusion of the contract which are not listed in the policy (*Vorsorgeversicherung*). The policyholder, at the request of the insurer, which may take the form of a printed note on the premium invoice, is obliged to notify the insurer, within one month of receiving such a request, of any new risk that has arisen in the meantime. If the policyholder fails to notify the insurer in good time, the insurance cover for that risk shall lapse retroactively from the inception of said risk. If an insured event occurs before the new risk has been notified to the insurer, the policyholder must prove that the new risk arose after conclusion of the insurance contract but before the time-limit for notification had elapsed (A1-9.1 AVB BHV).

B. Insured Event

400. The definition of the insured event is identical with the definition of the personal liability insurance (A1-3.1 AVB BHV) (*see* paragraph 396).

---

314. *Allgemeinen Versicherungsbedingungen für die Betriebs- und Berufshaftpflichtversicherung*, AVB BHV as of December 2016, https://www.gdv.de/resource/blob/6240/d304da17986df3b8cd3b70d6d8a35be5/02-avb-betriebs-und-berufshaftpflichtversicherung-dez-2016n-data.pdf (accessed 28 Mar. 2018).

C. Personal Scope of Coverage

401. According to § 102 paragraph 1 VVG the insurance extends to the liability of the policyholder's employees and personnel with the same status as employees (including temporary workers or subcontractor workers) (*see also* A1-2 AVB BHV).

III. Product Liability Insurance

A. Insured Risks and Damages

402. There are no specific rules on product liability insurance. Commercial general liability insurance policies cover damages caused by products produced or delivered by the policyholder, through work or other activities after implementation or after completion of the work (product liability). As mentioned before, the cover in principle does not include pure financial loss (*see* paragraph 398).

403. Suppliers, and in particular component manufacturers, therefore want to extend their standard product liability cover and to include financial losses incurred by their customers from industry and trade, caused by the supply of substances which when combined, mixed or processed created a defect in the final product. There is need for cover for:

- costs of the additional processing needed if a defective component is supplied;
- costs of replacement, dismantling and refitting;
- costs of defective products resulting from a defective machine; and
- costs for testing and sorting.

In response to these needs the GDV has issued model terms and conditions for product liability insurance (ProdHM[315]), which form the basis for product liability policies in the German market.

404. The ProdHM also provides cover for product warranties regarding the quality of manufactured goods (no. 3.2 ProdHM). Normally, the insurer accepts certain agreements between the policyholder and the buyer that go beyond any liability imposed by law such as the extension of limitation and warranty periods (warranty for defects), or the waiver to rely on the buyer's failure to examine the goods and to notify him within a reasonable time after he has discovered any defect or ought to have discovered it (*see* § 377 HGB, Articles 38, 39 CISG).

---

315. *Besondere Bedingungen und Risikobeschreibungen für die Produkthaftpflichtversicherung von Industrie- und Handelsbetrieben (Produkthaftpflicht-Modell)* – ProdHM as of January 2015, https://www.gdv.de/resource/blob/5966/e514308a3a39a5a801ccd0dbd01f237c/14-besondere-bedingungen-und-risikobeschreibungen-fuer-die-produkthaftpflichtversicherung-von-industrie--und-handelsbetrieben--produkthaftpflicht-modell--data.pdf (accessed 28 Mar. 2018).

405. The exclusion listed in no. 7 AHB (*see* paragraph 384), with some modifications, also apply to the product liability insurance. One variation of high practical relevance concerns the test exclusion clause (*Erprobungsklausel*) (no. 6.2.5 ProdHM). In the event of inadequate testing of the goods sold and/or manufactured there is no cover for damages caused by them.[316]

B. Insured Event

406. The insured event is the event when the loss occurs due to e.g., processing of the defective goods or the dismantling and installation of the defective goods (no. 8 ProdHM).

C. Personal Scope of Coverage

407. Like under the commercial general liability insurance, liability claims against the policyholder's employees and personnel with the same status as employees are covered (clause 2.2 ProdHM) (*see* paragraph 401).

IV. Environmental Liability Insurance

A. Insured Risks and Damages

408. There are no specific rules on environmental liability insurance. Environmental liability insurance policies follow with minor changes the GDV model terms and conditions (UmweltHM[317]). The UmweltHM provides coverage against liability for bodily injury or property damage caused by substances, vibrations, noises, pressure, radiation, gases, vapours, heat or other phenomena that have spread in the soil, air or water (environmental damage) (no. 1.2 sentence 1 UmweltHM). Pure financial loss resulting from the breach of rights of appropriation, the right to an established and operating business (*Recht am eingerichteten und ausgeuebten Gewerbebetrieb*), or rights granted under water legislation is also covered (no. 1.2 sentence 2 UmweltHM).

409. Environmental damage to persons and property is regularly included in the personal liability insurance. The commercial general liability insurance/product liability insurance only includes environmental damage to persons and property

316. For details, *see* R. Koch, in: Bruck/Moeller, Großkommentar zum VVG, 9 ed., vol. 4, DeGruyter 2013, no. 6 ProdHM n. 19 et seq.

317. *Besondere Bedingungen und Risikobeschreibungen für die Versicherung der Haftpflicht wegen Schäden durch Umwelteinwirkung (Umwelthaftpflicht-Modell)* – UmwHM as of September 2009, https://www.gdv.de/resource/blob/6204/072c0c9a3b5a3be826f31508b7aa2d80/19-besondere-bedingungen-und-risikobeschreibungen-fuer-die-versicherung-der-haftpflicht-wegen-schaeden-durch-umwelteinwirkung--umwelthaftpflicht-modell--data.pdf (accessed 28 Mar. 2018).

caused by products (also waste products). There is no cover in commercial general liability insurance/product liability insurance, however, for environmental damage *inter alia* resulting from the planning, production, delivery, assembly, dismantling, repair or maintenance of installations intended for the production, processing, storage, depositing, conveying or disposal of substances harmful to waterbodies or other related components which are clearly intended for use in such installations.

B. *Insured Event*

410. The insured event is the objectively verifiable first discovery of a loss by the injured party, a third party or the policyholder, e.g., when symptoms of an injured party's health impairment lead to a medical visit, when environmental damage resulting from a prior spill of pollutants is discovered (manifestation principle) (no. 4 UmweltHM) (*see* paragraph 379).[318]

C. *Personal Scope of Coverage*

411. Like under the commercial general liability insurance, liability claims against the policyholder's employees and personnel with the same status as employees are covered (no. 1.3 UmweltHM) (*see* paragraph 401).

V. Environmental Impairment Insurance

A. *Insured Risks and Damages*

412. There are no specific rules on environmental impairment insurance. According to no. 1 of GDV model terms and conditions (USV[319]) there is cover for the legal obligation under public law governed by the German environmental damage act (*Umweltschadensgesetz*, hereafter 'USchadG') or other national legislation based on the EU environmental liability Directive 2004/35/EC[320] to restore polluted environments in the case of damage to protected species and natural habitats, water bodies and soil. Such claims are not covered under commercial general liability insurance/product liability insurance (*see* paragraphs 398, 402).

318. *See* Tettamanti/Baer/Werz, Compulsory Liability Insurance in a Changing Legal Environment – An Insurance and Reinsurance Perspective, in: Fenyves/Kissling/Perner/Rubin (eds), Compulsory Liability Insurance from a European Perspective, DeGruyter 2016, p. 357.
319. *Allgemeine Versicherungsbedingungen für die Umweltschadensversicherung*, USV as of February 2016, https://www.gdv.de/resource/blob/6042/c993854e4cebb25737c149613a655244/22-allgemeine-versicherungsbedingungen-fuer-die-umweltschadensversicherung--usv--data.pdf (accessed 28 Mar. 2018).
320. O.J., 30 April 2004, L 143/56.

B. Insured Event

413. The insured event definition (no. 8 USV) is identical with the one of the environmental liability insurance (*see* paragraph 410).

C. Personal Scope of Coverage

414. Like under the commercial general liability insurance, liability claims against the policyholder's employees and personnel with the same status as employees are covered (no. 1.2 USV) (*see* paragraph 401).

VI. Professional Liability Insurance

A. Insured Risks and Damages

415. Professional liability insurance (also called E&O insurance) provides protection for professionals such as physicians, dentists, veterinary practitioners, non-medical practitioners, physiotherapists, midwives, massage therapists, psychologists, members of bar associations, patent agents, accountants, tax consultants, consultant economists and business economists, auditors, chartered accountants (attested auditors of books), tax agents, engineers, architects, brokers, real estate agents against liability incurred as a result of errors and omissions in performing their professional services. Except for physicians, architects, and engineers, most professional liability policies only cover pure financial losses suffered by third parties, as opposed to bodily injury and property damage claims.

416. Professional liability insurance is required int*er alia* for lawyers (§ 51 BRAO), tax advisers (§ 67 StBerG), auditors (§ 54 WPO), and notaries (§ 19a paragraph 1 sentence 1 BNotO). The rules on compulsory liability insurance in §§ 113–124 VVG apply as long as there are no special rules in the acts which require professionals to take out insurance (for more details on §§ 113–124 VVG *see* paragraph 432). The injured party has a direct claim against the insurer if the policyholder is insolvent or his/her whereabouts is unknown (*see* § 115 paragraph 1 sentence nos 2 and 3 VVG).

B. Insured Event

417. There are no GDV model terms and conditions on professional liability insurance. A uniform market standard, however, has been evolved.[321] The definition of the insured event is any loss which allegedly occurred as a result of an act, error

321. For the wording of the 'Allgemeine Versicherungsbedingungen zur Vermögensschaden-Haftpflichtversicherung', Proelss/Martin, VVG, 30th ed., C. H. Beck 2018, Ch. 250.

or omission of the policyholder during the policy period (§ 5 AVB Vermoegen). It is not necessary that the injured has already claimed the damage during the duration of the insurance contract. Thus, it might happen that even a long time after the termination of the insurance contract a third party evokes a claim for an event which happened during the duration of the insurance contract.

C. Personal Scope of Coverage

418. Co-insured are, e.g., the partners and associates e.g., of a law firm, if the law firm is the policyholder, or associates, if the partner is the policyholder.[322]

VII. Directors and Officers Insurance

A. Insured Risks and Damages

419. There are no specific rules on D&O insurance. D&O insurance offers liability cover for directors and officers. It is aimed to protect directors and officers from claims not only of third parties but also of their company which may arise from the decisions and actions taken within the scope of their regular duties. It is commonplace in Germany that cover is taken out and paid for by the company that ultimately benefits from the insurance coverage because it ensures that the claim will be enforceable. It needs to be emphasized that D&O policies only cover pure financial losses suffered by the company or a third party.

420. The vast majority claims against directors and officers are made by their own companies. Whenever the company suffers damages as a result of wrongdoing or compliance failings, the policyholder is at the same time the injured party. The dual role of the company may lead to conflicts once the insurer has decided to defend the directors and officers against the claim of the company. In such situation the company, in its capacity as policyholder, is no longer under the duties to seek and to follow instructions from the insurer (*see* paragraph 274).

421. Although the underwriting practice does not make use of the GDV model terms and conditions (AVB-AVG), a uniform market standard has somehow evolved. D&O policies cover the personal liability of company directors and officers as individuals (side A cover[323]), but also the reimbursement of the insured company in case it has paid the claim of a third party on behalf of its managers in order to protect them (side B or company reimbursement cover[324]). Listed stock companies can also obtain cover for claims against the company itself for a wrongful act

322. Diller, Berufshaftpflichtversicherung für Rechtsanwälte, 2nd ed., C. H. Beck 2017, § 7 AVB-RSW n. 8.
323. Cf. Lange, D&O-Versicherung und Managerhaftung, C. H. Beck 2014, § 6 n. 2 et seq.
324. *Ibid.*, n. 44.

in connection with the trading of its securities (side C or securities entity cover[325]). Except for the latter case, it is to be noted that the D&O insurance is a pure third-party insurance since only the interests of the directors and officers are insured.

422. As pointed out before, under D&O policies defence costs are included in the one sum insured (*see* paragraph 370). Many D&O policies also cover defence costs for the policyholder's company directors and officers caused by administrative and criminal proceedings or in the course of investigations by regulators or criminal prosecutors (with the reservation of the right to reclaim in case of a deliberate misconduct).[326]

423. D&O-insurance policies regularly provide that the directors and officers, by derogation from §§ 44 paragraph 1, 45 paragraph 1 VVG (*see* paragraph 225), have the right to demand payment and file an action against the insurer. They also have the right to assign the claim to be released from liability to the company. In that case the company, in its capacity as injured party, is entitled to demand payment from the insurer (*see* paragraph 387).[327]

424. D&O policies do not cover deliberate non-compliant acts (no. 5.1 AVB-AVG). Nevertheless, innocent directors and officers remain fully covered if they are – together with colleagues who acted deliberately – jointly and severally liable for damages to the company (*see* paragraph 315).

425. § 93 paragraph 2 sentence 3 AktG calls for an excess of at least ten percent of the loss up to at least one and a half times the fixed annual remuneration of the management board member of a corporation (*Aktiengesellschaft*) to be agreed. There is no such requirement for the corporation's supervisory board members and for management board members of a limited liability company (*Gesellschaft mit beschraenkter Haftung*).The mandatory retention set forth in § 93 paragraph 2 sentence 3 AktG does not apply to defence costs and settlement amounts. It is to be noted that the directors and officers of a corporation may insure the retention by taking out a D&O retention insurance.[328] In this case the respective directors and officers are policyholders.

B. Insured Event

426. D&O insurance grants cover on a claims-made basis (*see* paragraph 380). This means that claims are only covered if they are made while the policy is in effect or within a contractually agreed extended claim period, which can extend up to another 120 months for corporations. [329] Normally a policy will have an agreed-on,

325. *Ibid.*, n. 45.
326. *See* Lange, D&O-Versicherung und Managerhaftung, C.H. Beck 2014, § 14 n. 94 et seq.
327. *See* R. Koch.
328. Cf. Lange, D&O-Versicherung und Managerhaftung, C.H. Beck 2014, § 17.
329. *Ibid.*, § 10 n. 17.

often unlimited, retroactive period covering claims for wrongful acts that took place before the policy's inception (no. 3.1 AVB-AVG). Unlike as in other European countries such as France[330] or Spain,[331] there are no specific rules requiring an extended claim period. There are decisions, however, where the courts held that there must be a reasonable period of time following the policy's expiration date during which claims made against the policyholder are covered.[332]

C. Personal Scope of Coverage

1. Directors

427. (Co-)Insured persons are all current, future and past members of the management board and the supervisory board.

2. Officers (Executive Staff)

428. Moreover, executive staff (*leitende Angestellte*) is (co-)insured. In the absence of agreement of the contrary the qualification as executive staff member is assessed according to § 5 paragraph 3 BetrVG.[333] Hence all employees are considered as executive staff who, under their contract of employment and by their status in the company or establishment, are:

- are entitled on their own responsibility to engage and dismiss employees on behalf of the establishment or one of its departments;
- are endowed with general authority (power of procuration) or full power of representation or power to sign, the latter also being important in relation to the employer; or
- regularly carry out other duties which are important for the existence and development of the company or an establishment and fulfilment of which requires particular experience and knowledge, if, in doing so, they either essentially make decisions on their own responsibility or substantially influence these decisions.

---

330. Articles L. 124–125 French insurance contract act (five years after the end of the contract).
331. Article 73 para. 2 Spanish insurance contract act (one year after the end of the contract).
332. Cf. OLG Frankfurt/M., 5 Dec. 2012 – 7 U 73/11, RuS 2013, pp. 329, 332; *see also* OLG München, 8 May 2009 – 25 U 5136/08, RuS 2009, pp. 327, 330.
333. OLG München, 13 Sept. 2017 – 7 U 4126/13, RuS 2017, pp. 589. 591.

VIII. Cyber Risk Liability Insurance

A. *Insured Risks and Damages*

429. There are no specific rules on cyber risk liability insurance. Cyber insurance policies, in general, cover more than one class of insurance (multiline insurance). They provide coverage not only against first-party losses – i.e., own property damage and interruption loss – but also against liability for bodily injury, property damage and pure financial losses. The model terms and conditions issued by the GDV (AVB Cyber[334]), which are addressed to small and medium sized businesses, deal with cyber risk liability insurance in part 3 (*Abschnitt A3*). They provide protection against liability incurred as a result of the impairment of availability, integrity and/or confidentiality of the policyholder's data (including software and programmes) or the policyholder's information-processing system due to cyber-attacks (including malware) (A3-1 in conjunction with A1.2 AVB Cyber).

B. *Insured Event*

430. The definition of the insured event is the verifiable first discovery of the financial loss (A1-4 AVB Cyber) (*see* paragraph 379).

C. *Personal Scope of Coverage*

431. Like under the commercial general liability insurance, liability claims against the policyholder's employees and personnel with the same status as employees are covered (A1-7 AVB Cyber) (*see* paragraph 401).

IX. Motor Liability Insurance

432. *See* paragraphs 574–620.

§6. Compulsory Liability Insurance

I. General Remarks

433. The Compulsory liability insurance is subject to §§ 113–124 VVG. § 113 paragraph 1 VVG defines as compulsory liability insurance any legally required liability insurance. In Germany, both at federal and Laender level, there are more

334. *Allgemeine Versicherungsbedingungen für die Cyberrisiko-Versicherung*, AVB Cyber as of April 2017, https://www.gdv.de/resource/blob/6100/d4c013232e8b0a5722b7655b8c0cc207/01-allgemeine-versicherungsbedingungen-fuer-die-cyberrisiko-versicherung--avb-cyber--data.pdf (accessed 28 Mar. 2018).

than 100 laws stipulating an obligation to take out liability insurance.[335] Compulsory liability insurance is foreseen for claims arising out of or relating to keeping vehicles (e.g., cars), animals (e.g., dogs) or weapons, the operation of (potentially) hazardous activities (e.g., the operation of air carriers, aircraft suppliers and other airplane owner's, railway companies and railway network operators, hunting) or a specific professional practice (e.g., lawyers, notaries). The aim of such insurance is to protect third parties against damages resulting from injury to life and limb, property, and/or against damages for pure economic loss. There is no general rule that, in cases where there is strict liability, compulsory liability insurance has been introduced. Except for motor liability insurance (§ 5 paragraph 2 PflVG), there is no obligation of the insurer to accept an application for compulsory liability insurance (*see* paragraph 581).

434. It is important to emphasize that §§ 113–124 VVG do not establish the obligation to take out insurance but only provide a framework and determine *inter alia* the minimum content of cover whenever such obligation is imposed by a legal provision. Apart from this, there is no coherent regulatory regime of compulsory liability insurance, either at federal or Laender level in terms of the reasons why they were established or with regard to different standards of liability or different types of damages.

435. It is to be noted that pursuant to § 113 paragraph 3 VVG, the framework provisions on compulsory liability insurance also apply insofar as the contract of insurance grants cover in excess of the minimum requirements set forth in the rules stipulating the obligation to take out insurance (*see* paragraph 224). It follows from that provision *e contrario* that derogations as to the contents of the contract in favour of the policyholder are generally permitted. Even if there were no legal provision to that effect, such deviations, in light of the objectives of compulsory liability insurance, would be valid since they would not be detrimental to or, with regard to lower or higher deductibles, would be without effect on the victims. Within the limits set forth in § 114 paragraph 2 sentence 1 VVG the insurer and the policyholder are free to agree on clauses which exempt the insurer from coverage vis-à-vis the policyholder (in whole or in part).

II. Right of Direct Action Against the Insurer

436. The victim has a direct right of action against the insurer only in the case of compulsory liability insurance provided he/she has a claim against the policyholder (or any co-insured). Pursuant to § 115 paragraph 1 sentence 1 VVG in conjunction with § 1 PflVG this right, however, is limited to motor vehicle liability insurance cases (no. 1), or where insolvency proceedings have been instituted against the policyholder's assets, where the request for such proceedings has been

335. For a (non-exhaustive) list of federal and Laender level rules setting out a duty to take out liability insurance, *see* Attyla Fenyves/Christa Kissling/Stefan Perner/Daniel Rubin (eds), Compulsory Liablity Insurance from a European Perspective, DeGruyter 2016, pp. 479 et seq.

rejected due to lack of assets, where a temporary insolvency administrator has been appointed (no. 2), or where the policyholder's domicile is unknown (no. 3). Where the conditions for a direct right of action are not met, the victim only has a derived right of action where first, the policyholder has assigned his right against the insurer to be released from liability to the victim, second, the victim has obtained an order of attachment and transfer of the policyholder's right, or third, the policyholder becomes insolvent provided that the claim has been established in terms of § 106 sentence 1 VVG prior to the opening of the insolvency proceedings (*see* paragraph 387).[336]

III. Content of Insurance Cover

A. *Insured Risk*

437. The rules that impose an obligation to take out liability insurance are not related to extra-contractual or contractual liability. These rules generally require taking out insurance against liability claims on the grounds of statutory liability regardless of whether the liability is of an extra-/contractual nature. There are only few provisions aimed at the protection of absolutely protected rights as well as the compensation of pure economic loss. For example, § 1 PflVG requires the keeper of a vehicle to take out compulsory insurance coverage not only for personal injury and damage to property but also pure economic loss. The duties for legal advisors (lawyers (§ 51 BRAO), notaries (§ 19 paragraph 1 sentence 1 BNotO), tax advisors (§ 67 StBerG), and auditors (§ 54 WPO)) to take out professional liability insurance are directed only at the compensation of pure financial loss.

B. *Personal Scope of Cover*

438. There are provisions, such as § 1 PflVG, which require the keeper of a car to take out compulsory insurance coverage not only for himself but also for the owner and any driver of the car. § 6 paragraph 1 development aid workers act (*Entwicklungshelfer-Gesetz*, hereafter 'EhfG') imposes on development services the obligation to conclude liability insurance not only for the benefit of development aid workers but also for the benefit of their dependent spouses and children. Moreover, § 1908f BGB requires from social associations (*Betreuungsverein*) which have the task of finding and training voluntary citizens willing to become *Betreuer* (guardians of a disabled person) to insure its employees for any damage that they may cause to others in the course of their activity. Similar provisions exist for fairground workers (§ 55 f GewO in conjunction with § 1 ordinance on the liability of fairground workers, *Schaustellerhaftpflichtverordnung*, hereafter 'SchauHV'). According to § 19a paragraph 1 sentence 1 BNotO, notaries have a duty to maintain a professional liability insurance policy to cover the risks of liability for material

336. R. Koch, in: Bruck/Moeller, Großkommentar zum VVG, 9th ed., vol. 4, DeGruyter 2013, § 110 VVG n. 14 et seq.

damages arising out of the activity of persons for whom they are responsible (e.g., officially appointed representatives, notary clerks).

C. Restrictions of Cover

1. Statutory Exclusions from Coverage

439. According to § 103 VVG, which is applicable to both voluntary liability and compulsory liability insurance, there is no coverage to the extent the policyholder has intentionally and unlawfully caused the loss suffered by the victim.

2. Contractual Restrictions of Coverage

440. Contractual restrictions of coverage which are not prohibited by the rules requiring the conclusion of a liability insurance are subject to § 114 paragraph 2 sentence 1 VVG. Pursuant to this provision the contract of insurance may specify the content and scope of the compulsory insurance in more detail as long as it does not endanger the fulfilment of the respective objective of the compulsory insurance.

441. In order to eliminate long-tail claims, which only become apparent after many years and possibly after the expiration of the policy, liability insurers generally introduce clauses according to which there is no coverage for wrongful acts, errors or omissions that occurred during the period of insurance but for which a claim was not made and/or reported within a certain period of time (e.g., three or five years) after the expiration of the policy. Such *run-off coverage* clauses can be found not only in voluntary insurance policies (e.g., product liability insurance, environmental liability insurance)[337] but also in professional compulsory insurance contracts such as architects' liability insurance. They may endanger the purpose (not only) of the compulsory insurance contract if first, in reality, there is a considerable time lag between the date on which a professional's act, error or omission took place and the date of its discovery and, second, the run-off period is shorter than the prescription period for a claim.[338] In any event, the clause is void when coupled with a provision that the insurance cover for the entire run-off period is limited to the available cover of the last year of the insurance period since the rules on compulsory liability insurance require a minimum coverage for each breach that occurred during the insurance period, or on an aggregate basis.

337. For further details, *see* R. Koch, in: Bruck/Moeller, Großkommentar zum VVG, 9th ed., vol. 4, DeGruyter 2013, Produkthaftpflicht-Modell no. 7 n. 1 et seq.; Umwelthaftpflicht-Modell no. 8 n. 1 et seq.

338. Roland M. Beckmann, in: Bruck/Moeller, Großkommentar zum VVG, 9th ed., vol. 4, DeGruyter 2013, § 114 VVG n. 40; Claus von Rintelen, in: Beckmann/Matusche-Beckmann (eds), Versicherungsrechts-Handbuch, 3rd ed., C.H. Beck 2015, § 26 n. 215; for a somewhat different, very debatable view *see* OLG Stuttgart, 27 Nov. 2008 – 7 U 89/08, VersR 2009, pp. 669, 671 (held that a run-off clause shorter than the prescription was valid since the clause had to be so construed that the insurer could not invoke the limitation where the insurance holder acted without fault).

D. Insured Sum

1. Minimum Amount

442. The rules requiring the conclusion of a liability insurance policy often specify the minimum insurance sum but in no event the maximum one. For example, according to the annex to § 4 paragraph 2 PflVG, compulsory motor liability insurance requires as a minimum coverage EUR 7.5 million for personal injury, EUR 1.12 million for damage to property and EUR 50,000 for pure economic loss. § 19a paragraph 2 sentence 1 BNotO requires EUR 500,000 per claim as the minimum sum insured. Where there is no specification of the minimum sum, this sum is determined by § 114 paragraph 1 VVG according to which the minimum sum insured shall be EUR 250,000 per claim and EUR 1 million for all claims per insurance year.

2. Series Clauses

443. Like any other restrictions of coverage, claims series clauses must comply with the rules requiring the conclusion of liability insurance. § 51 paragraph 2 BRAO, § 19 paragraph 3 sentence 4 BNotO, § 45 paragraph 2 PatAnwO and § 5 paragraph 2 ordinance on the legal service act (*Verordnung zum Rechtsdienstleistungsgesetz*, hereafter 'RDV'), e.g., permit clauses according to which two or more claims arising from or relating to one and the same mandate are considered a single claim. § 53 paragraph 3 Regulation Implementing the Tax Consultants' Act (*Verordnung zur Durchfuehrung der Vorschriften über Steuerberater, Steuerbevollmaechtigte und Steuerberatungsgesellschaften*, hereafter 'DVStB') defines in more detail the permissible content of series clauses. According to this provision, the insurer is entitled to limit its liability to the sum insured for a single claim where the victim has a claim against more than one insured person (lit. a), or where the same damage results from multiple breaches (lit. b), or with regard to the consequences arising out of acts or omissions based on the same or a similar error if the matters concerned are legally or commercially related (lit. c). Series clauses modelled after § 53 paragraph 3 DVStB should be permissible where the rules requiring the conclusion of liability insurance keep silent on this issue. With regard to § 53 paragraph 3 lit. c) DVStB, it is to be noted that the BGH held that there is no legal or commercial connection where the policyholder continued to make the same mistakes in different matters for one and the same client (e.g., annual tax declaration).[339] Thus for each client who suffered damages the minimum coverage must be available.

339. BGH, 15 May 1991 – IV ZR 85/90, VersR 1991, pp. 873, 875.

3. Deductibles

444. According to § 114 paragraph 2 sentence 2 VVG, deductibles on the part of the policyholder cannot be invoked against the victim. As a consequence, clauses stipulating deductibles are permissible, albeit restricted to the internal relationship between insurer and policyholder. § 114 paragraph 2 sentence 2 VVG further states that deductibles cannot be asserted against a co-insured person. Hence, the employer/keeper of a car cannot demand from his employee reimbursement of the deductible in the case of an accident caused by the latter since, as a driver, he/she has co-insured status (§ 4 paragraph 2 PflVG in conjunction with § 2 paragraph 2 KfzPflVV).[340]

E. Settlement of Liability Claims

445. Except for motor liability insurance, there are no statutory provisions specifically establishing standards with regard to the settlement of liability claims. § 3a paragraph 1 PflVG, in accordance with Article 22 of the Directive 2009/103/EC,[341] requires the motor vehicle insurer or its claims representative to make, without undue delay and in all cases within three months of the date when the victim presented his/her claim for compensation, a reasoned offer of compensation in cases where liability is not contested and the damages have been quantified. Where liability is denied or has not been clearly determined or the damages have not been fully quantified, the insurer has to provide a reasoned reply to the points made in the claim. If the insurer fails to make an offer within three months, pursuant to § 3a paragraph 2 PflVG, default interest in the amount of five percentage points above the basic rate of interest per annum become due. The assertion of further damage is not excluded.

F. Protection Mechanism

1. Effects of Policyholder's Violation of Duties

446. According to § 117 paragraph 1 and paragraph 3 sentence 1 VVG, the insurer remains liable to the victim within the framework of the prescribed minimum sum insured and the risk assumed by it, even if it is wholly or partially released from liability vis-à-vis the policyholder due to a breach of an obligation (e.g., default in payment of the premium) (*see* paragraph 232) and/or a duty (e.g., duty of disclosure of risks prior to the conclusion of the contract, duty not to increase the risk insured, etc.) (*see* paragraphs 239, 249). The insurer must first compensate the victim and then has the right to recourse against the policyholder. This right follows from § 115 paragraph 1 sentence 4 VVG according to which the

340. *See* BAG, 13 Dec. 2012 – 8 AZR 432/11, NZA 2013, pp. 622, 623 et seq.
341. O.J., 7 October 2009, L 263/11.

insurer and the policyholder are liable towards the victim as joint and several debtors, and, second, as regards the relationship between them, from § 116 paragraph 1 sentence 2 VVG according to which the policyholder is solely liable. Pursuant to § 116 paragraph 1 sentence 3 VVG, the insurer is moreover entitled to claim for reimbursement of the expenses incurred (e.g., defence costs). The right to recourse against the policyholder, however, is limited in motor liability insurance (*see* paragraphs 619, 620).

2. Run-off Cover (*Nachhaftung*)

447. According to § 117 paragraph 2 sentence 1 VVG, circumstances, which result in the non-existence (e.g., due to lack of the policyholder's legal capacity,[342] (hidden) lack of consent), or the cessation of the insurance contract (e.g., due to a revocation of or termination of or withdrawal from the insurance contract[343]) are only effective vis-à-vis the victim one month after the insurer has notified the competent agency of this circumstance (so-called *Nachhaftung*). The competent agency will be generally identified by the rules requiring the conclusion of liability insurance (e.g., vehicle registration authorities for motor vehicle liability insurance, § 7 PflVG in conjunction with § 25 paragraph 1 FZV, or the bar association for liability insurance taken out by lawyers, § 51 paragraph 7 BRAO). The 'Nachhaftung' shall also apply if the insurance contract has expired (§ 117 paragraph 2 sentence 2 VVG).

448. The 'Nachhaftung' by no means commences before the insurance contract has ended (for one of the afore-mentioned reasons) (§ 117 paragraph 2 sentence 3 VVG). The liability insurer, however, can invoke that the insurance agreement had already ended by the time relevant in respect of the obligation to provide cover if, at that point in time, the competent agency has received confirmation that a new contract has been concluded (§ 117 paragraph 2 sentence 4 VVG). It needs to emphasised that there will be no 'Nachhaftung' where no competent agency has been appointed to receive the notification (§ 117 paragraph 2 sentence 5 VVG), as is the case, e.g., with development aid workers' liability insurance (*see* § 6 EhfG).

3. Subsidiary Liability of the Insurer

449. It is important to note that according to § 117 paragraph 3 sentence 2 VVG the insurer is not obligated to effect payment in the cases described in § 117 paragraph 1 and 2 VVG insofar as the victim may receive compensation for his loss from another indemnity insurer (e.g., his/her comprehensive motor vehicle insurer, *see* paragraph 622) or from a social security institution (*see* paragraph 757).

342. BGH, 2 Oct. 2002 – IV ZR 309/01, VersR 2002, p. 1501.
343. Klimke, in: Proelss/Martin, VVG, 30th ed., C.H. Beck 2018, § 117 VVG n. 7.

4. Order of Precedence of Several Claims

450. Where the claims for compensation to be paid on the basis of the same occurrence of loss are in excess of the sum insured, § 118 paragraph 1 VVG establishes a ranking system on how claims are to be settled in the following order: first, claims arising from personal injury, second, claims arising from other injuries to natural or legal persons, third, claims arising from personal injury or other injuries assigned to insurers or other third parties; fourth, claims assigned to social insurance agencies and fifth, all other claims. In the event of equal-ranking claims, they will be settled in proportion to their amount.

Chapter 5. Legal Expenses Insurance

§1. Legal Regime

451. Legal expense insurance is subject to §§ 125–129 VVG. § 125 VVG states that the insurer is obliged to safeguard the policyholder's legal interests and to cover the expenses required for this purpose. What expenses are covered depend on the policy wording. The GDV has issued model terms and conditions on legal expense insurance in 2012 (ARB 2012[344]) which have a different structure as previous versions and appear to be yet less accepted by the market.

452. Until the transposition of the Directive 87/344/EC of June 1987,[345] legal expenses policies could only be sold by an insurer whose business plan did not at the same time contain other insurance classes. The rationale behind that was that there is potential conflict of interest if, e.g., a liability policyholder causes harm to a third party who has a legal expenses insurance with the same insurer. The insurer would have to represent the interests of the legal expenses policyholder and also of the liability policyholder. In this situation there would be a doubt as to whether the insurer wholeheartedly is willing to defend its policyholder against the liability claim or to support the third party's liability claim.[346] Since 1 July 1990 the strict separation of insurance classes no longer has existed.

453. According to § 164 VAG an insurer, which carries on legal expenses insurance together with other classes of insurance, has to transfer the claims handling to a loss adjustment firm. The loss adjustment firm must have no other kind of insurance business apart from legal expenses insurance. In dealing with individual claims it must not be bound by instructions from the legal expenses insurer. According to § 126 paragraph 2 VVG, claims arising under a legal expenses insurance contract may only be asserted against the loss adjustment firm.

454. § 127 VVG grants the policyholder the free choice of a lawyer and § 128 VVG provides a process for calling in expert opinions in the event that the insurer denies his liability because looking after the legal interests does not have sufficient prospects of success or is wanton. §§ 126 to 128 VVG are semi-mandatory (§ 129 VVG).

455. It is important to note that under the legal services act (*Rechtsdienstleistungsgesetz*, hereafter 'RDG'), legal expenses insurers are not permitted to offer

344. *Allgemeine Bedingungen für die Rechtsschutzversicherung*, ARB 2012 as of June 2017, https://www.gdv.de/resource/blob/5904/48224b09423b3cac163e9cfdab5a50a5/01-allgemeine-bedingungen-fuer-die-rechtsschutzversicherung--arb-2012--data.pdf (accessed 28 Mar. 2018).
345. Directive 87/344/EC on the coordination of laws, regulations and administrative provisions relating to legal expenses insurance, O.J., 4 July 1987, L 185/77 (repealed by the solvency II Directive 2009/138/EG, O.J., 17 December 2009, L-335/1).
346. Harbauer/Bauer, Rechtsschutzversicherung, 8th ed., C.H. Beck 2010, § 126 VVG n. 1.

legal counselling as part of the claims handling process.[347] For that reason, legal expenses insurers have intensified their business relationships with the legal profession by offering to conclude fee agreements. Furthermore, they offer hotline counselling services and transfer the policyholder to lawyers who are members of the insurer's lawyer network.

§2. Types of Policy and Benefit

I. Modular Structure

456. Legal expenses insurance does not grant general coverage. Like the liability insurance, it is subject to the principle of speciality: insurance cover is based on a modular principle linked to certain characteristics of the policyholder or areas of activity of the policyholder, for which certain types of benefit and risks from certain legal fields can be insured (no.2 ARB 2012). The following types of policy (and combinations) are offered:

- legal expenses insurance for consumers;
- legal expenses insurance for self-employed and businesses;
- legal expenses insurance for non-profit-making associations;
- legal expenses insurance for farmers;
- legal expenses insurance for employees;
- traffic legal expenses insurance;
- vehicle legal expenses insurance;
- legal expenses insurance for owners and tenants of buildings or parts of buildings.

457. Each policy type contains a bundle of particular types of benefit (no. 2.2 ARB 2012). The following types of benefit (and combinations) are offered:

- legal expenses for damages;
- employment legal protection;
- legal protection for dwellings and property;
- legal expenses for contract and property law;
- fiscal legal expenses;
- Social Court legal expenses;
- administrative legal expenses for traffic matters;
- legal expenses in disciplinary and professional misconduct proceedings;
- legal expenses in criminal cases;
- legal expenses in administrative offence cases;
- legal expenses for counselling in family and inheritance law;
- legal expenses for accessory private prosecution of a crime of violence.

347. For further details, *see* Looschelders, Aktuelle Probleme der Rechtsschutzversicherung im deutschen und österreichischen Recht, VersR 2017, pp. 1234, 1237).

458. The extent of cover for these types of benefit is defined in more detail in nos 2.2.1–2.2.12 ARB 2012. For example, legal expenses for damages include damages for the enforcement of claims for damages insofar as these are not based on breach of contract or a violation of a property right (right in rem) on land, buildings or parts of buildings. Legal expenses in criminal cases include expenses for the defence against the charge of an offence pursuant to traffic law or any other offence caused by negligence.

459. It is important to note that not all of the afore-listed types of benefit are available for certain policy types. For example, for self-employed and businesses there is no coverage for legal expenses for contract and property law available, because this involves the typical entrepreneurial risk which should not be transferred to the insurer.

II. Legal Expenses Insurance for Consumers

460. This type of policy provides legal expenses coverage for the private sphere. There is no cover for expenses in connection with a commercial, freelance or other independent activity. The following persons are co-insured (no. 2.1.2 ARB 2012):

- spouse or unmarried life partner named in the insurance policy;
- minors up to the age of 18;
- children who have reached the legal age of majority, provided they are younger than 25 years and unmarried and they do not yet have a steady occupation for which they receive an income.

III. Legal Expenses Insurance for Self-employed and Businesses

461. This type of policy provides coverage for legal expenses in connection with commercial, freelance or other independent activity specified in the insurance certificate. The policyholder's employees are co-insured (no. 2.1.2 ARB 2012).

IV. Legal Expenses Insurance for Non-profit Associations

462. This type of policy provides coverage for the legal expenses of the non-profit association and their legal representatives (board of management), employees and members in connection with their activities for the association (no. 2.1.2 ARB 2012).

V. Legal Expenses Insurance for Farmers

463. This type of policy provides coverage for the policyholder's capacity as owner of the farm specified in the insurance certificate, for the policyholder's private sphere as well as his/her non-self-employed activities. The scope of cover includes traffic legal expenses insurance (*see* paragraph 466) for passenger vans and motorbikes, trucks use for agriculture and forestry.

464. The following persons are co-insured (no. 2.1.2 ARB 2012):

- employees;
- spouse or unmarried life partner named in the insurance policy;
- minors up to the age of 18;
- children who have reached the legal age of majority, provided they are younger than 25 years and unmarried and they do not yet have a steady occupation for which they receive an income.

VI. Legal Expenses Insurance for Employees

465. This type of policy provides coverage of legal expenses arising e.g., from the employer-employee relationship because of dismissal or wage claims. Disputes in public service due to job grading, transfer to another department or dismissal from public service are also covered.

VII. Traffic Legal Expenses Insurance

466. Legal protection for traffic matters is granted if the policyholders' legal interests need to be safeguarded in their capacity as owner or keeper, purchaser, lessee and/or driver of vehicles or trailers (no. 2.1.2 ARB 2012).

467. The vehicles and trailers must be registered in the name of the policyholder, or furnished in his/her name with an insurance license plate, or leased by the policyholder. Furthermore, the policyholder is insured in his/her capacity as a passenger as well as a pedestrian or a cyclist in taking part in traffic on public roads.

468. In the case the driver did not have a driving license at the time of a legal expenses claim, or he/she was not authorized to drive the motor vehicle, or the vehicle was not registered or furnished with an insurance license plate, the insurer is discharged from its liability towards those (co-)insureds who had knowledge or were unaware due to negligence of such circumstances. In cases of a grossly negligent unawareness, the insurer is only entitled to reduce the cover under the contract in proportion to the severity of gross negligence. If the (co-)insureds prove that the circumstances had no influence on the occurrence or determination of the insured event or on the determination or the extent of the insurer's obligation to pay, the insurer must provide full coverage (no. 4.2 ARB 2012).

VIII. Vehicle Legal Expenses Insurance

469. Vehicle legal expenses insurance provides coverage where policyholders take part in road traffic with vehicles they do not own. The policyholder is insured as a driver irrespective of whether the vehicle is registered in his name or have an insurance license plate. It is to be noted that only the policyholder himself is insured. The vehicle he/she uses is not insured. Thus, e.g., in a traffic accident involving bodily injury and vehicle damage, there is only insurance cover for the claim for damages of the driver against the tortfeasor for bodily injury. No. 4.2 ARB 2012 (*see* paragraph 468) applies *mutatits mutandis*.

IX. Legal Expenses Insurance for Owners and Tenants

470. This type of policy provides coverage of legal expenses arising e.g., out of disputes in connection with rental and lease contracts, the right to use a building or part of a building as a residence. The policyholder is insured in his/her capacity as the owner of the premise, building or parts of the building, as lessor and lessee or other beneficiary. Besides the accommodation unit itself, the garages or parking spaces that belong to it are also insured.

X. Other Types of Policy

471. Additional protection is offered to businesses. For example, some insurers offer – not based on the ARB 2012 – companies an extended form of criminal defence protection against the effects of criminal investigation proceedings. Criminal legal expenses insurance will be concluded by the company. All legal representatives, all members of the management board and supervisory board, and all employees of the company are co-insured against criminal proceedings instituted in conjunction with their professional activities. It is possible to limit the coverage for members of the management board as an individual solution.

472. Insurers also offer legal protection for travellers. The coverage is restricted to typical travel perils. If, e.g., the policyholder in his/her capacity as a tenant of a holiday home, as a pedestrian or as the driver of a vehicle after an accident, is involved in a dispute (e.g., a dispute regarding the size of a claim for damages, a dispute with a hotelier or the owner of a holiday home), the insurer provides legal advice and processes the legal case on behalf of the policyholder. In addition, the insurer may cover, among other charges, the advances for bail payments.

§3. Scope of Coverage

I. Policyholder's Expenses for a Lawyer

473. According to no. 2.3.1 ARB 2012 the insurer pays the statutory fees of a (one) lawyer acting on behalf of the policyholder in accordance with the lawyers' remuneration act (*Rechtsanwaltungsverguetungsgesetz*, hereafter 'RVG'). The remuneration schedule attached to the RVG (Annex 1 to the RVG) prescribes either fixed fees or fee ranges applicable to individual activities. A distinction is made between, e.g., civil, administrative and fiscal matters, criminal cases, fines and social law matters. In civil matters the fee level is determined by reference to the value of the claim. Lawyers must charge VAT at 19%. It is charged separately as an expense and is not included in their fees.

474. If the competent court is situated outside a radius of 100 km, as the crow flies, from the policyholder's place of domicile, the insurer pays an additional fee for an associate attorney in accordance with the RVG (no. 2.3.1.2 ARB 2012). For legal protection abroad the insurer pays for a foreign lawyer at the location of the competent court (no. 2.3.2 ARB 2012).

II. Court Fees

475. The insurer takes over the court fees, including costs for witnesses and experts appointed by the court and the costs for the bailiff (no. 2.3.3.1 ARB 2012). In Germany the court fees are laid down in the court costs act (*Gerichtskostengesetz*, hereafter 'GKG') and the court costs (family matters) act (*Gesetz ueber Gerichtskosten in Familiensachen*, hereafter 'FamGKG'). The fee rates are set out in the schedule of costs (Annex 1 of the GKG/FamGKG). The fees are set out by claim value in the table of fees (Annex 2 of the GKG/FamGKG). In civil law cases the fees are related to the value of the claim, as with the lawyer's costs. Proceedings before social courts involve no costs for insured persons (§ 183 SGG). Costs for arbitration or conciliation are covered up to the amount of corresponding costs for the Court of First Instance. Costs for mediation are insured up to an agreed amount (no. 2.3.1.1 ARB 2012).

476. Experts called by the court receive a fee based on an hourly rate that is fixed by law in the judicial remuneration and compensation act (*Justizverguetungs- und Justizentschaedigungsgesetz*, hereafter 'JVEG'), and is paid by the parties to the proceedings. Bailiffs (*Gerichtsvollzieher*) only charge the costs stipulated in the bailiffs' costs act (*Gerichtsvollzieherkostengesetz*, hereafter 'GvKostG'). A set fee is prescribed for each individual activity carried out by the bailiff. Court fees and bailiff fees are not subject to VAT.

III. Costs of the Opposing Lawyer

477. The insurer also pays the fees of the opponent's lawyer when the policyholder lost the litigation as well as the opponent's court fees to the extent required by law and/or in accordance with the judgment (no. 2.3.3.3 ARB 2012). It needs to be emphasized that these costs are also covered under liability insurance policies if the opponent sues the policyholder for damages e.g., for bodily harm.

IV. Costs of Enforced Debt Collection Proceedings

478. If the losing party does not meet its obligations despite a final judgment or a settlement in favour of the policyholder, the costs for up to three enforcement measures within five years of the title being legally effective (the lawyer's fees and the cost of the bailiff) are covered by the insurer (no. 3.3.5 ARB 2012).

V. Costs of out of Court Experts

479. For cases involving criminal and/or administrative criminal proceedings or cases related to purchase or repair contracts of motor land vehicles or trailers the costs of an expert who is appointed in an out of court procedure are insured provided that the expert has the required technical expertise evidenced by a certificate of the competent authority (no. 2.3.1.3 ARB 2012).

VI. Further Costs

480. If the policyholder is required to appear before a foreign court as a defendant or a party, the legal expenses insurer pays for the foreign travel expenses (no. 2.3.2.3 ARB 2012). The costs for translation of written documents are also insured (no. 2.3.2.4 ARB 2012). Moreover, the insurer takes over the payment of bail, to spare the policyholder interim prosecution measures. This takes the form of an interest free loan (no. 2.3.3.5 ARB 2012). Depending on the insurer, the limit lies between EUR 60,000 and EUR 200,000.

481. Some insurers cover – not based on the ARB 2012 – the costs for public relations work, costs incurred for investigative custody, and costs for litigation services (e.g., forensic services, reinstatement of reputation) and all advances on these.

VII. Limits of Indemnification

482. For each case the insurer pays at most the agreed sum insured. For many insurance companies this is EUR 1 million. Some insurers offer unlimited coverage. Bail, which is granted as a loan, is not included in the sum insured. Most insurers offer tariffs with and without excesses.

§4. INSURED EVENT

483. Legal expenses insurance policies grant insurance coverage only for future disputes. There is no insurance cover for legal disputes having been caused or occasioned at a time before the inception of the policy as well as during a waiting period.

I. Occurrence During the Period of Insurance

484. The legal expenses insurer is only obligated to reimburse the policyholder (or a co-insured person) if the insured event has occurred after the inception of the policy and prior to the expiry of the cover (no. 2.4 ARB 2012). The definition of the insured event depends on the individual types of benefit. If the policyholder claims legal expenses for counselling in family and inheritance law, the relevant point in time is the event that resulted in a change in the policyholder's legal position (no. 2.4.1 ARB 2012). The change in the legal position, e.g., the death of a family member, must have actually occurred.

485. Where the policyholder claims for legal expenses for a compensation claim against a third person, the point in time is the first event (*erstes Ereignis*) when the damage (or injury) occurred or is supposed to have occurred (no. 2.4.2 ARB 2012). According to the BGH the question of whether or not the insured event is triggered depends on the facts set out in the policyholder's claim. The earliest point in time is the breach of the opposing party on which the policyholder rests his/her claim.[348] For all other types of benefit relevant is the point in time when the policyholder or a third person has breached or is alleged to have breached legal obligations or legal regulations (no. 2.4.3 ARB 2012). Therefore the allegation of a claim for compensation or a breach of an obligation is sufficient to entitle the policyholder to claim reimbursement of the legal expenses incurred by him/her.[349]

II. Waiting Period

486. No. 3.1.1 ARB 2012 provides for a waiting period of three months after the inception of the policy. The waiting period reflects the fact that insurance events occurring shortly after the commencement of insurance generally reflect the materialisation of an elevated risk existing already upon commencement of insurance. The purpose of the waiting period is to avoid the policy being taken out when the reason for the claim has existed prior to the inception of the policy.[350]

487. There is not a waiting period for all types of benefit. A waiting period must only be observed for the following types of benefit:

348. BGH, 30 Apr. 2014 – IV ZR 47/13, RuS 2014, p. 354 para. 17 et seq.
349. For further details, *see* Armbruester, in: Proelss/Martin, VVG, 30th ed., C.H. Beck 2018, § 3 ARB 2010 ns 15, 41.
350. OLG Hamm, 4 Jul. 2014 – 20 U 114/14, RuS 2015, pp. 196, 197.

- legal expenses for damages;
- legal expenses in disciplinary and professional misconduct proceedings;
- legal expenses in criminal cases;
- legal expenses in administrative offence cases;
- legal expenses resulting from disputes over contract of sale or lease of a new vehicle;
- legal expenses for counselling in family and inheritance law;
- legal expenses for accessory private prosecution of a crime of violence.

488. The actual date of the legal expenses claim is always the determining factor. It can happen that the loss already occurred years ago and the policyholder has only now learnt about it.

III. Declaration of Intent

489. There is no legal protection if a declaration of intent or a legal act that was carried out before the beginning of the insurance coverage triggers the insured event (no. 3.1.2 ARB 2012). Such a declaration of intent can be, e.g., the notice of claim, the application for a driving licence or a warning notice. While the notice of claim always triggers the insured event,[351] the situation is different in the event of an application or a warning notice, where there might be later disputes when the authority refuses to issue the licence, or the debtor claims that the claim was not yet due. According to decisions of the OLG Koeln and OLG Duesseldorf the insurer is obliged to provide coverage where a defective notice concerning the right to withdraw from the consumer credit agreement was given prior to the conclusion of the legal insurance contract. The appellate courts held that only the denial of the bank to accept the withdrawal triggers the insured event not the defective notice of the policyholder.[352]

IV. Notification Period

490. For events occurring within the policy period but that are reported later than three years after the termination of the policy there is no insurance cover (no.3.1.3 ARB 2012).

§5. Exclusions

491. There are exclusions which apply to all types of policy and benefit and there are exclusions which apply to individual types of policy and specific types of

351. *Ibid.*
352. OLG Köln, 16 Feb. 2016 – 9 U 159/15, zfs 2016, p. 335; OLG Düsseldorf, 22 Jul. 2016 – 4 U 213/14, RuS 2016, p. 514.

benefit only. Relevant for all types of policy and benefit are the exclusions to provide cover for legal expenses in conjunction with:

- war, hostilities, rebellion, civil unrest, strike, lock out or earthquake (no. 3.2.1 ARB 2012);
- nuclear and genetic damage (except as a result of medical treatment) (no. 3.2.1 ARB 2012);
- defence of claims for damages (no. 3.2.3 ARB 2012);
- claims against the insurer or the loss adjustment firm (no. 3.2.11 ARB 2012);
- proceedings before constitutional courts or international courts of justice (no. 3.2.13 ARB 2012);
- opening of insolvency proceedings over the policyholder's assets (no. 3.2.14 ARB 2012);
- disputes between insured persons (no. 3.2.17 ARB 2012);
- claims or liabilities that have been transferred or passed over to the policyholder after a legal expenses claim has occurred (e.g., assignment) (no. 3.2.18 ARB 2012);
- third party claims made by the policyholder in his own name (no. 3.2.20 ARB 2012);
- the unlawful and deliberate causation of the insured event (no. 3.2.21 ARB 2012).

492. Relevant for individual types of policy and benefit are the exclusions to provide cover for legal expenses in disputes concerning:

- subsidence affecting property and buildings (no. 3.2.1 ARB 2012);
- purchase or sale of a plot of land for construction development (no. 3.2.2 ARB 2012);
- planning or the construction of a building that is either owned by or in the possession of the policyholder or which he/she intends to purchase (no. 3.2.2 ARB 2012);
- financing of the purchase of a plot of land or the construction of a building (no. 3.2.2 ARB 2012);
- collective agreements or public service law (no. 3.2.4 ARB 2012);
- company law or service contracts between the company and their legal representatives (no. 3.2.5 ARB 2012);
- patent law, copyright, trade mark law, industrial design law, utility model law or other rights deriving from intellectual property (no. 3.2.6 ARB 2012);
- cartel law or unfair competition law (no. 3.2.7 ARB 2012);
- capital investments management (no. 3.2.8 ARB 2012);
- granting loans (no. 3.2.9 ARB 2012);
- gaming or betting contracts as well as forward transactions or similar speculative activities (no. 3.2.9 ARB 2012);
- family and inheritance law (cf. legal expenses insurance for counselling) (no. 3.2.10 ARB 2012);
- tax evaluations of property and one-off development taxes and other residential taxes (no. 3.2.12 ARB 2012);
- expropriation, planning permission, land consolidation (no. 3.2.15 ARB 2012);

- infringement and administrative proceedings because of a violation of a stop or parking restriction (no. 3.2.16 ARB 2012);
- unmarried life partners in connection with the unmarried partnership (no. 3.2.18 ARB 2012);
- commercial, freelance or self-employed activities (no. 3.2.22 ARB 2012);
- timesharing (no. 3.2.23 ARB 2012).

§6. Examining the Prospects of Success

493. As indicated above (*see* paragraph 454) the insurer has the right to examine the case and may deny coverage because of the poor prospects of success. There is sufficient prospect of success if there is certain likelihood of a positive outcome because e.g., the policyholder can rely on case law which supports his/her claim.[353]

494. According to no. 3.4.1.1 ARB 2012 insurance protection cannot be declined due to poor prospects of success with the following types of benefit:

- legal expenses in disciplinary and professional misconduct proceedings;
- legal expenses in criminal cases;
- legal expenses in administrative offence cases;
- legal expenses for counselling in family and inheritance law;
- legal expenses for accessory private prosecution of a crime of violence.

495. Furthermore the insurer may decline insurance protection if the claim is wanton. This is the case if the likely costs involved are out of proportion to the objective in mind (3.4.1.2 ARB 2012). Whether or not the costs are out of proportion depends on the individual circumstances of the case. As a general rule, a claim is wanton if a reasonable person would not pursue the claim if he/she had to bear all costs at his/her own expense.[354] According to no. 3.4.1.2 ARB 2012 the insurer must deny coverage without undue delay otherwise the insurer will be barred from denying its liability.[355]

496. If the parties have different opinions on the prospects of success or the wantonness of the claim, within a month the policyholder can demand the initiation of expert determination proceedings (no. 3.4.3 ARB 2012). According to no. 3.4.4 ARB 2012 the expert must be a lawyer who has been admitted to the bar for at least 5 years. The expert will be appointed by the president of the bar association competent at the place where the policyholder has his/her domicile. It needs to be emphasized that the appointee acts as an expert and not as an arbitrator when he/she establishes whether or not the decision to refuse legal protection was justified. Only the insurer is bound by the decision of the expert. If the expert finds for the insurer,

353. Cf. OLG Düsseldorf, 21 Sept. 2017 – 4 U 87/17, RuS 2017, pp. 633, 635.
354. Cf. BGH, 16 Oct. 2002 – XII ZR 73/02, NJW-RR 2003, pp. 228, 229.
355. *See also* BGH, 20 Jul. 2016 – IV ZR 245/15, RuS 2016, pp. 462, 464; BGH, 9 Mar. 2003 – IV ZR 139/01, RuS 2003, pp. 363, 365 (with regard to an older version of the ARB).

the policyholder bears the costs of the expert proceedings as well as those of the expert. The insurer bears its own costs in any case. If the expert comes to the conclusion that the refusal to provide protection was completely or partially unjustified, the insurer carries the complete costs of the arbitration procedure.

Chapter 6. Marine Insurance

§1. LEGAL REGIME

497. According to § 209 VVG the VVG does not apply to insurance against the perils of an ocean voyage. Insurance against the perils of an ocean voyage include *inter alia* hull insurance, machinery insurance, cargo insurance and protection & indemnity (P&I) insurance.[356] These types of marine insurance contracts are governed by the HGB and the BGB when the policyholder and the insurer have agreed on German law as the applicable law. The Transport-Informations-Service of the GDV (abbreviated 'TIS-GDV') offers English versions of various marine insurance model terms and conditions, e.g., the DTV standard terms and conditions of insurance for ocean-going vessels 2009 (DTV-ADS 2009[357]) and the DTV cargo insurance conditions 2000/2011 (DTV-Cargo 2000/2011). Although the VVG does not apply to marine insurance the model terms and conditions closely follow the VVG provisions applying to all classes of insurance.

§2. DTV-ADS 2009

498. The origin of the DTV-ADS 2009 goes back to the *Allgemeine Deutsche Seeversicherung* clauses (ADS) of 1919. When those clauses no longer met the market requirements they were partly replaced and amended by the DTV Hull Clauses in 1978, 1992 and 2004. In 2007 the GDV set up a working group to modernize and streamline the ADS and to increase their transparency. Initially the task of the working group was confined to hull insurance. In the course of the reform, loss of hire, increased value and war risk insurance were included into the ADS.[358]

499. The DTV-ADS 2009 have generally kept the structure of the ADS 1919 by setting out general clauses in part one (nos 1–53). Whenever there is a reference to DTV-ADS 2009 in a policy, these provisions will apply. Provisions in all other parts of the DTV-ADS 2009 – hull and machinery insurance (nos 54–66), additional insurances (nos 67–69), loss of hire insurance (nos 70 – 81), mines clause (no. 82) and war insurance (nos 83–88) are only applicable where there is an express agreement between the parties to that effect.

I. General Clauses

500. Number 1 DTV-ADS 2009 provides details of all risks insured. Unless otherwise agreed, in hull insurance the proprietary interest of the policyholder as the

356. Cf. Looschelders, in: Langheid/Wandt (eds), Münchener Kommentar zum VVG, 2nd ed., vol. 2, C.H. Beck 2017, § 209 n. 3).
357. *See* http://www.tis-gdv.de/tis/bedingungen/avb/see/see.html (accessed 28 Mar. 2018).
358. *See* Schwampe/Guth, Revised German Marine Insurance Clauses, The Swedish Club Triton 3-2011, pp. 30–31.

vessel's registered owner and his/her liability interest is insured. The same is true for the war risk insurance and the mines risk insurance. In additional insurances the policyholder's monetary interest in the cases of abandonment, total loss, vessel beyond or unworthy of repair, and in loss of hire insurance the interest of the policyholder in the vessel's income is insured.

501. The right of the insurer to reduce the agreed value in cases of an overvaluation is no longer dependent on a 'material overvaluation' (§ 6 paragraph 2 ADS 1919) but on an overvaluation of at least 20%. According to clause 10.4 DTV-ADS 2009 this right is excluded if either the policyholder had no knowledge, or the insurer had knowledge, of the overvaluation.

502. Unlike the ADS 1919/DTV Hull Clauses, wilful misconduct or gross negligence is required on the policyholder's side to forfeit his rights under the respective insurance. Only in connection with the pre-contractual disclosure duty (no. 22 DTV-ADS 2009) is ordinary negligence sufficient. On this point the DTV-ADS 2009 clauses are more favourable for the policyholder compared to the ADS 1919/ DTV Hull Clauses. Within the area of risk alteration, on the other side, the DTV-ADS 2009 clauses are disadvantageous for policyholders since gross negligence is now enough to forfeit the policyholder's rights (no. 24 DTV-ADS 2009). Under no. 11 DTV Hull Clauses, the policyholder only forfeited his rights when he acted with wilful misconduct.

503. Pursuant to no. 26.2 DTV-ADS 2009 the insurance ends once the vessel continues or resumes its voyage without the consent of the classification society in cases where the class expires, is restricted or withdrawn. In the case of general average, the insurer no longer can limit its liability when the contributing value of the vessel exceeds the agreed value. § 30 paragraph 8 ADS 1919 has not been adopted within the DTV-ADS.

504. Number 33.1 DTV-ADS 2009 introduces as a new concept the duty to comply with ship safety/security regulations which is applicable insofar as no. 33.2 DTV-ADS 2009 – seaworthiness, hazardous cargo, bulk cargo – has not been explicitly included in the insurance. According to clause 33.1.2 DTV-ADS 2009 the insurer is not relieved from cover in the case of a breach of ship safety regulations. The burden of proof of (lack of) causation has been moved to the policyholder´s side. If he can prove that failure to comply with the regulation had no bearing on the type or scale of the loss or damage that occurred, and was the result neither of a deliberate nor grossly negligent act, the insurer is not discharged from liability. ADS 1919/DTV Hull Clauses, in comparison, put the burden of proof of cause on the insurer's side, but relieve the insurer if the policyholder cannot exonerate himself from ordinary negligence. There has been a lot of debate on the new concept of the DTV-ADS 2009 with ship owners, which finally prompted the GDV to maintain the old unseaworthiness concept as an alternative option (no. 33.2 DTV-ADS 2009). It is to be noted that pursuant to no. 33.1.3 DTV-ADS 2009 the captain's failure to comply with the ship safety/security regulations will not discharge the insurer from the provision of coverage if the policyholder can prove that the omission was the result neither of a deliberate nor grossly negligent act during management of the ship's operations.

505. Another important change concerns the insurance of the risk of piracy, which had been part of the traditional all-risk cover under § 28 ADS 1919. Clause 35.1.4 DTV-ADS 2009 shifts the piracy risk from hull insurance to war risk insurance (no. 84.1.6 DTV-ADS 2009). Cyber-attacks and any chemical, biological, biochemical, electromagnetic, nuclear or atomic weapon are excluded from cover (no. 36 DTV-ADS 2009).

II. Hull and Machinery Insurance

506. According to no. 59 DTV-ADS 2009 the cover for loss or damage due to latent defects, errors or defects in construction or breakage of the vessel's shaft, which is confined to machinery damage under ADS 1919/ DTV Hull Clauses, has been extended to damage to the hull. The defective part itself is insured as long as it was classified by a classification society. No. 62.1 DTV-ADS 2009 requires, in cases of partial loss, the involvement of a surveyor only when the parties disagree on the amount of damage. According to § 74 ADS 1919, a surveyor had to be involved in every case. In cases of constructive total loss it is only necessary to sell the vessel by way of a public auction when the parties cannot agree on the value of the vessel in damaged condition (no. 61.2.2 DTV-ADS 2009). Under § 77 paragraph 1 ADS 1919, the sale by public auction had to be carried out in every case.

III. Liability Insurance

507. Pursuant to no. 65.1 DTV-ADS 2009 the insurer indemnifies the policyholder for third-party liability claims based on statutory liability provisions and caused by movements of the vessel or by any navigational measures directly connected therewith. There is no cover, however, *inter alia,* for liability claims arising from death or injury to persons and other bodily injury (no. 65.4.1.1 DTV-ADS 2009), loss of or damage to property on board the insured vessel (no. 65.4.1.3 DTV-ADS).

IV. Additional Insurances

508. Numbers 67–69 DTV-ADS 2009 contain, besides the increased value provisions, provisions as to freight and the insurance premium paid in the cases of abandonment, total loss and vessel beyond or unworthy of repair. According to no. 67.2 DTV-ADS 2009 the insurer indemnifies for claims brought by third parties insured under the hull policy for the amount by which the third-party indemnity exceeds the agreed value for hull insurance, but only in the proportion of the sum insured to the total sum insured on collision excess-of-loss basis. No. 68 DTV-ADS 2009 states that the insurer pays the sum insured agreed in the policy for freight.

V. Loss of Hire Insurance

509. Numbers 70–81 DTV-ADS 2009 contain provisions for a loss of hire insurance. These clauses were drafted on the basis of Chapter 16 of the Norwegian Marine Insurance Plan. The insurer indemnifies for loss of income from the insured vessel for the period during which the vessel is unable to earn the full freight or hire due to an indemnifiable hull loss (no. 70.1 DTV-ADS 2009). Therefore a damage to the ship is required. The insurance also covers cases where the loss under the hull insurance is within the deductible, or where the loss of income is due to the vessel having run aground without a hull loss having materialized (no. 70.2 DTV-ADS 2009). There is no cover in the case of abandonment, to loss of income arising from total loss and equivalent cases or where the vessel is beyond or unworthy of repair (no. 71.1 DTV-ADS 2009).

VI. Mines Clause

510. The provisions of the DTV Mines Clause have been adopted in no. 82 DTV-ADS 2009. The cover is extended to damage caused by derelict weapons left behind after a war (no. 82.2 DTV-ADS 2009). According to no. 84.1.3 DTV-ADS 2009, the same is insured under the war risks insurance.

VII. War Risk Insurance

511. The newly introduced standard clauses within part 6 of the DTV-ADS 2009 for war risk insurance are based on the institute war and strike clauses-hulls. Since the World War II no war risk insurance has been written in Germany and it is the first time since then that the German market has been provided with a set of standard clauses on this. Coverage will be provided for loss of or damage to the vessel e.g., arising from events resulting from war, war operations conducted by or against a belligerent power, as well as the hostile use of weapons of war, irrespective of whether war is declared or not. There is also cover for loss or damage to the vessel caused by terrorist attacks and pirates.

VIII. Concluding Clauses

512. The closing provisions contain a five-year preclusion period (no. 89 DTV-ADS 2009), stipulating that German law applies to the contract (no. 90 DTV-ADS 2009) and gives the court at the insurer's place of business the exclusive jurisdiction for any dispute (no. 91 DTV-ADS 2009).

§3. DTV-Cargo 2000/2011

513. Like the Institute Cargo Clauses (I.C.C.) the DTV Cargo 2000/2011 provides cover for all risks of loss or damage to cargo and general average and liability in a 'both to blame' clause (DTV-Cargo 2000/2011 *Volle Deckung*) and limited cover for named perils (DTV-Cargo 2000/2011 *Eingeschraenkte Deckung*) from warehouse to warehouse.

I. DTV Cargo 2000/2011 (*Volle Deckung*)

A. *Perils Not Covered*

514. There are a number of perils not covered. e.g., loss or damage to cargo due to:

- war, civil war or similar hostilities (2.4.1.1 DTV-Cargo 2000/2011);
- strikes, lock-outs, industrial unrest, acts of violence by terrorist or political groups riots and other form of civil unrest (2.4.1.2 DTV-Cargo 2000/2011);
- confiscation, deprivation of possession or other acts of authorities (2.4.1.3 DTV-Cargo 2000/2011);
- the use of chemical, biological, biochemical sub-stances or electromagnetic waves as weapons which constitute a public danger, irrespective of other contributory causes (2.4.1.4);
- nuclear energy or other ionising radiation (2.4.1.5 DTV-Cargo 2000/2011).

515. There are supplementary clauses for war, strikes, riots, civil unrest, and confiscation. For example, the war clause covers loss of or damage to the insured goods caused by:

- war, civil war or warlike events, as well as events arising – irrespective of a state of war – from the hostile use of weapons of war and the presence of derelict weapons of war as a consequence of one of these risks;
- confiscation, capture, seizure, deprivation and other acts of authorities as a result of the afore-mentioned risks.

B. *Exclusions*

516. The insurer is not liable for loss or damage to cargo arising from:

- delay in the transport (no. 2.5.1.1 DTV-Cargo 2000/2011);
- inherent vice or the nature of the goods (no. 2.5.1.2 DTV-Cargo 2000/2011);
- customary differences or losses in number, weight or measure of the goods (no. 2.5.1.3 DTV-Cargo 2000/2011);
- ordinary humidity or fluctuations in temperature (no. 2.5.1.4 DTV-Cargo 2000/2011);

- inappropriate and inadequate packaging or incorrect stowage insofar as the policyholder acted wilfully or with gross negligence (no. 2.5.1.5 DTV-Cargo 2000/2011).

II. DTV Cargo 2000/2011 (*Eingeschraenkte Deckung*)

A. *Named Perils*

517. The following perils are covered:

- loss or damage to cargo due to an accident of the ship (no. 2.1 lit. a) paragraph 1 DTV-Cargo 2000/2011);
- collapse of warehouse buildings (no. 2.1 lit. b) DTV-Cargo 2000/2011);
- fire, lightning, explosion, earthquakes, sea-quakes, volcanic eruptions and other natural disasters; strike or crashing of a flying object or parts thereof including its cargo (no. 2.1 lit. c) DTV-Cargo 2000/2011);
- jettison, washing overboard or otherwise being lost overboard as a result of heavy weather (no. 2.1 lit. d) DTV-Cargo 2000/2011);
- general average sacrifice (no. 2.1 lit. e) DTV-Cargo 2000/2011);
- discharging, interim storage and loading of goods at a port or airport of distress entered as a result of an insured event or following an emergency landing (no. 2.1 lit. f) DTV-Cargo 2000/2011);
- total loss of entire packages during loading on-to or unloading from a means of transport, or during transhipment to or from a means of transport (no. 2.1 lit. g) DTV-Cargo 2000/2011).

518. It is important to note that an accident of the ship is also said to exist when the ship or vessel carrying the goods is stranded, strikes ground or runs aground, capsizes, sinks, founders, or is damaged by ice (no. 2.1 lit. a) paragraph 2 DTV-Cargo 2000/2011). As with the DTV-Cargo 2000/2011 'Volle Deckung' the coverage can be extended to loss of and damage to the cargo caused by war, strikes, riots and civil unrest, and confiscation

B. *Exclusions*

519. The exclusions under no. 2.5 DTV-Cargo 2000/2011 *Eingeschraenkte Deckung*) are identical with the exclusions under no. 2.5 DTV-Cargo 2000/2011 *Volle Deckung*.

§4. P&I Insurance

520. The P&I Insurance for ship owners of seagoing vessels covers their third party liability resulting *inter alia* from:

- damage to cargo;
- collision with/damage to another vessel/object;
- personal injury or loss of life to crew members and to passengers;
- stowaways, deserters and refugees;
- costs of life salvage;
- quarantine expenses;
- wreck liabilities;
- towage contracts;
- general average contribution to the cargo and/or the vessel; and
- oil and other polluting substances.

521. P&I Insurance for charterers, in addition, covers liability for damage to or loss of the chartered vessel. At present, in Germany there is only the (co-insurance) consortium of Hanseatic P&I that offers, *inter alia*, P&I Insurance for small and medium sized seagoing feeder and coastal tonnage.

Chapter 7. Aviation and Aerospace Insurance

§1. Legal Regime

522. There are no specific rules on aviation and aerospace insurance. Aviation (airlines) insurance includes hull coverage (physical damage) and liability protection for passenger and cargo. *Aerospace insurance provides* physical damage and liability cover for manufacturers and suppliers as well as for airports, airfields, refuellers and associated service providers. Besides the rules applying to all classes of insurance (§§ 1–73 VVG), depending on the risk insured the provisions on indemnity insurance (§§ 74–87 VVG), property insurance (§§ 88–99 VVG), liability insurance §§ 100–124 VVG), and accident insurance (§§ 178–191 VVG) are applicable. It is important to note that the provisions on transport insurance (§§ 130–141 VVG) do not apply to the risks of air transportation of goods (*see* paragraph 347).

523. Aviation and aerospace hull insurance and liability insurance qualify by definition as large risk (§ 210 paragraph 2 no. 1 VVG in conjunction with VAG Annex 1 nos 5 and 11) and are therefore exempted from the restraints of the (semi-)mandatory VVG provisions on contractual freedom. The TIS-GDV offers English versions of various aviation insurance model terms and conditions, e.g., Aviation Liability Insurance Conditions for Aircraft Operators and Carriers (LHB 2008[359]), Aviation Hull Insurance Conditions (LKB 2008[360]), Aviation Accident Insurance Conditions (LUB 2008[361]).

§2. Aviation Hull Insurance

I. Scope of Coverage

524. Subject to aviation hull insurance are airplanes, helicopters and other aircraft. (Worldwide) insurance cover is provided for standard equipment levels or aircraft variants. Cover for special equipment is subject to separate agreement. Accessories defined as movable items which, while not components of the aircraft, are intended to support its operation on an ongoing basis and are located in or on the aircraft, are not covered (no. 1.1 LKB 2008).

525. Aviation hull insurance provides cover up to the amount of the sum insured for any external loss event impacting the aircraft while taking off, landing or ruling the aircraft and leading to total or partial damage (no. 1.2 LKB 2008).

---

359. Aviation Liability Insurance Conditions for Aircraft Operators and Carriers, LHB 2008 as of December 2007, http://www.tis-gdv.de/tis/bedingungen/avb/luftfahrt/Luftfahrt_Haftpflicht.pdf (accessed 28 Mar. 2018).
360. Aviation Hull Insurance Conditions, LKB 2008 as of February 2008, http://www.tis-gdv.de/tis/bedingungen/avb/luftfahrt/Luftfahrt_Kasko_en.pdf (accessed 28 Mar. 2018).
361. Aviation Accident Insurance Conditions, LUB 2008 as of November 2007), http://www.tis-gdv.de/tis/bedingungen/avb/luftfahrt/Luftfahrt_Kasko_en.pdf (accessed 28 Mar. 2018).

II. Scope of Indemnification

526. In the event of a total loss, the insurer indemnifies the policyholder for the replacement value of the aircraft (excluding the costs of replacement) at the time of the loss event, but only up to the sum insured. The replacement value is defined as the purchase price the policyholder has to pay to acquire a comparable aircraft up to the level of the agreed sum insured (no. 3.1.1 sentence 3 LKB 2008).

527. Agreed Value policies are the usual way of insuring large airlines. Under an agreed value policy the insurer agrees with the policyholder, for the policy period, the value of the aircraft, and in the event of total loss, this agreed value is payable in full (no. 3.1.1 sentence 2 LKB 2008).

528. If an aircraft is partially damaged, the insurer indemnifies the policyholder for the cost of repairing the damage to the aircraft caused by the loss event, less the agreed deductible (no. 3.2.1 LKB 2008)

III. Exclusions

529. According to clause 4.1 LKB 2008 no insurance is provided, *inter alia*, for damage:

- in connection with war or civil war, other hostilities, uprising, revolution, rebellion, strike, lockout, insurrection, civil unrest, industrial unrest, acts of terror or sabotage, aircraft hijackings, confiscation and other acts of authorities;
- arising out of the fact that the parked aircraft was not secured in accordance with the manufacturer's instructions or in another reasonable manner;
- caused by the policyholder or its personnel while carrying out work on the aircraft, i.e., damage to that part of an aircraft component (technical unit) on which they were working (error in workmanship). If work is being carried out on the aircraft as a whole, this exclusion applies only to those parts directly impacted by the workers;
- directly attributable to faulty operation or internal operating procedures or which, given the nature of the operations, is the result of impacts that are either unavoidable, necessary or accepted as a matter of course (operational damage);
- caused by an internal problem with the aircraft engine or through objects left in the engine intake area;
- due to wear and tear, dilapidation, gradual impacts, ageing, corrosion, moisture or frost;
- due to errors or defects in the aircraft of which the policyholder was or should have been aware;
- attributable to wilful acts or gross negligence on the part of the policyholder;
- due to explosive or auto-igniting objects or liquids on board, with the exception of aviation fuel and fluids, and signal and emergency flares;
- during the transport or aircraft or parts thereof, including loading/unloading; transport of this kind can be included in the insurance by separate agreement;

– due to the misappropriation or theft of aircraft parts and instruments that are not firmly installed in the aircraft.

§3. AVIATION LIABILITY INSURANCE

I. Insured Risks and Damages

530. Aviation liability insurance provides cover for claims of third-parties outside the aircraft and by passengers for damages brought against the policyholder on the basis of statutory liability provisions under private law arising out of a loss event occurring during the policy period (insured event) and resulting in property damage, bodily injury or consequential financial loss (no. 1 sentence 1 LHB 2008).

531. The insurance cover comprises the policyholder's statutory liability arising out of:

– the operation of aircraft for bodily injury or damage to persons or property not being carried in the air-craft (Air Operators' Liability Insurance) (no. 2.1 LHB 2008),
– the contractually agreed carriage of persons (exception: flight training) and the property they have on or with them as well as their luggage and air freight of undeclared value (Air Carriers' Liability Insurance) (no. 2.2 LHB 2008) and
– as a contracting air carrier from the self-arranged carriage of persons including luggage of undeclared value (tour operators' liability insurance) (no 2.3 LHB 2008).

532. There is worldwide coverage on a 'cost-inclusive' basis for claims based on foreign law and brought before foreign courts (no. 6.1.2 LHB 2008). Insured events occurring in the USA, US territories or Canada are covered only subject to special agreement (no. 6.2.1 LHB 2008).

II. Insured Event

533. A loss event is defined as the event that directly resulted in damage to or injury of the third party. It is immaterial when the actual cause leading to the loss event occurred (no. 1 sentence 2 LHB 2008).

III. Personal Scope of Coverage

534. Co-insured are:

– the operator and all persons who, with the knowledge and approval of the operator, are involved in guiding and operating the aircraft, including persons who are authorized to operate the remote controls of model aircraft (no 3.1.1 LHB 2008);

- the policyholder's personnel, to the extent that they are authorized to carry out work or activities in connection with aircraft insured under this policy (no 3.1.2 LHB 2008);
- personnel working for the contracting air carrier, with the exception of the executing air carrier and its personnel (no. 3.1.3 LHB 2008).

IV. Exclusions

535. According to no. 7 LHB 2008 coverage is excluded, *inter alia*, for:

- liability in cases where, at the time of the loss event, the aircraft in question was not in a condition that complied with the legal provisions or official regulations governing the ownership and operation of aircraft and/or if any necessary official licences had not been granted;
- liability claims in cases where, at the time of the loss event, the aviation company did not have the official approvals prescribed by law;
- liability claims in cases where, at the time of the loss event, the pilot(s) of the aircraft did not possess the prescribed permits, required authorizations or professional qualifications;
- liability for damage caused in connection with war, civil war or other hostilities, any detonation of a weapon of war employing nuclear fission and/or fusion or radiation of another kind, strike, lockout, insurrection, civil commotion, industrial unrest, hijacking and acts of terror or sabotage;
- liability for damage caused through the unlawful misappropriation of aircraft or in connection with acts of authorities or any act of government powers.

§4. Aviation Accident Insurance

I. Scope of Coverage

536. Insurance based on the GDV model terms and condition of aviation accident insurance (LUB 2008) provides worldwide cover for accidents suffered by the policyholder and/or any another insured person named in the application. Cover is granted from boarding to de-boarding of an aircraft, including accidents that occur in the process of boarding/de-boarding. Cover also extends to accidents during stopovers at airports and landing fields, in the immediate vicinity of the aircraft after emergency landings, when using aerial sports equipment (including during landing) and during the necessary alternative conveyance of passengers on behalf of airlines (no. 1.2 LUB 2008).

II. Types and Amount of Benefit

537. Aviation accident insurance follows the rules on general accident insurance (*see* paragraph 653). According to the LUB 2008 it is a fixed sum insurance which does not cover the costs of medical treatment.

538. There are two types of benefits: the disability benefits and the accident annuity (no. 2 LUB 2008). If the policyholder suffers permanent impairment as a result of an accident (e.g., restrictions in movement, paralysis or amputation), the insurer will pay either a lump sum (disability benefit) and/or an annuity (accident annuity), depending on what is agreed in advance. The amount of the disability benefits is determined by the sum insured and degree of impairment. The accident annuity is paid in cases of very serious impairment. As usual under accident insurance policies, the benefits will be reduced if existing illnesses or infirmities contribute towards the consequences of the accident (no. 2.1.2.2.3 LUB 2008).

III. Exclusions

539. No cover is provided pursuant clause 4 LUB 2008, in particular, for accidents:

- suffered by insured persons who were not in possession of the prescribed permits required authorizations or professional qualifications (no. 4.1.1 LUB 2008);
- involving aircraft which were not in proper condition (no. 4.1.1 LUB 2008);
- resulting from drunkenness (no. 4.1.2 LUB 2008);
- caused by wilful criminal acts committed by the insured person (no. 4.1.3 LUB 2008);
- arising out of war or civil war (no. 4.1.4 LUB 2008).

§5. Satellite Insurance

540. Only few German first insurers offer satellite insurance, also sometimes called space insurance. From an insurance perspective the life-cycle of a satellite falls into four phases. The launch is the most dangerous stage. The cause of loss is most commonly explosion or failure to orbit. If the launch is successful, there follow the post separation phase after the booster rockets have fallen away and then the in-orbit phase. The final phase is the return of the satellite to the earth.

541. Satellite insurers offer hull coverage for physical loss of or damage to the satellite not only while in the in-orbit phase of the satellite but already during the manufacturing and testing phase and the transport to the launch pad, at the launch pad before launch or in storage. Satellite insurers also offer property cover for manufacturing and storage facilities and for the launch systems and commissioning equipment. Satellite insurance always includes third party liability cover during a launch or in-orbit activities as well as the return of the satellite.

Chapter 8. Theft and Embezzlement Insurance

542. The VVG does not contain specific rules on theft and embezzlement insurance. Therefore these types of insurance are subject to the VVG provisions applying to all classes of insurance (§§ 1–73 VVG) and to indemnity insurance (§§ 74–99 VVG).

§1. THEFT

543. There is separate cover against theft available. In practice, however, coverage against theft is included in comprehensive contents insurance contracts, e.g., comprehensive motor vehicle insurance (*see* paragraph 623). Burglary is covered under the extended coverage contract for the insurance of additional perils to fire insurance for industrial and commercial enterprises (§ 7 ECB 2010, *see* paragraph 335) and under the comprehensive household insurance (A 1.2 VHB[362]). According to the rules of interpretation theft is to be construed according to its meaning in § 242 StGB (*see* paragraph 164). § 242 StGB defines theft as the taking away of chattels belonging to another with the intention of unlawfully appropriating them for himself or a third person. Burglary is an aggravated form of theft which requires an unlawful entry into a building (§ 243 paragraph 1 no. 1 StGB).

544. In case of burglary and/or theft the policyholder has the duty to report the loss at the next police station immediately (e.g., E.1.3.3 AKB 2015), and to submit a list of stolen items to the police without delay (e.g., § 8 no. 2 lit. a) ee) ECB 2010).

§2. EMBEZZLEMENT

545. There are no separate policies insuring property against embezzlement. Coverage against embezzlement is available under comprehensive motor vehicle insurance policies (*see* paragraph 623). There, embezzlement – this term is to be construed according to its meaning in § 246 StGB – is insured provided that the car is not left to the perpetrator (1) for use in his/her own interest, (2) for the sale of the car or (3) under retention of title (*see* A.2.2.1.2 lit. b) AKB 2015). § 246 StGB defines embezzlement as unlawful appropriation of chattels belonging to another for himself or a third person. Moreover, fidelity insurance policies provide cover against losses caused by tortious acts or omissions of trusted persons in a company (*see* paragraph 555).

362. 'Allgemeine Hausrat Versicherungsbedingungen (VHB 2016 – Quadratmetermodell)', VHB 2016 as of 26 May 2017, https://www.gdv.de/resource/blob/6114/2d6b8855f1102c0006655438aa0f3a5d/01-allgemeine-hausrat-versicherungsbedingungen--vhb-2016---quadratmetermodell--data.pdf (accessed 28 Mar. 2018).

Chapter 9. Agricultural Insurance, Hail Insurance, Livestock Insurance

§1. Agricultural Insurance and Livestock Insurance

546. There are no provisions in the VVG dealing with agricultural insurance. Prior to the reform of the VVG in 2008 there were special provisions in the VVG dealing with animal business insurance (§§ 116–128 VVG 1908). The German legislator considered regulation no longer as necessary since these insurances were only a particular type of property insurance to which the usual general principles should apply. There are, however, model terms and conditions of the GDV which reflect market standards (ABL).[363] The ABL provide coverage against the usual risks of fire, lightning, explosion, airplane crash, water damage, storm and hail causing damages to the buildings and/or movable property including animals (e.g., horses, cattle) and crops (except maize, potatoes, beets, fruit and vegetables) (§§ 1–4 and 6 ABL). § 8 ABL provides for a harvest failure insurance which protects the policyholder against loss of earnings. Clearance, demolition, fire extinguishing, movement and safety costs are also insured (§ 10 ABL).

§2. Hail Insurance

547. Prior to the reform of the VVG in 2008 there were special provisions in the VVG dealing with hail insurance (§§ 108–115a VVG 1908). Like with the animal business insurance, the German legislator considered regulation no longer as necessary. After the reform hail insurance is only specifically addressed in § 92 VVG which deals with the termination of the contract after an insured event. According to § 92 paragraph 3 VVG in the case of hail insurance, the insurer may only terminate the contract to the end of the period of insurance in which the insured event occurred. In all other types of property insurance the insurer has the right to terminate the contract on one month's notice.

548. There are GDV model terms and conditions for hail insurance which reflect market standards (AHagB[364]). The AHagB define hail as solid precipitation in form of ice pellets (§ 1 no. 1 AHagB). The cover includes damage to the crop (§ 1 no. 2 AHagB). There is no protection against a downward movement of commodity prices between policy inception and harvesting.

363. *Allgemeine Bedingungen für die Sachversicherung landwirtschaftlicher Betriebe, Wirtschaftsgebäude und deren Inhalt sowie Wohngebäude*, ABL 2010 as of 1 Apr. 2014, https://www.gdv.de/resource/blob/5894/e85bec4d4bb00bdcf7aef976db59ad14/01-allgemeine-bedingungen-fuer-die-sachversicherung-landwirtschaftlicher-betriebe--wirtschaftsgebaeude-und-deren-inhalt-sowie-wohngebaeude--abl-2010--data.pdf (accessed 28 Mar. 2018).

364. *Allgemeine Hagelversicherungsbedingungen*, AHagB 2010 as of 1 Jan. 2011, https://www.gdv.de/resource/blob/5898/fcd629ef529bc2e9d537840d25a4e2da/03-allgemeine-hagelversicherungs-bedingungen--ahagb-2010--data.pdf (accessed 28 Mar. 2018).

Chapter 10. Catastrophe Insurance

§1. Natural Hazards

549. There are no rules in the VVG dealing with the insurance of catastrophic risks such as earthquakes, floods and storms, volcanic eruption. Until the transposition of the Directive 92/49/EEC[365] in 1994, house owners in Hamburg und Baden-Wuerttemberg were obliged to take out insurance against damages caused by flood and hail (Hamburg), storm, hail, flood, landslide, avalanches, snow pressure, rock avalanches (Baden-Wuerttemberg).

550. While storm and hail is generally included as insured peril under a standard building (*see* paragraph 337), comprehensive household (*see* paragraph 339) or comprehensive motor vehicle insurance (*see* paragraph 623) other natural hazards may be added as an extra risk to such policies. Alternatively, it is possible take out a separate insurance against natural hazards. There are GDV model terms and conditions for natural hazard insurance (BWE[366]) which reflect market standards. They include damage to property caused by floods, avalanches, snow pressure, earthquake, landslide and volcanic eruption (§ 2 BWE).

§2. Terror Acts

551. In September 2002, 16 insurance companies have founded Extremus Versicherungs-AG (Extremus) which provides coverage for property damage and associated business interruption claims resulting from terrorist acts over EUR 25 million up to an amount of EUR 2.5 billion. The first 25 million are covered by 15 fire and fire business interruption insurer which are the shareholder of Extremus and in this capacity act like a coinsurance group.[367] A government guarantee, which was in 2015 renewed for further four years until the end of 2019, covers damages in excess of that amount. The maximum compensation amount available for covering terrorism damages amounts to EUR 10 billion per annum. It needs to be emphasized that Extremus does not provide compensation for victims of terrorist attacks. The insurance standard terms of Extremus are available on the internet (ATB 2016[368]).

---

365. Directive 92/49/EEC of 18 June 1992 on the coordination of laws, regulations and administrative provisions relating to direct insurance other than life assurance and amending Directives 73/239/EEC and 88/357/EEC (Third Non-life Insurance Directive) (O.J., 11 August 1992, L 228/1).
366. *Besondere Bedingungen für die Versicherung weiterer Elementarschäden*, BWE 2010 as of 1 Apr. 2010), https://www.gdv.de/resource/blob/6080/4b0881f581b2c15ce3d99f11e6cc087f/05-elementarversicherung-data.pdf (accessed 28 Mar. 2018).
367. For further information, *see* http://www.extremus.de/index.php/ueber-uns/aktionaere (accessed 28 Mar. 2018).
368. *Allgemeine Bedingungen für die Terrorversicherung*, (ATB 2016) http://www.extremus.de/templates/extremus_unterseiten/downloads/ATB2016.pdf (accessed 28 Mar. 2018).

552. Terror acts are defined under A 1 no. 2 ATB as any acts committed by persons or groups of persons to achieve political, religious, ethnic or ideological purposes that are likely to spread anxiety or fear amongst the population or parts of the population and thereby influence any government or government institution.

§3. Nuclear Risks

553. There is a nuclear insurance pool of first insurers and reinsurers (*Deutsche Kernreaktor-Versicherungsgemeinschaf*). The so-called Atompool has been founded in 1957 and has 35 first insurers and reinsurers as members.[369] It provides reinsurance coverage for first insurers against damages caused by nuclear risks up to EUR 256 million. Damages over EUR 256 million up to the maximum insured sum of EUR 2.5 billion required by § 34 of the Atomic Energy Act (*Atomgesetz*, hereafter 'AtG') are covered by the nuclear power plant operators in Germany as a whole. Damages above that amount have to be paid by the operator of the nuclear power plant that caused the damage.[370]

369. GDV AssekuranzAgenda, issue no. 20 (April 2011), p. 6; available in German at https://www.gdv.de/resource/blob/8482/12ed60926d5ea0c1f4b5235076365305/ausgabe-20---april-2011--1695950230-data.pdf.

370. For details, *see* Diekmann, Verstärkte Haftung und Deckungsvorsorge für Schäden nuklearer Unfälle – Notwendige Schritte zur Internalisierung externer Effekte, ZfU 2011, pp. 119 et seq.

Chapter 11. Credit and Caution Insurance

554. There are no specific rules on credit insurance or caution insurance. These types of insurance are subject to the VVG provisions applying to all classes of insurance (§§ 1–73 VVG) and to indemnity insurance (§§ 74–87 VVG). There are no model terms and conditions for these types insurance provided by the GDV. Both credit insurance and caution insurance qualify by definition as a large risk insurance (§ 210 paragraph 2 no. 2 VVG in conjunction with VAG Annex 1 nos 14 and 15). For that reason deviations from (semi-)mandatory rules are permitted. Any deviation in standard policy wordings, however, is subject to unfairness control (*see* paragraph 186).

§1. Credit Insurance

I. Trade Credit Insurance

555. Credit insurance in the narrow sense provides protection against the failure of the policyholder's customers (purchaser) to pay trade credit debts owed to the policyholder (supplier). The insured event occurs if a purchaser becomes insolvent or fails to pay the purchase price within the agreed terms and conditions (protracted default).

II. Fidelity Insurance

556. In a broader sense credit insurance includes fidelity insurance which provides cover against losses caused by tortious acts or omissions of trusted persons in a company.[371] Tortious acts include theft, fraud and embezzlement.

557. Fidelity insurance can be taken out by the trusted person for the account of the company or an individual person (*Personenkautionsversicherung*). As a consequence §§ 43–48 VVG apply (*see* paragraph 313) with the particularity that, by derogation from §§ 44 paragraph 1, 45 paragraph 1 VVG (*see* paragraph 314), in the case of fraud only the company/individual person is entitled to assert the claim against the insurer. The insurer, in turn, takes recourse against the policyholder. In the vast majority of cases, however, it is the company that takes out the insurance and claims for compensation (*Personengarantieversicherung*, also called *Vertrauensschadensversicherung*).[372]

---

371. For a qualification of the fidelity as credit insurance, *see* OLG Koeln, 9 Jan. 1978 – 5 U 2/77, RuS 1978, pp. 153 et seq.

372. For the different types of fidelity insurance, *see* R. Koch, Vertrauensschadensversicherung, Verlag Versicherungswirtschaft 2006, n. 49 et seq.

558. Apart from the company's employees, external staff, temporary workers and external service providers may qualify as trusted persons. It is not required that their names are being listed or functions are being defined.

559. Fidelity insurance policies regularly provide indemnification for financial loss due to unauthorized computer interference by third parties (computer crimes). There is an aggregate sum insured for this cover which will be reduced over the year as each claim is reported.

§2. Caution Insurance

560. Caution Insurance (*Kautionsversicherung*), which is also called surety insurance or bond insurance, is written by credit insurers in Germany. While credit insurance compensates a supplier whose customers have become insolvent and cannot pay for the goods or services delivered, surety insurer protect customers if their suppliers fail to deliver goods or services as contractually agreed. The caution insurance is taken out by the supplier for the account of its customers.

561. The surety insurer is the warrantor, because it warrants (guarantees) payment on default; the supplier pays the premium, and the customer is the beneficiary in the event of supplier's failure to perform. Alternatively, a supplier could provide a guarantee by depositing cash with the principal or arranging a bank guarantee. Since the caution insurance has the same economic as a bank guarantee the BGH has held that caution insurance does not qualify as insurance but as a contract of service.[373]

§3. Payment Protection Insurance

562. Credit insurance and caution insurance must not be confused with payment protection insurance which protects borrowers from not being able to repay mortgages or consumer credits in the event of death and, e.g., sickness, disability or their becoming unemployed. Payment protection insurance is regularly a group policy with the bank being the policyholder and at the same time the beneficiary, to which the borrowers have the opportunity to accede as co-insured persons. In the event of death, sickness, disability or becoming unemployed the lending bank has the right to demand payment from the insurer. Such policies qualify as personal insurance. Depending on the risk insured they are subject to the rules on life insurance (*see* paragraph 710) or occupational disability insurance (*see* paragraph 644).

563. In the case the consumer borrower becomes the policyholder the rules on 'connected contracts' apply. Whenever the loan agreement serves the financing of the payment protection insurance contract and both contracts constitute an economic unit in that they are connected in such a way that one contract would not have

373. BGH, 6 Jul. 2006 – IX ZR 121/05, BGHZ 168, pp. 276, 282.

been concluded without the other (§ 358 paragraph 3 BGB), the consumer exercising his right to withdraw from the loan agreement will also no longer be bound by the connected payment protection insurance contract, and *vice versa*.[374]

374. BGH, 15 Dec. 2009 – XI ZR 45/09, NJW 2010, p. 531, paras 17 et seq.

Chapter 12. Technical Insurance

§1. Terminology

564. In German practice, technical insurance is an umbrella term covering all risks to which projects under construction, installed machinery or equipment are exposed during installation and commissioning. The term technical insurance includes property policies as well as business interruption policies, the purpose of which is to insure loss of earnings and/or additional costs as a result of property damage, and insurance of extra costs incurred while normal business operations are disrupted. There are no specific rules governing technical insurances since they are only a particular type of property insurance to which the general rules to all classes of insurance (§§ 1–73 VVG), to indemnity insurance (§§ 74–87 VVG) and property insurance (§§ 88–99 VVG) apply.

§2. Types of Technical Insurance

565. The GDV provides model terms and conditions for:

- machinery breakdown insurance, which covers damage to stationary(AMB[375]) and mobile machines, mechanical equipment and technical systems ready for operation (ABMG[376]) resulting from destruction or damage due to an unforeseen event;
- electronic equipment insurance (ABE[377]), which covers damages to electronical equipment and devices ready for operation, caused, e.g., by excess voltage, short-circuit, operation mistakes, as well as faults in material or constructional flaw;
- assembly insurance (AMoB[378]), which covers damage to and the loss of the objects to be assembled such as machines, mechanical and electronic equipment and associated spare parts;

375. *Allgemeine Bedingungen für die Maschinenversicherung von stationären Maschinen*, AMB 2011 as of 1 Jan. 2011, https://www.gdv.de/resource/blob/5988/a5626ac351cc3f74c4455144e46fdab1/01-allgemeine-bedingungen-fuer-die-maschinenversicherung-von-stationaeren-maschinen--amb-2011--data.pdf (accessed 28 Mar. 2018).
376. *Allgemeine Bedingungen für die Maschinen- und Kaskoversicherung von fahrbaren oder transportablen Geräten*, ABMG 2011 as of 1 Jan. 2011, https://www.gdv.de/resource/blob/6274/c4f802fdb5260630c386e7383947d2f5/03-allgemeine-bedingungen-fuer-die-maschinen--und-kaskoversicherung-von-fahrbaren-oder-transportablen-geraeten--abmg-2011--data.pdf (accessed 28 Mar. 2018).
377. *Allgemeine Bedingungen für die Elektronikversicherung*, ABE 2011 as of 1 Jan. 2011, https://www.gdv.de/resource/blob/6154/bfec8b863b9c6ba3c6175b8517f2acb5/05-allgemeine-bedingungen-fuer-die-elektronikversicherung--abe-2011--data.pdf (accessed 28 Mar. 2018).
378. *Allgemeine Bedingungen für die Montageversicherung*, AMoB 2011 as of 1 Jan. 2011, https://www.gdv.de/resource/blob/6236/642eaa397e1194b90aaa26e3a074f11e/07-allgemeine-bedingungen-fuer-die-montageversicherung--amob-2011--data.pdf (accessed 28 Mar. 2018).

- construction insurance (ABBL[379]), which covers damage to building construction projects;
- business building stock insurance (ABBV[380]), which covers damages to building and civil engineering projects occurred after the completion and acceptance of the works;
- warranty insurance (MGar[381]), which covers consequential damages within the agreed warranty period resulting from defects in the construction, in the materials or workmanship of the machines, mechanical and electronic equipment delivered by the policyholder.

566. The coverage of most of the afore-mentioned types of technical insurance can be extended to include loss due to business interruption or extra costs as a consequence of covered property damage. The GDV only provides model terms and conditions for machinery loss of profits insurance.[382]

§3. Exclusions

567. It needs to be emphasized that technical insurances even though they are considered as all risks insurances, in fact, do not cover all risks. For example, under the machinery insurance, irrespective of other contributory causes, there is no cover for damages caused, e.g., by:

- wilful acts of the policyholder or his/her 'Repraesentant' (*see* paragraph 58) (§ 2 no. 4 lit. a) AMB 2011);
- war, war-like events, civil war, revolution, rebellion, insurrection (§ 2 no. 4 lit. b) AMB 2011);
- civil unrest (§ 2 no. 4 lit. c) AMB 2011);
- nuclear energy (§ 2 no. 4 lit. d) AMB 2011);
- earthquakes (§ 2 no. 4 lit. e) AMB 2011);
- floods (§ 2 no. 4 lit. f) AMB 2011);
- faults or defects existing at the time of commencement of the policy with the knowledge of the policyholder or his/her representatives (§ 2 no. 4 lit. h) AMB 2011);

379. *Allgemeine Bedingungen für die Versicherung von Bauleistungen*, ABBL 2018 as of 1 Jan. 2018, https://www.gdv.de/resource/blob/6230/e42af42f4b77944a5161f02dcc98771d/11-allgemeine-bedingungen-fuer-die-versicherung-von-bauleistungen--abbl-2018--data.pdf (accessed 28 Mar. 2018).
380. *Allgemeine Bedingungen für die Baubestandsversicherung*, ABBV 2011 as of 1 Jan. 2011, https://www.gdv.de/resource/blob/6286/7ed53a4f42effc06848063dac12c577a/13-allgemeine-bedingungen-fuer-die-baubestandsversicherung--abbv-2011--data.pdf (accessed 28 Mar. 2018).
381. *Allgemeine Bedingungen für die Garantieversicherung*, MGar 2014 as of 1 Jan. 2014, https://www.gdv.de/resource/blob/6040/210b776994aa3290238ebbc7271b0122/15-allgemeine-bedingungen-fuer-die-garantieversicherung--mgar-2014--data.pdf (accessed 28 Mar. 2018).
382. *Allgemeine Bedingungen für die Maschinen-Betriebsunterbrechungsversicherung*, AMBUB 2011 as of 1 Jan. 2011, https://www.gdv.de/resource/blob/6084/35ac5155d0d0ca67d249de73f51e9e21/01-allgemeine-bedingungen-fuer-die-maschinen-betriebsunterbrechungsversicherung--ambub-2011--data.pdf (accessed 28 Mar. 2018).

- routine consequences of continual operation (e.g., wear and tear, cavitation, erosion, corrosion, incrustation) (§ 2 no. 4 lit. i) AMB 2011),
- theft (§ 2 no. 4 lit. k) AMB 2011).

There is also no cover if the policyholder has a claim against the manufacturer or supplier of the electronic equipment (§ 2 no. 4 lit. l) AMB 2011).

568. It is important to note that machinery breakdown insurance and electronic equipment insurance only covers machinery and electronic equipment that is ready for operation – i.e., after successful completion of performance acceptance tests and launch of its operation (*betriebsfertig*) (§ 1 No. 1 sentence 2 AMB 2011).

Chapter 13. Miscellaneous Insurance

569. Since the turn of the millennium first insurers have started to write stand-alone cyber policies. Before that, coverage for losses and damages resulting from cyber incidents had been provided as a specific endorsement on property policies and on fidelity insurance policies, or as a result of a court-imposed legal interpretation of the concept of thing in respect of the question as to whether electronic data qualify as a tangible movable item in terms of § 90 BGB.[383] At present, the German market for cyber insurance still may be best described as being in its infancy although all insurers have started to offer cyber policies.

570. The GDV has identified as one reason for the reluctance of potential policyholders to take out cyber insurance the very different coverage approaches taken by different insurers which make it difficult for the market to compare the coverage. For that reason the GDV has issued model terms and conditions for cyber products (AVB Cyber[384]). The model wording is designed for small and mid-sized companies with revenue of up to EUR 50 million and up to 250 employees.

571. The GDV model wording is divided into four modules: module one contains general information about the scope of coverage. Financial losses caused by an information security breach are covered (A1-1 AVB Cyber). An information security breach is defined as an impairment of the availability, integrity and the confidentiality of electronic data or an information processing system (A1-2.1 AVB Cyber). The information security breach has to be the result of specific events, like unauthorised access to electronic data of the policyholder.

572. The insured event is defined as the damage that is verifiably identified for the first time (A1-4 AVB Cyber). Module two implements certain cyber-related services, such as forensic and call centre services as well as crisis communication (A2-1 AVB Cyber). Module three deals with the coverage of financial loss resulting from third party damage claims based on statutory liability provisions (A3-1 AVB Cyber), and module four deals with certain first party-losses, such as business interruption losses and costs incurred for data recovery (A.4-1 AVB Cyber).

383. For the discussion, *see* R. Koch, Versicherbarkeit von IT-Risken, Verlag Erich Schmidt 2004, n. 357 et seq.

384. *Allgemeine Versicherungsbedingungen für die Cyberrisiko-Versicherung*, AVB Cyber as of April 2017, https://www.gdv.de/resource/blob/6100/d4c013232e8b0a5722b7655b8c0cc207/01-allgemeine-versicherungsbedingungen-fuer-die-cyberrisiko-versicherung--avb-cyber--data.pdf (accessed 28 Mar. 2018), *see also* Achenbach, Die Cyber-Versicherung – Überblick und Analyse, VersR 2017, 1493.

Part IV. Motor Vehicle Insurance

Chapter 1. Introduction

573. All motor vehicle insurance policies issued in Germany are based on the GDV model terms and conditions (AKB[385]). The AKB include all types of motor vehicle insurance: liability insurance, comprehensive insurance, roadside assistance insurance, accident insurance and driver protection insurance. In the application form for the conclusion of motor vehicle insurance the applicant must choose the type of coverage according to his/her need.

574. It is important to note that the different types of insurance are concluded as legally independent contracts. As a result, they may have different dates of inception of cover, and in case of an accident caused by the policyholder the insurer may terminate the liability insurance or the comprehensive insurance only, or both. For example, if the policyholder is in default with the payment of a renewal premium for the roadside assistance insurance, the insurer is still obliged to compensate the policyholder under the comprehensive insurance for the damage he/she caused to his/her car.

385. *Allgemeine Bedingungen für die Kfz-Versicherung*, AKB 2015 as of 12 Oct. 2017, https://www.gdv.de/resource/blob/6178/d28c3de7b24b415ad67976ff4c0bf1e5/01-allgemeine-bedingungen-fuer-die-kfz-versicherung--akb-2015--data.pdf (accessed 28 Mar. 2018).

Chapter 2. Motor Liability Insurance

§1. Legal Regime

575. Motor Liability Insurance is subject to the PflVG (*see* paragraph 42) and the KfzPflVV (*see* paragraph 45) or, if the car is registered abroad, the AuslPflVG (*see* paragraph 43), and the AuslKfzPflVV, respectively. Besides the rules applicable to all classes of insurance (§§ 1–73 VVG), the VVG provisions on indemnity insurance (§§ 74–87 VVG) and (compulsory) liability insurance (§§ 100–124 VVG) apply.

I. Insurance Requirement

576. Before a person can register a car in Germany he/she must have proof of third party liability coverage which meets the requirements set forth by the PflVG and, in more detail, in the KfzPflVV. The statutory requirements concern, *inter alia*, the following areas:

- § 1 Geographical limits
- § 2 Scope of cover
- § 3 Trailers
- § 4 Exclusions
- § 5 Duties to be observed before the occurrence of the insured event
- § 6 Duties to be observed after the occurrence of the insured event
- § 7 Serious breaches of duty
- § 8 Calculation of annuities
- § 9 Provisional cover
- §10 Change of regulation
- §11 Coming into force

577. The AKB model terms and conditions dealing with liability insurance comply with the statutory requirements of the KfzPflVV and in some cases provide even broader coverage. For this reason the AKB are described in more detail below (*see* paragraph 584).

II. Provisional Cover

578. The proof of liability coverage must be provided by the electronic confirmation of insurance coverage issued by the motor vehicle insurer. This is a code, the so-called eVB number. By issuing the eVB the policyholder has provisional insurance cover immediately. This provisional coverage begins at the latest with the registration of the vehicle and only relates to the motor liability insurance and roadside assistance cover (B.2.1 AKB 2015). Once the policyholder has paid the premium the provisional cover is converted to final insurance cover (B.2.3 AKB 2015).

III. Exemptions from the Insurance Requirement

579. § 2 paragraph 1 nos 1–5 PflVG exempts the following legal entities of public law from the requirement to take out motor liability insurance for their motor vehicles on the grounds that they are in a position to cope with the financial consequences of a motor accident:

- Federal Public of Germany;
- Laender (e.g., Bavaria, Hamburg, Lowern Saxony);
- municipalities having more than 100,000 residents;
- associations of municipalities and special-purpose associations (*Zweckverbaende*) having exclusively public law corporations as members;
- legal person that receives coverage from a non-legal associations of municipalities the purpose of which is to balance, via cost allocation, losses resulting from risks taken by their members and by undertakings operated to provide public services, in which one or several members or other regional and/or local authorities hold a share of at least 50%.

580. According to § 2 paragraph 1 no. 6 PflVG the following motor vehicles are not subject to the insurance requirement since they do not present a particular danger (operational hazard):

- motor vehicles with a maximum speed of 6 kph;
- self-propelled working machines with a maximum speed of 20 kph;
- trailers that do not need to be registered.

§2. Insurer's Obligation to Provide Insurance

I. Obligation to Contract

581. Pursuant to § 5 paragraph 2 PflVG the insurer is obliged to accept an application for compulsory motor liability insurance (obligation to contract or *Kontrahierungszwang*). [386] § 5 paragraph 3 PflVG states that the application for motor vehicle insurance deemed to have been accepted in accordance with the principles governing the insurer's business and the insurer's general business tariff unless the insurer has rejected the application within two weeks or the insurer has asked for a higher insurance premium due to a verifiable increase of risk (counter-offer).[387]

386. For details *see* R. Koch, in: Bruck/Moeller, Großkommentar zum VVG, 9th ed., vol. 12, DeGruyter 2018, § 5 PflVG n. 2 et seq.
387. *Ibid.*, n. 21 et seq.

II. Exceptions to the Obligation to Contract

582. Pursuant to § 5 paragraph 4 PflVG the insurer is only entitled to reject the application if there are territorial or material restrictions in the principles governing his business, or the applicant was already insured by him and the insurer:

- has contested the insurance contract because of threat or fraudulent misrepresentation by the applicant (no. 1), or
- has rescinded the contract because of an intentional breach of the obligation to provide information prior to conclusion of contract or because of non-payment of the first insurance premium (no. 2), or
- has terminated the contract due to delayed payment of (subsequent) premiums or because of the occurrence of an insured event (no. 3).

583. The automatic acceptance applies only up to the (minimum) coverage prescribed by § 4 paragraph 2 PflVG (*see* paragraph 442). An application for insurance coverage that goes beyond this, such as unlimited cover can be declined by the insurer, also after the two-week period is over.[388]

§3. Insured Risks and Geographical Limits

I. Insured Risks

584. A.1.1 AKB 2015 provides coverage if insured or additionally insured persons cause damage by the use of a motor vehicle or the use of a trailer that is subject to compulsory registration. The insurer is obliged to exempt the policyholder (and co-insureds) from claims for damages if the use:

- causes injury to or the death of a person;
- damages or destroys property, or such property is lost;
- causes economic losses which are neither directly or indirectly connected with damage to persons or property (pure economic loss).

It needs to be emphasized that it is not sufficient that the damage is the result of the use of the car. Rather the damage must be the result of potential danger inherent in the typical use of the car (*Zurechnungszusammenhang*).[389] For example, if prior to loading with cement the silo tanker has not been effectively cleaned, the damage caused by the residues of the previous cargo and other soiling is not the result of potential danger inherent in the typical use of the car.[390]

388. *Ibid.*, n. 10 et seq.
389. Cf. BGH, 8.12.2015 – VI ZR 139/15, BGHZ 208, p. 140 para. 22; BGH, 27.10.1993 – IV ZR 243/92, NJW-RR 1994, pp. 218 et seq.
390. BGH, 27.10.1993 – IV ZR 243/92, NJW-RR 1994, pp. 218 et seq.

585. The term 'use' has a broad meaning and extends far beyond the operation of the vehicle. It includes not only driving, but also getting into and out of the vehicle, loading and unloading the vehicle, parking, washing, pushing an obstacle aside that is blocking the road, dis-/assembling vehicle components or roof/luggage racks, painting the vehicle, refuelling, storing goods in the vehicle, or the use as a machine, e.g., a pump for the purpose of filling a tank with oil.[391]

586. Towing a trailer with a vehicle means is not only a use of the trailer but also of the vehicle. According to a judgment of the *BGH* of 27 October 2010, the liability insurer of a motor vehicle pulling a trailer as well as the liability insurer of the trailer, both are equally liable towards the injured party.[392] If damage is caused by the trailer at a time when vehicle and trailer are not coupled together, the liability insurer of the trailer alone is responsible for the indemnification.

II. Geographical Limits

587. According to A.1.4 AKB coverage is provided for the use of the vehicle within the geographical boundaries of Europe, plus the non-European areas that are included within the scope of the EU. It must provide an amount of coverage legally specified by the country the policyholder is visiting, however, at least the amount specified in Germany, i.e., EUR 7.5 million for bodily injury, EUR 1.22 million for property damage and EUR 50,000 for pure economic loss (*see* § 4 paragraph 2 PflVG, *see* paragraph 441). If the insurer has issued an international insurance card, coverage also includes the non-European countries specified therein, provided country names have not been scored out.[393]

§4. (Co-)Insured Persons

588. Besides the policyholder the following persons are (co-)insured (A.1.2 AKB in conjunction with § 2 paragraph 2 KfzPflVV):

- keeper of the vehicle;
- owner of the vehicle;
- driver of the vehicle;
- passenger who is in the course of his/her employment supposed to take over driving or (un-)loading the vehicle;
- policyholder's employer (private or public) if the vehicle insured is used for business reasons with the approval of the policyholder; and
- bus conductor.

391. For further details *see* R. Koch, in: Bruck/Moeller, Großkommentar zum VVG, 9th ed., vol. 12, DeGruyter 2018, A.1 AKB n. 12 et seq.
392. BGH, 27.10.2010 – IV ZR 279/08, BGHZ 187 pp. 211, 213.
393. For details, *see* R. Koch, in: Bruck/Moeller, Großkommentar zum VVG, 9th ed., vol. 12, DeGruyter 2018, A.1 AKB n. 10 et seq.

It is important to note that in order to protect traffic accident victims the insurer must also provide compensation for losses caused by an unauthorized driver (joy-rider or thief). The insurer can subsequently exercise (limited) recourse against the unauthorized driver (*see* paragraphs 618, 619). Moreover, F.2 AKB provides that the co-insured persons, by derogation from §§ 44 paragraph 1, 45 paragraph 1 VVG (*see* paragraph 225), have the right to demand performance and file an action against the insurer.

§5. Exclusions

I. Regulatory Framework

589. According to § 115 paragraph 1 sentence 2 VVG the injured party's claim against the insurer exist within the framework of the insurer's liability under the insurance agreement. For that reason, the insurer is not liable towards the injured party whenever a contractual exclusion from cover applies. In order to protect the interests of injured parties the legislator has, however, first, limited possible contractual restrictions of cover by means of exclusions, and, second, provided for a compensation scheme (guarantee fund funded by the all motor vehicle insurers) which compensates injured parties in the case of:

- hit-and-run driving (§ 12 paragraph 1 sentence 1 no. 1 PflVG);
- there was no insurance coverage (§ 12 paragraph 1 sentence 1 no. 2 PflVG);
- the driver acted with intent (§ 12 paragraph 1 sentence 1 no. 3 PflVG).

II. Permissible Exclusions

A. *KfzPflVV and VVG*

590. § 4 KfzPflVV contains a list of exclusions the insurer is permitted to include into the policy. The motor vehicle insurer is only allowed to exclude liability claims for damage:

- to property or on account of pure economic loss of the policyholder, keeper or owner of the vehicle against co-insured persons (§ 4 no. 1 KfzPflVV);
- to or destruction of or loss of the insured car except for the damage to an inoperable car during towing (§ 4 no. 2 KfzPflVV);
- to or destruction of or loss of items carried in the car except for such items normally used by passengers or intended for satisfying personal needs (§ 4 no. 3 KfzPflVV);
- that occurs during the participation in car races or during test-drives for car races (§ 4 no. 4 KfzPflVV);
- resulting from the failure to meet delivery deadlines (§ 4 no. 5 KfzPflVV); and
- damage due to nuclear energy (§ 4 no. 6 KfzPflVV).

Exclusions clauses that go beyond these options are void according to § 134 BGB with one exception: the wilful infliction of damage. Even though it is not expressly mentioned in § 4 KfzPflVV, it follows from § 103 VVG that such exclusion is permitted.

591. It is worth to be noted that there are some discussions in the legal literature, even in the cases where the guarantee fund provides for compensation, whether § 4 KfzPflVV and § 103 VVG are compatible with the Directive 2009/103/EC. Some authors take the view that the directive does not allow limitations of the insurer's liability towards the injured party but only allows recourse against the policyholder and any co-insured person.[394] As far as the exclusions are based on Article 4 of Annex I of the European Convention on Compulsory Insurance against Civil Liability in Respect of Motor Vehicles (*see* paragraph 31) or justified by the possible reservations listed in Annex II, i.e., § 103 VVG, § 4 nos 1, 5 and 5 KfzPflVV, the relationship between the Convention and the Directive 2009/103/EC needs clarification by the European Court of Justice.[395]

B. Motor Vehicle Insurance

592. In line with § 4 KfzPflVV and § 103 VVG, A.1.5 AKB 2015 provides a list of all exclusions.

1. Intent

593. There is no coverage for damages caused intentionally and unlawfully (A.1.5.1 AKB 2015).

2. Officially Authorized Racing

594. Damages arising from participation in officially approved motor sport competitions, including the associated practice drives, are not covered (A.1.5.2 AKB 2015). It is to be noted, however, that the authorities in line with Article 6 paragraph 1 of the European Convention on Compulsory Insurance against Civil Liability in Respect of Motor Vehicles (*see* paragraph 31) only give their authorisation to such competition under the condition that the organiser has taken out adequate organiser's liability insurance.

394. For details, *see* R. Koch, in: Bruck/Moeller, Großkommentar zum VVG, 9th ed., vol. 12, DeGruyter 2018, § 4 KfzPflVV n. 10 et seq.
395. *Ibid.,* n. 21 et seq.

3. Damage to the Insured Vehicle

595. There is no insurance cover for damage to, the destruction or loss of the insured vehicle (A.1.5.3 AKB 2015). This exclusion is primarily of declaratory nature since claims for damages of the owner or the keeper of the vehicle are not subject to liability insurance but covered by the comprehensive insurance.

4. Damage to Trailers or Towed Vehicles

596. Damage to, the destruction or loss of a trailer, semi-trailer or a vehicle towed or towed away by the insured vehicle is excluded from cover. If an inoperable vehicle is towed away, as simple assistance, damages occurring thereby to the towed vehicle are covered (A.1.5.4 AKB 2015). This exclusion is for the aforementioned reason also of declaratory nature.

5. Damage to Transported Property

597. There is no insurance cover for losses due to damage to, the destruction or loss of property transported with the insured vehicle. However, there is insurance cover for property usually carried by passengers in the motor vehicle for personal use (e.g., clothing, spectacles, briefcase, and food). There is no insurance coverage for unauthorized passengers (A.1.5.5 AKB 2015).

6. Claim for Damages Against a Co-insured Person

598. Property or economic losses caused to the policyholder, the keeper or the owner of the vehicle by a co-insured person are excluded from cover. Bodily injury, however, is insured (A.1.5.6 AKB 2015).

7. Non-observation of Delivery and Transport Deadlines

599. Pure economic losses arising from non-observation of delivery and transport deadlines are excluded from cover (A.1.5.7 AKB 2015).

8. Contractual Claims

600. There is no insurance cover for liability claims, insofar as these according to the contract or a specific agreement are beyond the scope of legal liability (A.1.5.8 AKB 2015).

9. Damage by Nuclear Energy

601. Damages caused by nuclear energy are excluded from cover (A.1.5.9 AKB 2015).

§6. Policyholder's Non-Compliance with Duties

I. Regulatory Framework

602. Unlike exclusions which exempt the insurer from liability towards the injured party, according to § 117 paragraph 1 and paragraph 3 sentence 1 VVG the insurer remains liable to the victim, even if it is wholly or partially released from liability vis-à-vis the policyholder due to a breach of a statutory or contractual duty (*see* paragraph 445). The insurer must first compensate the victim and then has the right to limited recourse against the policyholder (*see* paragraphs 619, 620).

603. In order to protect the interests not only of the injured parties but in particular the interests of the policyholder (and co-insureds), the legislator has limited the contractual freedom of the parties to agree, first, on duties to be observed prior to the insured event, and, second, on the consequences following from a breach of duties to be observed prior to and after the insured event.

II. Permissible Duties to Be Observed prior to the Insured Event

604. § 5 KfzPflVV contains a list of duties to be observed prior to the insured event the insurer is permitted to include into the policy. These duties have been included almost verbatim in D.1.1 and D.1.2 AKB.

A. *Intended Purpose*

605. The vehicle may only be used for the purpose specified in the insurance certificate (§ 5 paragraph 1 no. 1 KfzPflVV/D.1.1.1 AKB 2015). For example: A private car may not be used as a taxi.

B. *Authorized Driver*

606. The vehicle may only be used by an authorized driver. Authorized is a person who uses the vehicle with the permission of the keeper or the owner of the vehicle. Neither the policyholder nor the keeper or the owner of the vehicle may permit an unauthorized driver to use the vehicle (§ 5 paragraph 1 no. 3 KfzPflVV/D.1.1.2 AKB 2015).

C. Driving License

607. The driver of the vehicle may only drive the car with the required driving license. Neither the policyholder nor the keeper or the owner of the vehicle may allow the vehicle to be used by a driver without the required driving license (§ 5 paragraph 1 no. 4 KfzPflVV/D.1.1.3 AKB 2015).

D. Unauthorized Racing

608. The driver may not use the vehicle for an unauthorized race event, including the associated practice drives (§ 5 paragraph 1 no. 2 KfzPflVV/D.1.1.4 AKB 2015).

E. Transferable License Plates

609. The driver may only use a vehicle authorized to bear transferable license plates if the respective license plate is completely and properly attached to the vehicle. Neither the policyholder nor the keeper or the owner of the vehicle may allow the vehicle to be used by a driver if the license plate is not completely and properly attached (§ 5 paragraph 1 no. 6 KfzPflVV/D.1.1.5 AKB 2015).

F. Alcohol and Other Drugs

610. The vehicle may not be used if the driver, under the influence of alcohol or other drugs, is not in a position to drive the vehicle safely. Neither the policyholder nor the keeper or the owner of the vehicle may allow the vehicle to be used by a driver who, under the influence of alcohol or other drugs, is not in a position to drive the vehicle safely (§ 5 paragraph 1 no. 5 KfzPflVV/D.1.2 AKB 2015).

III. Contractual Duties to Be Observed after the Occurrence of the Insured Event

611. There is no exclusive list on permissible duties to be observed after the occurrence of the insured event. Nor are there any restrictions on the contractual freedom of the parties to agree on duties.

A. Notifying Duties

612. The policyholder must notify the insurer in writing within one week of the occurrence of every insured event. If the policyholder fails to do so, the insurer can reject the insurance coverage unless he did learn of the occurrence of the insured event in another way within the notification period (e.g., from witnesses' reports or an excerpt from a file of the fine payment authority or from the public prosecutor) (E.1.1.1 AKB 2015).

613. The policyholder is under the duty to inform the insurer in the case that the police, the public prosecutor, or another authority investigates the insured event, even if the policyholder has already notified the insurer of the loss (E.1.1.2 AKB 2015).

614. The policyholder has permission to regulate small property damage claims that presumably do not exceed an agreed amount (e.g., 500 Euro). In that case the policyholder must notify the insurer of the claim if the self-regulation was not successful (E.1.2.2 AKB 2015). In case of a legal claim is made against the policyholder (court order or enforcement order) he/she must notify the insurer immediately (E.1.2.3 AKB 2015).

B. Duty to Cooperate and Mitigate Loss

615. The policyholder must answer questions of the insurer as to the circumstances of the insured event truthfully and in their entirety and may not leave the place of accident before he/she has facilitated, on behalf of the other parties to the accident and any persons suffering injury or damage, the determination of his identity, his/her vehicle and the nature of his/her involvement through his/her presence and an statement that he/she was involved in the accident.

616. The policyholder must moreover follow the instructions of the insurer which are necessary to clarify the loss occurrence (E.1.1.3 AKB 2015) and to avert or minimize the loss (E.1.1.4 AKB 2015).

C. Court Claim

617. If the injured party has filed a lawsuit, the policyholder must let the insurer handle the case: i.e., the insurer appoints a lawyer to represent the interests of itself and at the same time the interests of the policyholder (E.1.2.4 AKB 2015). If a court payment order has been issued against the policyholder, he/she must appeal against it immediately (E.1.2.5 AKB 2015).

IV. Consequences of Non-compliance with Duties

618. In line with the consequences provided for in § 28 VVG (*see* paragraph 267), the insurer is vis-à-vis the policyholder partly or fully released from its obligation to provide coverage depending first, on the degree of the policyholder's fault and, second, except the policyholder acted fraudulently, the causal link between the non-compliance and the loss. In any event the insurer remains liable towards the injured party (*see* paragraph 602).

619. In case of partial or full release the insurer may take recourse against the policyholder. However, according to § 5 paragraph 3 KfzPflVV/D.2.3 AKB 2015 the recourse is limited to EUR 5,000 in the case of a breach of duty to be observed before the occurrence of the insured event.

620. In the case of a breach of duty to be observed after the occurrence of the insured event the limitation of recourse depends on the type of duty and on the gravity of the breach. If the policyholder has deliberately and seriously violated the duty to assist the insurer and to reduce the damage (in particular leaving the scene of the accident, failure to render assistance, deliberate false statements), the insurer may take recourse up to a maximum amount of EUR 5,000 (§ 6 paragraph 3 KfzPflVV/E.2.3 AKB 2015). In all other cases the recourse is limited to EUR 2,500 (§ 6 paragraph 1 KfzPflVV/E.2.4 AKB 2015).

621. If the policyholder breach duties to be observed prior and after the occurrence of the insured event the recourse may amount up to a maximum of EUR 10,000.[396]

---

396. BGH, 14 Sept. 2005 – IV ZR 216/04, RuS 2006, pp. 100, 101; OLG Frankfurt/M., 27 Dec. 2017 – 0 U 218/16, VersR 2018, p. 477; OLG Celle, 26 Jul. 2012 – 8 W 39/12, RuS 2014, pp. 59, 60.

Chapter 3. Comprehensive Motor Vehicle Insurance

§1. Legal Regime

622. There are no specific rules on comprehensive motor vehicle insurance that provides coverage in the case of damage, destruction, loss or total loss of the vehicle including its co-insured parts. Besides the rules applying to all classes of insurance (§§ 1–73 VVG), the provisions on indemnity insurance (§§ 74–87 VVG) and property insurance (§§ 88–99 VVG) are applicable.

§2. Scope of Coverage

623. There is partially and fully comprehensive motor vehicle insurance. The partial comprehensive insurance (*Teilkaskoversicherung*) covers damage caused by fire/explosion, theft, robbery, misappropriation, storm, hail, lightning and flooding, by collisions with game, glass breakage and due to scorching of wiring because of a short circuit (A.2.2.1 AKB 2015). Fully comprehensive insurance (*Vollkaskoversicherung*) includes in addition all damage to the vehicle caused by accidents, as well as damage due to the wilful and malicious acts of third parties (A.2.2.2 AKB 2015).

§3. Scope of Indemnification

I. Repair

624. In (partially and fully) comprehensive motor vehicle insurance the insurer pays the repair costs up to a maximum of the replacement value and the costs for towage from the place of damage to the nearest garage for repair. If the repair entails replacing old parts with new, or the vehicle is completely or partly newly painted, the insurer deducts an amount from the costs of the spare parts and paintwork corresponding to the age and wear of the old parts (new-for-old). If the vehicle is not or not completely repaired, the insurer pay the cost required for a complete repair up to the amount of the replacement value minus the residual value (*Restwert*) (A.2.5.2 AKB 2015).

II. Total Write-off, Destruction or Loss

625. In the case of a total write-off, destruction or loss of the vehicle the insurer pays the replacement value (purchase price) with the deduction of a residual value of the vehicle. If the total write-off, destruction or loss occurs within an agreed period (e.g., 15 months) of the initial registration, and the policyholder is the first owner i.e., has acquired the vehicle from a car dealer or manufacturer, the insurer pays the original price of the vehicle minus any residual value of the vehicle (A.2.5.1 AKB 2015).

626. The insurer pays the original price or purchase price compensation beyond the replacement value only up to the amount ensured that the reimbursement is used for the repair of the vehicle or for the purchase of another vehicle within two years of the determination of the loss (A.2.5.1.3 AKB 2015). Not included in in the insurance coverage are alterations, improvements and wear-and-tear repairs (A.2.5.7 AKB 2015).

§4. Insured Persons

627. Provided that the policyholder is not identical with the owner of the car, according to A.2.3 AKB not only the policyholder's interest to be discharged from any liability towards the owner (e.g., lessor) is insured but also the owner's interest to get compensated (*see* paragraph 213).

§5. Exclusions

I. Intent and Gross Negligence

628. There is no coverage for damage intentionally caused by the policyholder. In the case of gross negligence the insurer, in line with § 81 paragraph 2 VVG (*see* paragraph 362), is entitled to reduce the compensation in relation to the seriousness of the policyholder's fault (A.2.9.1 AKB 2015).

II. Officially Authorized Racing

629. Damage arising out from participation in officially approved motor sport events, including associated practice drives, is excluded (A.2.9.2 AKB 2015).

III. Tire Damage

630. There is no coverage for damaged or destroyed tires. Insurance coverage is, however, in place if the tires are damaged or destroyed due to an event that at the same time caused other damage to the insured vehicle that is covered under the comprehensive motor vehicle insurance (A.2.9.3 AKB 2015).

IV. Earthquake, War, Civil Unrest, State Authority Measures

631. Damage caused directly or indirectly by earthquakes, war, civil unrest or state authority measures is excluded (A.2.9.4 AKB 2015).

V. Damage by Atomic Energy

632. Excluded from coverage is damage caused by atomic energy (A.2.9.5 AKB 2015).

§6. Policyholder's Non-Compliance with Duties

633. The (partially or fully) comprehensive motor vehicle insurer may be released from his obligation to indemnify the policyholder where the latter has not complied with contractual or statutory duties. For the statutory duties *see* paragraphs 249–279.

634. With regard to the contractual duties the AKB provisions on comprehensive motor vehicle insurance like the ones on motor liability insurance distinguish between duties to be observed prior to (D.2 AKB 2015) and after the occurrence (E.2 AKB 2015) of the insured event. The duties to be observed prior to the occurrence of an insured event are identical to the ones for motor liability insurance (*see* paragraphs 603–609). The duties to be observed after the insured event occurred, i.e., to notify the insurer of the insured event (E.1.1.1 AKB 2015), to inform the insurer about official investigations (E.1.1.2 AKB 2015), to cooperate with the insurer and to mitigate losses (E.1.1.3 and 1.1.4 AKB 2015) are also identical to the ones for motor liability insurance (*see* paragraphs 611–615). For example, the policyholder must give correct information about the state of the vehicle, the mileage and what happened in the accident. Before the repair of the damaged vehicle, the policyholder must seek for instructions from the insurer where circumstances permit (E.1.3.2 AKB 2015). In the case of theft, fire or game damage, the policyholder must inform the police if the damage or loss exceeds the agreed amount (E.1.3.3 AKB 2015).

Chapter 4. Roadside Assistance Insurance

§1. Legal Regime

635. There are no specific rules on roadside assistance insurance. Besides the rules applying to all classes of insurance (§§ 1–73 VVG) the provisions on indemnity insurance (§§ 74–87 VVG) and property insurance (§§ 88–99 VVG) apply.

§2. Scope of Coverage and Indemnification

636. Roadside assistance insurance provides cover in the case of breakdown, accident or theft of the insured car and in the case of illness, injury or death of the policyholder (or a co-insured person) on a journey (A.3 AKB 2015). The insurer organizes a service to reinstate the ability to drive at the location of damage and cover the costs for the service (including costs for towage and repair) (A.3.5 AKB 2015). In the case of a breakdown, accident or theft of the insured car at a location in Germany at least 50 km from the policyholder's permanent residence in Germany, the insurer further organizes the continuation of the journey or the return journey, accommodation, hiring a car and, if necessary the storage of the insured car (A.3.6 AKB 2015).

637. In the case of illness, injury or death of the policyholder (or a co-insured person) on a journey the insurer organizes his return transport, the return transport of accompanying children and of the insured car. In case of the policyholder's death on a journey abroad the insurer covers the funeral costs abroad or repatriation of the remains of policyholder (A.3.7 and 3.8 AKB 2015).

§3. Insured Persons

638. Insured are the authorized drivers and passengers of the insured vehicle (A.3.2 AKB).

Chapter 5. Motor Vehicle Accident Insurance

§1. Legal Regime

639. The motor vehicle accident insurance follows the rules on general, non-motor vehicle related accident insurance (*see* paragraph 654). It provides cover whenever an insured person suffers damage to his/her health by an accident occurred during the use of the vehicle (A.4.1 AKB 2015).

§2. Insured Persons

640. Insured are the driver and all passengers who are authorized by the policyholder to use the vehicle except for professional (co-)drivers employed by the policyholder if they use the car in this capacity (A.4.2 AKB 2015). In the case of invalidity depending on the sum agreed and the degree of invalidity the insurer pays the agreed benefit to the insured person (A.4.5 AKB 2015). In the case of death the insurer pays the agreed sum to the beneficiary (A.4.8 AKB 2015).

Chapter 6. Driver Protection Insurance

641. The driver protection insurance is a kind of accident insurance (A.5 AKB 2015). The driver insurance is only offered in connection with motor liability insurance. In contrast to the non-motor vehicle related accident insurance, the benefit of the driver protection insurance does not depend on the degree of invalidity but on the compensation amount for personal injury or death of the driver (A.5.4 AKB 2015). The insurer pays the sum the driver (or his/her surviving dependants) would be entitled to under German liability law if a third party was liable for the accident.[397]

397. For details, *see* R. Koch, in: Bruck/Moeller, Großkommentar zum VVG, 9th ed., vol. 12, DeGruyter 2018, A.5 AKB n. 6 et seq.

Part V. Insurance of the Person

642. Insurance of the person, or personal insurance, is characterized in that the insured risk (of e.g., death, occupational disability, accident, medical treatment) materializes in harm to the policyholder or another person. Under the VVG there are rules on live insurance (*see* paragraph 710), occupational disability (*see* paragraph 644), accident insurance (*see* paragraph 654) and health insurance (*see* paragraph 684).

Chapter 1. Workmen's Compensation and Occupational Disease

§1. Statutory Workmen's Compensation and Occupational Disease Insurance

643. Workmen's compensation for work-related accidents and diseases is subject to the seventh book of the social law book (SGB VII), which deals not only with accidents at work (*see* paragraph 653) but also with occupational diseases. Occupational diseases are diseases suffered by insured persons as a result of their work (§ 9 paragraph 1 SGB VIII). They are listed in the annex 1 of the ordinance on occupational diseases (*Berufskrankheiten-Verordnung*, hereafter 'BKV'). Statutory workmen's compensation and occupational disease insurance contributions are paid by the employer who registers all employees with the respective employer's liability insurance association (*Berufsgenossenschaft*).

§2. Private Occupational Disability Insurance

I. Legal Regime

644. The private occupational disability insurance (*Berufsunfaehigkeitsversicherung*) is subject to §§ 172–176 VVG and the provision applicable to all classes of insurance (§§ 1–73 VVG). Moreover, according to § 177 VVG the rules on life insurance (§§ 150–170 VVG) apply *mutatis mutandis* to occupational disability insurance insofar as this does not conflict with the specific nature of this insurance. The GDV provides model terms and conditions (BUV[398]).

II. Scope of Coverage

645. The private occupational disability insurance covers the policyholder against an occupational disability resulting from sickness, physical injury or loss of strength over and above what is normal for his/her age that incapacitates him/her to such a degree that he/she can presumably no longer wholly or partially exercise his/her profession (§ 172 paragraph 2 VVG).

III. Requirements for Indemnification

646. In practice, insurers require that it is probable that the policyholder cannot exercise his/her profession less than 50% of his/her workload for at least six consecutive months (*see* § 2 paragraph 1 and 2 BUV). There may be a waiting period up to five or more years. According to § 172 paragraph 2 VVG the insurer may

398. *Allgemeine Bedingungen für die Berufsunfähigkeitsversicherung*, BUV as of 25 Oct. 2017, https://www.gdv.de/resource/blob/6326/f73151d2ad0d7f8f1925201abfd17bf6/01-allgemeine-bedingungen-fur-die-berufsunfahigkeits-versicherung-0-pdf-data.pdf (accessed 28 Mar. 2018).

agree as a further requirement for its liability that the policyholder does not or cannot exercise another profession which he/she is in a position to take on based on his/her training and skills and which corresponds to his/her previous occupational status (abstract referral-clause). The latter is the case where the alternative profession is not significantly below the income and social esteem of the profession that has been exercised prior the insured event. According to case law, as a general line, a reduction of the income up to 20% must be accepted by the policyholder.[399]

647. The need for long-term care (*Pflegebeduerftigkeit*) is another trigger for occupational disability Insurance. If on the basis of a medical examination the policyholder is presumably permanently incapable, or if there is the prospect that for six consecutive months the insured will not be able to perform one or two of six activities of daily living – depending on the policy – the claim will be admitted (*see* § 2 paragraph 4 and 7 BUV). Some policies also cover mental illness and dementia.

IV. Benefits

648. On the German insurance market there are no disability policies that pay out a lump sum where the disablement is so serious that the policyholder would be unable to pursue his/her previous profession. The benefit is rather paid in the form of an annuity, which may be indexed and ceases if the policyholder recovers, and the policy is converted to premium-free insurance (§ 1 BUV). The amount of the annuity must not exceed the monthly net income. Many policies offer occupational rehabilitation and/or retraining or other forms of assistance benefits such as making contacts with educational institutions or helping in the search for employment.

649. According to § 173 VVG the insurer must declare in text form (§ 126b BGB) whether it acknowledges its obligation to effect payment. The insurer may once limit its acknowledgement to a certain period. It is binding on the insurer up to the end of the time limit. Where the requirements for the insurer's liability are no longer met, pursuant to § 174 VVG the insurer is only released from its liability if it has notified the policyholder in text form.

650. As pointed out before (*see* paragraph 644), the life insurance provisions apply mutatis mutandis to occupational disability insurance.[400] For this reason the insurers are obliged to forward a proportion of the surpluses to the policyholders. The surpluses are generally used to decrease the premiums. The gross premium then equals the actual premium and the net premium is reduced by the surpluses. If the surpluses are not used in order to reduce the premium, they can be paid at the end of the term (*see* § 3 BUV).

399. Cf. BGH 8 Feb. 2012 – IV ZR 287/10, RuS 2012, p. 193; *see also* BGH, 7 Dec. 2016 – IV ZR 434/15, RuS 2017, pp. 87, 89.

400. *See also* BGH, 5 Dec. 1990 – IV ZR 13/90, VersR 1991, p. 289; BGH, 5 Oct. 1988 – IVa ZR 317/86, VersR 1988, p. 1233.

V. Exclusions

651. There is no insurance coverage for occupational disease caused by the policyholder with intent or in the course of an attempted criminal offence, by civil unrest where the policyholder supported the troublemaker, by atomic energy or by war (§ 5 BUV).

VI. Risk Groups/Tariffs

652. Besides individually agreed benefits and sums insured, the activity of the person to be insured is important for calculating the premium. For the premium calculation the various activities/occupations are split into so-called risk groups. Individual insurers can decide themselves on the composition and classification of the risk groups. For example, risk groups might be split as follows:

- Risk group 1: comparatively low risk (e.g., lawyers, professors, tax advisers).
- Risk group 2 und 3: moderate risk (e.g., dentists, teachers, tax officers).
- Risk group 4: high risk (e.g., soldiers, carpenters, chauffeurs, farmers, butchers).
- Risk group 5 and 6: dangerous professions, insured only against the payment of a premium surcharge (e.g., dancers, vocal coaches, broadcasters, fitness coaches).

Chapter 2. Accident Insurance

§1. Statutory Accident Insurance

653. Statutory accident insurance is part of the social security system. The legal basis is the SGB VII. Statutory accident insurance provides cover for accidents at work; it does not apply to non-work related accidents. The insurance contributions are paid by the employer (*see* paragraph 643).

§2. Private Accident Insurance

I. Legal Regime

654. The private accident insurance (*Unfallversicherung*) is subject to §§ 178–191 VVG and the provision applicable to all classes of insurance (§§ 1–73 VVG). The GDV provides model terms and conditions (AUB[401]). The rules on indemnity insurance (§§ 74–87 VVG) do not apply since the accident insurance, as provided for under §§ 178–191 VVG, is a fixed sum insurance.

II. Forms of Accident Insurance

655. Private accident insurance is offered in various forms. In the case of accident insurance for individuals it is always an individual person who is insured. The cover includes all kind of accidents round the clock worldwide (no. 1.2 AUB 2014). Group accident insurance is taken out, e.g., by sports associations, organizers of sporting events or employers for their members, participants or employees. If the insurance against accidents involving another person is taken out by the policyholder for his own account, pursuant to § 179 paragraph 2 VVG the written consent of the other person shall be required for the contract to become effective.

III. Scope of Coverage

656. According to § 178 paragraph 2 sentence 1 VVG an accident shall be deemed to have occurred where the insured person involuntarily suffers health impairment on account of a sudden event having an external impact on his/her body. The GDV model terms and conditions copy this definition (no. 1.3 AUB 2014). An external impact requires that the impairment results from forces which lie outside the body. There must be a not necessarily physical but also psychological external event causing personal injury or loss of life. Personal injury triggered by a shock, however, is expressly excluded from coverage (no. 5.2.6 AUB 2014).

401. *Allgemeine Bedingungen für die Unfallversicherung*, AUB as of 25 Mar. 2014, https://www.gdv.de/resource/blob/6252/4a457aede06ffdde37c5865d23df7be6/01-allgemeine-unfallversicherungsbedingungen--aub-2014--data.pdf (accessed 28 Mar. 2018).

657. The requirement of an external physical event is not met, e.g., if the policyholder plays tennis and twists his knee while in motion without any physical contact with the ground. If the knee rotation is the result from a hollow in the ground, however, the injury will be covered.[402] In principle, this distinction would have to be made whenever, e.g., a joint is dislocated or muscles, tendons, ligaments or capsules are wrenched or torn. To avoid disputes about whether or not such injury was the result of an external impact, accident insurance policies provide for an 'extended accident definition', which includes physical injuries caused by extraordinary exertion to limbs or the spine in the coverage (no. 1.4 AUB 2014).

658. According to case law damage to health or death caused by fumes or gases,[403] frostbites or drowning,[404] intake of allergens or toxin,[405] diving,[406] rock climbing, tick bites,[407] or flying are accidents in terms of § 178 paragraph 2 sentence 1 VVG. Many insurers, moreover, provide cover in the case of damage to health and death caused by a stroke or heart attack, rabies, tetanus or infected wounds as the result of an accident, and during the lawful defence of or attempts to rescue people or things.

IV. Types of Benefits

659. First and foremost, accident insurances are taken out to protect the policyholder against the risk of disability and death as a result of an accident. Other benefits generally available under an accident insurance policy are interim payment, daily allowance, daily hospital allowance, cosmetic surgery and search and rescue operations.

A. *Disablement Benefits*

1. Precondition for the Benefits

660. The physical or mental capacity of the insured person must be permanently impaired as the result of an accident. An impairment is permanent if it is likely to exist for more than three years and a change to the person's state of health cannot be expected (no. 2.1.1.1 AUB 2014). The invalidity must occur within 15 months after the accident and be diagnosed by a doctor in written form (no. 2.1.1.2 AUB 2014). Within this period the policyholder has to assert a claim against the insurer

402. *See* e.g., BGH, 6 Jul. 2011 – IV ZR 29/09, RuS 2011, p. 400, para. 14 et seq.
403. OLG Düsseldorf, 5 Dec. 1995 – 4 U 190/93, VersR 1997, p. 174.
404. BGH, 13 Dec. 2011 – VI ZR 177/10, VersR 2012, p. 249.
405. BGH, 16 Oct. 2013 – IV ZR 390/13, RuS 2014, p. 34; OLG München, 1 Mar. 2012 – 14 U 2523/11, VersR 2012, p. 895.
406. OLG Karlsruhe, 16 May 1995 – 19 U 283/94, VersR 1996, p. 364.
407. OLG Düsseldorf, 7 Apr. 2009 – 4 U 39/08, VersR 2010, p. 61; OLG Hamm, 21 Nov. 1980 – 20 U 76/79, VersR 1981, p. 673.

(no. 2.1.1.3 AUB 2014). The policyholder must proof the health impairment, causation between the accident and the health impairment, the invalidity and its degree, and causation between the health impairment and the invalidity.[408]

2. Type and Amount of Benefits

a. Capital Sum

661. The disablement benefit is paid as a capital sum. The amount of benefit is calculated based on the insured sum and the degree of disablement caused by the accident in accordance with a so-called disability percentage table. In this table, which forms part of the contract, the degree of disability is determined if certain limbs are permanently impaired or disabled. For example, for the loss of an eye there is a fixed degree of 50% disability. If the policyholder has a disability sum insured of EUR 100,000, he/she thus receives compensation of EUR 50,000 as a lump sum payment for the loss of an eye.

662. According to no. 2.1.2.2.3 AUB 2014 the degree of invalidity is reduced by a pre-invalidity of the impaired body part or sense or their function. The burden of proof lies on the insurer.[409] No. 3.2 AUB 2014 provides that where illness or ailment contributed to the health impairments or their consequences following from the accident, the claim is reduced according to the weight of the illness or the ailment. § 182 VVG rules that the burden of proof lies on the insurer.

b. Annuity

663. The parties may agree on an annuity if the degree of disability amounts to a certain percentage according to the disability percentage table (2.2 AUB 2014).

B. Death Benefits

664. If the policyholder dies within a year of the accident, according to no. 2.6 AUB 2014 the death benefit will be paid out in the amount of the agreed sum to the beneficiary designated by the policyholder (§§ 185, 159 VVG).

C. Interim Benefits

665. In the case of that the policyholder is still disable of more than 50% due to the accident, and if this impairment has existed without interruption for at least six months after the accident, the interim benefit agreed in the policy will be paid (no.

---

408. *See* Knappmann, in: Proelss/Martin, VVG, 30th ed., C.H. Beck 2018, § 178 n. 24.
409. *Ibid.,* § 182 n. 1.

2.3 AUB 2014). The quick first disbursement is useful in those situations where the degree of disability is difficult to ascertain due to the severity of the injuries.[410]

D. Daily Benefits

666. The policyholder is entitled to daily benefit if his/her ability to work is impaired due to the accident (in-ability to work, wholly or partially) and if in addition he/she is being medically treated. The daily benefit is calculated in accordance with the sum insured agreed. The amount is determined by the degree to which the impairment affects the policyholder's performance of the occupational activity or employment. It is paid for the duration of medical treatment up to one year from the date of the accident (no. 2.4 AUB 2014).

E. Daily Hospital Benefits

667. Daily hospital benefit is paid for medically necessary inpatient treatment in a hospital as a result of the accident, from the day of admission to the day of discharge. It is also paid in the case of ambulatory surgery if the policyholder is unable to work due to the surgery. There are time limitations on this benefit, e.g., for a maximum of 2 years (no. 2.5 AUB 2014).

F. Cosmetic Surgery

668. It is a precondition for the benefit that the policyholder has undergone a cosmetic surgery in order to rectify any impairment to his/her external appearance caused by the accident. The cosmetic operation must take place within three years after the accident; for accidents suffered by minors by no later than upon attaining the age of 21. Up to a total of the agreed sum (e.g., EUR 10,000) compensation for doctor's fees, surgery costs, necessary costs of accommodation and care in the hospital and for costs for dental treatment and dental prostheses (no. 2.7 AUB 2014).

G. Search and Rescue Costs

669. The costs for search and rescue operations are covered if the policyholder has suffered an accident or such an incident was imminent or suspected according to the specific circumstances (no. 2.8 AUB 2014). It is worth noting that rescue activities are generally also paid by statutory health insurance or private health insurance.[411]

---

410. Cf. Leverenz, in: Bruck/Moeller, Großkommentar zum VVG, 9th ed., vol. 9, DeGruyter 2010, no.2.2 AUB 2008 n. 2.
411. Cf. OLG Hamburg, 24 Aug. 1978 – 5 U 42/77, VersR 1978, p. 814.

V. Exclusions

670. There are a number of incidents, which though satisfying the definition of an accident, are excluded from coverage (*see* no. 5.1 AUB 2014). Moreover certain injuries to health are not covered (*see* no. 5.2 AUB 2014).

A. Mental or Cognitive Disorders

671. Accidents caused by mental disturbances or impaired consciousness, also if these are due to drunkenness, or due to stroke, epileptic fits or other seizures, which affect the whole body of the policyholder, are excluded from cover. Insurance, however, is in place if these disorders or attacks are caused by an accident (*see* no. 5.1.1 AUB 2014).

B. Crime Related Accidents

672. There is no cover for accidents that happen to the policyholder in the course of committing or attempting a crime (e.g., a burglar plummets through the ceiling of a supermarket and seriously injures himself) (*see* no. 5.1.2 AUB 2014).

C. War or Civil War

673. Accidents caused directly or indirectly by (civil) war are generally excluded. Where the (civil) war has come unexpectedly for the policyholder whilst staying abroad, however, there is temporary insurance cover for up to 7 days after the beginning of the war in the territory of the state in which the policyholder is staying (no. 5.1.3 AUB 2014). For example, there is no cover in the case that the policyholder, during a trip in Middle East, passes through a land in which there is civil war, gets involved in combat action between rival warring parties and is wounded. If he had only fallen and injured himself due to carelessness, there would be insurance cover since the accident is neither directly nor indirectly due to the state of (civil) war.

D. Aircraft Pilot and Crew

674. There is no cover for accidents of the policyholder in his/her capacity as an aircraft pilot (also air sportsman) or as a flight attendant or in the course of professional activities during flights (e.g., taking aerial photographs) (no. 5.1.4 AUB 2014).

E. Participation in Car Races

675. Accidents of the policyholder when participation in race events for motor vehicles, including practice driving sessions, are excluded from cover (no. 5.1.5 AUB 2014).

F. Nuclear Power

676. Accidents caused directly or indirectly by nuclear energy are not insured (no. 5.1.6 AUB 2014).

G. Excluded Injuries

677. There is no coverage for the following injuries:[412]

- Injury to inter-vertebral disks and bleeding from internal organs and cerebral haemorrhages. Insurance cover exists, however, if an accident event is the predominant cause (no. 5.2.1 AUB 2014).
- Damage to health caused by radiation. Insurance cover exists, however, for damage to health caused by exposure as a result of an accident to X-rays, laser radiation, maser radiation and artificially generated ultraviolet radiation (no. 5.2.2 AUB 2014).
- Damage to health caused by therapeutic treatments or surgery to the body of the policyholder. Insurance cover exists, however, if the therapeutic treatments or surgery, including radio-diagnostic and radio-therapeutic treatment or surgery, are carried out as the result of an accident (no. 5.2.3 AUB 2014).
- Infections with the exception of rabies and tetanus or infected wounds which results from an accident (no. 5.2.4 AUB 2014).
- Poisoning as a result of taking solid or liquid substances through the gullet (no. 5.2.5 AUB 2014).
- Abnormal disorders as a result of psychological reactions which cannot be directly and causally attributed to a physical injury/a physical loss, even if these are caused by an accident (no. 5.2.6 AUB 2014).
- Abdominal or hypogastric hernias, unless they are directly caused by external mechanical effects (no. 5.2.7 AUB 2014).

H. Extensions of Cover

678. Insurers depart from the GDV's model terms and conditions and include in the coverage accidents caused by drunkenness if the blood alcohol level does not

---

412. For further details, *see* Leverenz, in: Bruck/Moeller, Großkommentar zum VVG, 9th ed., vol. 9, DeGruyter 2010, no. 5.2.1–5.2.7 AUB 2008.

exceed 0.8 per mille for drivers of motorized vehicles, 1.3 per mille in all other cases. They generally provide cover for lyme disease resulting from tick bites and poisoning for children up to the 10th birthday.

Chapter 3. Health Insurance

§1. Statutory Health Insurance

679. Statutory health insurance is part of the social security system. The legal basis of statutory health insurance is the SGB V. Statutory health insurance provides cover for pregnancy and maternity, inpatient or outpatient treatment and prevention of diseases and their deterioration, contraception, sterilisations, abortions, medical rehabilitation, dental care etc. (*see* § 11 SGB V).

680. Statutory health insurance contributions are dependent on income. Up to a monthly payment of EUR 4,425 (as of 2018), the basis is the gross income of the employee, from which a uniform contribution rate of 14.6% is levied. This is divided equally between the insured party and the employer, i.e., 7.3% each. Each health insurer also levies a different amount of additional contribution, which is paid only by the employee. If the gross income exceeds EUR 4,425 per month, income above it plays no role in calculating the contribution. Statutory health insurance includes into coverage the employee's spouse or unmarried partner and children.

681. Self-employed, freelancer, public servants and employees whose annual gross income for three consecutive calendar years exceeds EUR 59,400 (as of 2018) can choose between insuring themselves with a social health insurer (*gesetzliche Krankenkasse*) or long-term care insurer as an optional member (*freiwilliges Mitglied*) or taking out health insurance and long-term care insurance with one of the many private health and long-term care insurers (§ 6 paragraph 1 SGB V).

682. It is possible to return to the statutory health insurance scheme if a person's individual income falls below this limit. In such a case, the policyholder has one-off (and irrevocable) option to remain privately insured or to switch to the statutory health insurance scheme. Policyholder's over the age of 55, however, can no longer switch to the statutory health insurance scheme if they have not held statutory insurance in the preceding five years (§ 6 paragraph 3a SGB V). This rule is aimed at making it difficult for privately insured persons who have not participated for some time in the pay-as-you-go financing system within the statutory health insurance scheme to return to the scheme.

683. It is to be noted that the statutory health insurance is complemented by the statutory long-term care insurance which is subject to §§ 110 et seq. SGB XI. Long-term care insurance was introduced as the fifth pillar of social insurance system after health insurance, accident insurance, pensions and unemployment insurance (*see* paragraph 757).

§2. Private Health Insurance

684. Unlike the statutory health insurance scheme, private health insurance is financed by premiums that have been calculated on actuarial principles. As a consequence, private health insurance does not include families. Premiums of private health insurance are not based on the policyholder's income but on his/her age, medical condition and tariff. The premiums will be calculated separately for each insured person.

685. The premiums include an ageing reserve which is build up from the inception of the insurance and is drawn on if the annual premium is not sufficient to cover the increased cost of medical care when the policyholder gets older. To prevent the insurance premiums from increasing too steeply with age and the associated higher expenses, the private insurers charge younger members a higher contribution rate than necessary for their age and condition of health.

I. Legal Regime

686. The private health insurance is subject to §§ 192–208 VVG. Except for the rules on risk increase (§§ 23–27 VVG), the provisions relevant for all classes of insurance (§§ 1–73 VVG) apply. Depending on the type of the health insurance the provision of indemnity insurance (§§ 74–87 VVG), with the exception of § 81 VVG, are applicable. To the extent that health insurance is suitable as a full or partial substitute to statutory health insurance (substitutive health insurance) the health insurer must comply with special regulatory requirements laid down in §§ 146–160 VAG. In that case the insurer must operate the health insurance in accordance with the technical principles of life insurance.

II. Types of Health Insurance

687. The VVG distinguishes between comprehensive health insurance (§ 192 paragraph 1 VVG), daily hospital allowance insurance (§ 192 paragraph 4 VVG) and the daily sickness allowance insurance (§ 192 paragraph 5 VVG). While the comprehensive health insurance is an indemnity insurance the daily hospital allowance insurance (§ 192 paragraph 4 VVG) and the daily sickness allowance insurance are fixed sum insurances. They may be offered either in addition to the comprehensive health insurance or as a separate cover (supplementing the statutory health insurance). The PKV provides model terms and conditions for the various types of health insurance (MB/KK 2009 for comprehensive health insurance and daily hospital allowance insurance,[413] MB/KT 2009 for daily sickness allowance insurance[414]).

688. Analogous to the statutory insurance schemes the private health insurance is complemented by the private long-term nursing care insurance. According to § 192 paragraph 6 VVG the insurer is obligated, in the event of the need for long-term nursing care, to reimburse the expenses for caring for the insured person or to pay the agreed daily allowance.

III. Scope of Coverage

A. Comprehensive Health Insurance

689. Pursuant to § 192 paragraph 1 VVG the insurer provides the policyholder with cash benefits, in the form of reimbursement for medically necessary treatment due to sickness or in consequence of an accident and for other agreed services, including those expenses associated with pregnancy and childbirth, as well as out-patient medical check-ups for the early diagnosis of diseases in accordance with statutory programmes. The level of these reimbursements (e.g., single or two-bed rooms in the hospital, treatment by head physician, private clinics) depends on the individual insurance contract.

690. It is to be emphasized that the policyholder, not the insurer, is the contractual partner of the individual health service providers (e.g., doctor, dentist, hospital, and midwife). The policyholder chooses the service provider and meets the incurred costs, which are later reimbursed by the insurer (based on the individual contract, either in full or in part). The service provider's fee may be up 3.5 times that of the statutory health insurance fee schedule rate, depending on the type of service and the time required. In the case of comprehensive health insurance in the basic tariff (*see* paragraph 696), the service-provider pursuant to § 192 paragraph 7 VVG may assert its claim to remuneration for services provided against the insurer.

691. Pursuant to § 192 paragraph 2 VVG the insurer is not liable to pay claims insofar as the expenses for treatment or other services are obviously disproportionate to the services performed. It is to be noted, however, that the insurer has to provide cover for medically necessary treatment irrespective of its costs. According to the BGH the necessity of a treatment is to be determined on the basis of an objective medical assessment. Whenever a treatment was acceptable in the light of an

413. 'Musterbedingungen für die Krankheitskosten- und Krankenhaustagegeldversicherung, MB/KK 2009 as of January 2017; https://www.pkv.de/service/broschueren/musterbedingungen/mb-kk-2009.pdb.pdf (accessed 28 Mar. 2018).

414. 'Musterbedingungen 2009 für die Krankentagegeldversicherung', MB/KT 2009 as of Juni 2017, https://www.pkv.de/service/broschueren/musterbedingungen/mb-kt-2009.pdb.pdf (accessed 28 Mar. 2018).

objective medical assessment the insurer is liable.[415] Economic considerations must not be taken into consideration.[416] The burden of proof that the expenses are disproportionate rests on the insurer.[417]

692. § 1 paragraph 4 MB/KK 2009 limits the standard coverage to medical treatment within Europe. There is cover, however, during the first month of a temporary stay outside of Europe.

B. Daily Hospital Allowance Insurance

693. According to § 192 paragraph 4 VVG in the case of daily hospital allowance insurance, the insurer must pay the agreed daily hospital allowance for medically necessary inpatient treatment. As is the case in comprehensive health insurance, the need for inpatient treatment is to be determined on the basis of an objective medical assessment.

C. Daily Sickness Allowance Insurance

694. In the case of daily sickness allowance insurance, § 192 paragraph 5 VVG states that the insurer is obligated to reimburse the loss of earnings resulting from the illness or accident due to the incapacity to work by paying the agreed daily sickness allowance. § 1 paragraph 3 MB/KT defines incapacity to work as a situation where the policyholder, according to medical assessment, is temporary unable to pursue his/her professional activity and in fact does not pursue this activity nor another activity.

IV. Obligation to Contract

695. According to § 193 paragraph 3 sentence 1 VVG any person domiciled in Germany and not insured in statutory health insurance, is obliged to conclude and maintain with an insurer for herself/himself and for the persons legally represented by him/her, insofar as they are not themselves able to conclude contracts, a comprehensive health insurance.

696. The insurer, in turn, is obliged to accept an application for comprehensive health insurance not in the premium tariff but in the basic tariff (§ 193 paragraph 5 sentence 1 VVG) (*Kontrahierungszwang*). Pursuant to § 152 VAG the basic tariff

415. BGH, 10 Jul. 1996 – IV ZR 133/95, NJW 1996, pp. 3074, 3075.
416. BGH, 12 Mar. 2003 – IV ZR 278/01, NJW 2003, pp. 1596. 1599.
417. BGH, 12 Mar. 2003 – IV ZR 278/01, NJW 2003, pp. 1596. 1599.

must correspond to the statutory health insurance benefits catalogue. The PKV provides model terms and conditions for the basic tariff (AVB/BT[418]). In the basic tariff the service provider's fee may be up 2.0 times that of the statutory health insurance fee schedule rate (Teil II A.1 paragraph 2 AVB/BT).

697. The insurer is entitled to reject the application if the applicant was already insured by the insurer and the insurer has contested the contract of insurance because of threat or fraudulent misrepresentation, or has rescinded the contract of insurance because of an intentional breach of the obligation to provide information prior to conclusion of contract (§ 193 paragraph 5 sentence 4 VVG).

698. § 197 paragraph 1 VVG entitles insurers to stipulate a waiting period up to three months in respect of comprehensive health insurance, daily hospital allowance insurance and daily sickness allowance insurance and up to eight months in respect of childbirth, psychotherapy, dental treatment, dental prostheses and orthodontics. In the case of long-term nursing care insurance, the waiting period may not exceed three years. According to § 198 VVG new-born babies are to be included in the cover without waiting periods.

V. Limited Rights of the Insurer to Terminate the Contract

699. Private health insurers are in principle not allowed to terminate comprehensive health insurance contracts with or without notice period (§ 206 paragraph 1 sentence 1 VVG). The same is true for daily hospital allowance insurance taken out alongside a comprehensive health insurance contracts (§ 206 paragraph 1 sentence 3 VVG). Daily sickness allowance insurance contracts may be terminated by the insurer to the end of each insured year in the first three years, subject to a notice period of three months.

700. The BGH, however, held that this ban only applies to termination due to non-payment or delayed payment to the premium but do not prevent the insurer to terminate the contract for good cause without notice period in accordance with general contract law rules set forth in § 314 paragraph 1 BGB.[419] According to this provision there is good cause if, when considering all circumstances and taking into account the parties' mutual interests, continuation of the agreement is unacceptable for the terminating party. The courts have found for a good cause where the policyholder committed insurance fraud by submitting falsified documents[420] or beat up

418. *Allgemeine Versicherungsbedingungen für den Baistarif*, AVB/BT 2009 as of Juli 2017, https://www.pkv.de/service/broschueren/musterbedingungen/avb-bt-2009.pdb.pdf (accessed 28 Mar. 2018).
419. BGH, 7 Dec. 2011 – IV ZR 50/11, NJW 2012, p. 376, paras 9 et seq.
420. *Ibid.*, para. 29.

one of the insurer's employees who house visited the allegedly disabled policyholder.[421] It needs to be emphasized that the long-term care insurance cannot be terminated for good cause. [422]

701. If the policyholder is in arrears with payment in the amount of premium shares for two months, the insurer shall issue him with a reminder. If after two weeks after receipt of the reprimand the arrears are still higher than the premium share for one month, the insurer is entitled to suspend the benefits. During the period of suspension, however, the insurer is liable for expenses necessary to treat acute illness and pain, as well as in case of pregnancy and maternity (§ 193 paragraph 6 VVG).

VI. Right of the Insurer to Adjust the Premium and the Terms and Conditions of the Contract

702. As compensation for the limited rights of the insurer to terminate the contract, the insurer is under certain conditions entitled to adjust the premium and the terms and conditions of the contract.

A. Right of the Insurer to Adjust the Premium

703. According to § 203 paragraph 2 VVG the insurer may, in the event of a not only temporary change to one of the bases of calculation necessary for calculating the premium, re-determine the premium in accordance with the adjusted bases of calculation for existing insurance agreements insofar as an independent trustee has reviewed the technical bases of calculation and has agreed to the adjustment of the insurance premium. The amount of an excess may also be adjusted and an agreed risk premium amended accordingly insofar as this has been agreed.

704. According to § 157 paragraph 1 sentence 1 VAG only persons are eligible as trustee who are reliable, qualified and independent, i.e., must not have concluded an employment contract or other service contract with the insurer or any affiliated undertaking, and must have no claims against the undertaking under such a contract.

705. The trustee, regularly an actuary, is appointed by the insurer. Before the appointment, however, the insurer must inform the BaFin and provide it with the information necessary to evaluate whether the designated trustee meets the requirements set forth in § 157 paragraph 1 VAG. If there is evidence to suggest that the designated trustee is not reliable, qualified and independent, the BaFin pursuant to § 157 paragraph 2 VAG may require that another person be appointed.

---

421. BGH, 7 Dec. 2011 – IV ZR 105/11, NJW 2012, 1365, paras 9 et seq.
422. *Ibid.*, paras 28 et seq.

706. Recently, there have been a number of cases dealing with the independence of trustees where the courts held that a trustee who receives from a health insurer more than 30% of his/her annual income could not be considered as independent.[423] The judgments have not yet become res judicata and the appeals are pending before the BGH. Should the BGH uphold the decisions the premium adjustments approved by the trustee would be ineffective and the health insurer might be obligated to refund premiums.

B. Right of the Insurer to Adjust the Terms and Conditions of the Contract

707. The insurer is according to § 203 paragraph 3 VVG entitled to adjust the general terms and conditions of insurance and the conditions of the tariff in the case of a non-temporary change in the conditions in the health care sector if the changes appear necessary to sufficiently safeguard the policyholders' concerns, and an independent legal trustee has reviewed the conditions on which the change is based and has confirmed their appropriateness. The appointment proceeding is identical with the one of the trustee for premium adjustments. To meet the qualification requirement the trustee must have legal knowledge, relating in particular to the field of health insurance (§ 157 paragraph 3 sentence 2 VAG). In practice insurers often appoint lawyers and professors specialised in (health) insurance law.

VII. Exclusions

708. The following exclusions can be found in the comprehensive health insurance and in the daily hospital allowance insurance (§ 5 MB/KK). There is no cover for:

- illness, the consequences of illnesses or accidents and deaths attributable to warlike events (§ 5 paragraph 1 lit. a) MB/KK);
- illnesses and accidents based on intent as wells as treatment cures (§ 5 paragraph 1 lit. b) MB/KK);
- treatment by doctors, dentists, healing practitioners and hospitals whose bills have been excluded from remuneration for important reasons by the insurer if the insurance claim arises following notification of the policyholder as regards this exclusion from benefits (§ 5 paragraph 1 lit. c) MB/KK);
- for cures, recuperative treatments and rehabilitation measures administered by the statutory rehabilitation authorities, save as otherwise envisaged by the tariff (§ 5 paragraph 1 lit. d) MB/KK);– out-patient curative treatment in curative spas or health resorts (§ 5 paragraph 1 lit. e) MB/KK);

423. LG Offenburg, 27 July 2018 – 2 O 379/17, BeckRS 2018, 16523; LG Berlin, 10 Jan. 2018 – 23 O 78/16, BeckRS 2018, 1805; LG Potsdam, 27 Sept. 2017 – 6 S 80/16, RuS 2018, p. 24; LG Neuruppin, 25 Aug. 2017 – 1 O 338/16, VersR 2018, p. 469; AG Potsdam, 18 Oct. 2016 – 29 C 122/16, RuS 2017, p. 309.

- treatment of spouses/official partners, parents or children (§ 5 paragraph 1 lit. g) MB/KK);
- accommodation which is necessary due to a need of nursing care (§ 5 paragraph 1 lit. h) MB/KK).

709. There are some additional exclusions in the daily sickness allowance policies (§ 5 MB/KT). Besides the exclusion under § 5 MB/KK there is, e.g., no cover for the loss of earnings resulting from the illness or accident due to the incapacity to work in the case of:

- excessive consumption of alcohol (§ 5 paragraph 1 lit. c) MB/KT);
- pregnancy, childbirth, miscarriage and abortion (§ 5 paragraph 1 lit. d) MB/KT);
- maternity leave (§ 5 paragraph 1 lit. e) MB/KT);
- the policyholder reside not at his/her place of residence (§ 5 paragraph 1 lit. f) MB/KT).

Chapter 4. Life Insurance

§1. Legal Regime

710. The life insurance is subject to §§ 150–171 VVG. Except for a few deviations from the rules on revocation (§§ 8, 9 VVG), the duty of disclosure (§ 19 paragraph 2 VVG), risk increase (§§ 23–27 VVG) and delayed payment of renewal premiums (§ 38 VVG) the provisions relevant for all classes of insurance (§§ 1–73 VVG) apply. Clauses deviating from § 152 paragraph 1 and 2 VVG and §§ 153 to 155 VVG, §§ 157, 158, 161 VVG and §§ 163 to 170 VVG to the detriment of the policyholder, the insured person or the beneficiary are not permitted. At the supervisory level, life insurers must comply with special regulatory requirements laid down in §§ 102, 138 to 145 VAG concerning *inter alia* premium calculation, equal treatment, policyholders' profit participation.

§2. Types of Life Insurance

711. Life insurance may be offered as an endowment policy (*Kapitallebensversicherung*), term life policy (*Risikolebensversicherung*) or fixed date policy. The GDV provides model terms and conditions for endowment policies (ALB[424] and ABR[425]) and term life policies (ALR[426]).

I. Endowment Policies

A. Classical Form

712. In case of an endowment policy in its classical form, the insurers pay out the sum insured on maturity of the contract to the policyholder or other beneficiary (§ 1 ALB). In the case of death of the policyholder prior to the maturity of the contract the pay-out will be made to the beneficiary (§ 9 ALB).[427]

424. *Allgemeine Bedingungen für die kapitalbildende Lebensversicherung*, ALB as of 25 Oct. 2017, https://www.gdv.de/resource/blob/6348/5827a5492cca6aa1147852c30f10247b/allgemeine-bedingungen-fuer-die-kapitalbildende-lebensversicherung-0-pdf-data.pdf (accessed 28 Mar. 2018).

425. *Allgemeine Bedingungen für die Rentenversicherungmit aufgeschobener Rentenzahlung*, ABR as of 25 Oct. 2017, https://www.gdv.de/resource/blob/6294/7f9e88e35e4617cf16575e95d7ade8a7/02-gdv-musterbedingung-lv-rentenversicherung-mit-aufgeschobener-rentenzahlung-2016-data.pdf (accessed 28 Mar. 2018).

426. *Allgemeine Bedingungen für die Risikolebensversicherung*, ALR as of 25 Oct. 2017, https://www.gdv.de/resource/blob/6324/c9b5120d820db45c2776f7b91d552fb6/allgemeine-bedingungen-fur-die-risikolebensversicherung-0-pdf-data.pdf (accessed 28 Mar. 2018).

427. For details, *see* Winter, in: Bruck/Moeller, Großkommentar zum VVG, 9th ed., vol. 8/1, DeGruyter 2013, Einf n. 37.

B. Pension Insurance

713. Another type of an endowment policy is private pension insurance. The parties may agree on a fixed sum or on a periodical payment (annuity) on retirement. Pension payments in form of an annuity can be divided into life annuities and annuities certain. In the former case the annuity will be paid as long as the retiree lives (§ 1 paragraph 1 ABR), in the latter case as long as the retiree lives, maximally however, until an agreed point of time (§ 1 paragraph 2 ABR). In practice, in addition to the annuity a death benefit is often included in the policy which is of relevance in the event that the policyholder dies before he/she has reached the retirement age (e.g., 65 or 67 years). In the alternative, the parties agree that at least the premiums paid in by the policyholder must be paid out to eligible beneficiary survivors to avoid that the insurer acquires the policyholder's considerable capital saving without having to provide a benefit.[428]

C. Unit-Linked Life Insurance

714. In the variant of unit-linked life insurance, the only guaranteed sum is the one payable in the event of death. The sum payable on survival (the sum payable on maturity of the policy or, if the policy is terminated before the maturity date, the surrender value), depends on the performance of the investment funds in question and may consequently fluctuate. Hence, there is no guaranteed sum insured on survival. As with classical endowment insurance, parts of the premiums are used to pay the acquisition costs and for the life cover. The savings portions of the premiums do not earn interest at a particular rate but are used to buy units (or shares) in investment funds.[429]

D. Insurance of Joint Lives

715. In the case of a joint life policy, the death benefit is due on the death of the first insured person, at the latest at policy maturity (§ 1 paragraph 1 sentence 1 ALB). If both lives die at the same time, the sum is paid only once (§ 1 paragraph 1 sentence 2 ALB).[430]

428. *Ibid.*, n. 47 et seq.
429. *Ibid.*, n. 71 et seq.
430. *Ibid.*, Einf n. 38.

E. Dread Disease

716. In addition to death or maturity benefits the parties may agree on payment if the policyholder becomes critically ill (as defined in the policy, e.g., heart infarction, cancer, bypass operation, stroke, multiple sclerosis) before attaining the maturity date.[431]

II. Term Life Policies

A. Classical Form

717. Term life insurance is only due if the life insured dies during the term of the policy (§ 1 paragraph 1 ALR). As with all forms of term insurance, the premiums are paid until the death of the insured, at the latest to the policy expiry date. If the insured person does not die during the policy term, the premiums paid for carrying the risk will have been used up.[432]

718. Term insurance policies generally contain an option that the policyholder is granted the right within a certain period (generally 10 years) to convert the term insurance as a pure death benefit into an endowment policy with maximally the same sum insured (§ 10 ALR). The premium for the converted policy is then calculated, based on the age of the life insured at conversion and the remaining policy period. The advantage for the policyholder is that there is no new medical examination.[433]

B. Credit Life Insurance

719. Credit life insurance is a particular type of death benefit (see also payment protection insurance, *see* paragraph 561). The sum insured falls at regular intervals (e.g., annually) and thus matches the falling loan debt. The bank is irrevocable designated by the policyholder of the credit life policy as beneficiary if the policyholder dies, and uses the benefit to pay off the outstanding loan.[434]

III. Fixed Date Policies

720. In the case of a policy with a savings component with a predetermined payment date, insurance benefit is due on a fixed agreed date/event no matter whether

431. *Ibid.*, ns. 101, 102.
432. *Ibid.*, n. 43.
433. *Ibid.*, n. 44.
434. *Ibid.*, n. 46.

the policyholder is alive at that point in time. The obligation to pay the premium payment, however, ceases on the death of the life insured, at the latest on the fixed agreed date/event.[435]

A. Education Policy

721. This policy is designated to finance tertiary education of the policyholder's children. If the policyholder dies before the policy matures, further premiums are waived. Irrespective of this the insurer pays the full insurance benefit at the agreed time.[436]

B. Insurance for Marriage

722. Dowry insurance includes the marriage of the policyholder's child as an additional benefit to the basic form of fixed date insurance. The benefit is due on the child's marriage, at the latest, in general at the end of the policy year in which the child becomes 24 years old. If the child dies before the due date, the insurer reimburses the premiums paid up to the value of the sum insured including any bonuses: at the very least, however, the policy surrender value. The highest age of entry of the insured child insurance is usually 10 years.[437]

§3. The Contract of Life Insurance

I. Formation of the Contract

723. Prior to the conclusion of the contract the insurer must provide the prospective insured with the information in writing about the contents of the life insurance contract (§ 7 paragraph 2 VVG in conjunction with § 2 VVG-InfoV), particularly about costs included in the premium, the method of calculating bonuses and the distribution of bonuses, surrender values and surplus participation. Due to the nature particularly of the life endowment insurance contract as a long-term investment, § 151 paragraph 1 VVG extends the policyholder's right to revoke the contract to 30 days (instead of 14 days as provided for in § 8 paragraph 1 VVG for all other types of insurances).

724. Where the life insurance is taken out against the death of another person and the agreed benefit exceeds funeral costs, pursuant to § 150 paragraph 2 VVG the written agreement of the other person is required for the contract to become effective. However, no agreement is necessary in the case of group life insurances in company pension schemes.

435. *Ibid.*, n. 39.
436. *Ibid.*
437. *Ibid.*, n. 40.

II. Parties and Beneficiaries

725. According to § 150 paragraph 1 VVG life insurance may be taken out for the death of the policyholder or for the death of another person. In the vast majority of cases the policyholder takes out the life insurance for his/her own death. Obviously, in the case of the death there must be a natural or a legal person that is entitled to the sum insured. Pursuant to § 159 VVG the policyholder is entitled to designate the beneficiary without the consent of the insurer. The appointment of the beneficiary can be revocable or irrevocable; it can apply on death but also on survival. A revocable appointment can be revoked at any time by the policyholder. Only upon on his/her death it becomes an effective legal title. An irrevocable appointment can only be changed with the agreement of the designated beneficiary.[438]

726. The beneficiary may demand from the policyholder or his/her heirs the handover of the insurance certificate.[439] If the policyholder terminates the policy, the beneficiary is entitled to the surrender value in terms of § 169 paragraph 3 VVG.[440] Where no beneficiary is designated, the policyholder's spouse or life partner or children are entitled to the benefit if they are qualified as heirs at the time of death.

727. Beneficiaries enjoy special protection in the case that creditors of the policyholder seize their insurance claims or if insolvency proceedings are instituted in the policyholder's assets. Pursuant to § 170 VVG in this case the designated beneficiaries may, with the consent of the policyholder, substitute the policyholder in the insurance contract provided that they satisfy the claims up to the amount the policyholder could demand from the insurer upon termination of the insurance contract.[441]

III. Surplus Participation

728. Life insurance policies run on average for a term of more than 20 years. During such a long period the assumptions underlying the premium calculation, such as capital market interest rates, life expectancy and the mortality experience of the population or the insurance company's expenses may change. Since the life insurers are only entitled under exceptional circumstances set forth in § 163 VVG to increase the premium during the policy duration, they must calculate the premiums with regard to risk profits, interest profits and profits on expenses with safety margins. At least before the era of low interest rate has started, this strategy led too considerable surpluses the greatest part of which the insurers returned to their policyholders.

438. *Ibid.*, § 159 n. 164 et seq.

439. AG Mölln, 10 Jun. 1976 – C 458/75, VersR 1978, p. 131; *see also* OLG Hamm, 19 Nov. 1996 – 29 U 65/96, VersR 1997, p. 1386.

440. BGH, 18 Jun. 2003 – IV ZR 59/02, VersR 2003, p. 1021; BGH, 20 May 1992 – XII ZR 255/909, NJW 1992, pp. 2154, 2156; BGH, 17 Feb. 1966 – II ZR 286/63, NJW 1966, pp. 1071, 1073.

441. For details, *see* Winter, in: Bruck/Moeller, Großkommentar zum VVG, 9th ed., vol. 8/1, DeGruyter 2013, § 170 n. 43 et seq.

729. In its decision of 26 July 2005 the BVerfG criticised the then practice in the life insurance sector of withholding unrealised hidden reserves from surrendering policyholders when allocating their final bonus. The court held that the interests of remaining and surrendering policyholders should be weighed against one another. This means that the assets accumulated with the help of policyholder premiums must be adequately taken into account for the calculation of a policyholder's final bonus. [442] The BVerfG also disapproved the practice among life insurance companies of reducing surplus by offsetting several surplus components against each other. The surplus derives from three income components: cost, risk and investment. In principle, all of these components must be positive; if not, the question arises as to whether or not a negative component can be offset against a positive one. If the answer is yes, this lead to a reduction of any surplus participation and, as a result, the final bonus allocated to the policyholder.[443]

730. The BVerfG found that the calculation of the final bonus was not transparent enough. Neither BaFin nor the civil courts would be in a position to examine them.[444] The BVerfG had given the legislator until the end of 2007 at the latest to safeguard the protection of the policyholders' legitimate interests. In response the German legislator, in the course of the reform of the VVG 2008, obligated life insurers to pay out half of their valuation reserves to policyholders whose contracts expired or had been terminated. The insurers had to take into account not only valuation reserves on equities and real estate but also those on fixed-income securities. Due to extremely low interest rates, the value of fixed-income securities ballooned, and as a result, life insurers were forced to pay more and more money to the small group of leaving policyholders instead of keeping it for the remaining ones.

731. To safeguard stable and fair benefits for all policyholders and to ensure the ongoing viability of life insurers, the legislator has limited the share of the valuation reserves which policyholders receive upon expiry of their contract by the life insurance reform act, which became effective on 1 January 2015.[445] Life insurers must only pass on certain valuation reserves to withdrawing policyholders if the insurer does not have any security requirements under insurance contracts with an interest rate guarantee. Unaffected by these changes are unit-linked and term assurance policies.

IV. Premature Termination

732. As pointed out before, life insurance policies are taken out for several years. In many cases, the policyholder's personal circumstances change during the

442. BVerfG, 26 Jul. 2005 – BvR 80/95, RuS 2005, pp. 429, 431.
443. *Ibid.*, pp. 429, 432.
444. *Ibid.*
445. *Gesetz zur Absicherung stabiler und fairer Leistungen für Lebensversicherte (Lebensversicherungsreformgesetz)*, hereafter 'LVRG', BGBl. 2014 I p. 1330.

term of the policy, which may have financial consequences and forces the policyholder to terminate the life insurance contract. The premature termination is disadvantageous for both the policyholder and the insurer. The policyholder will receive only the surrender value of the policy, and the insurer has calculated its premiums and expenses on the expectation of full compliance with the terms of the contract.

733. According to § 168 VVG a life insurance contract can be terminated by the policyholder in text form (§ 126b BGB) at any time during the period of insurance for no reasons. After termination of the policy the insurer pays out the surrender value (*see* paragraph 7343) and the surplus participation (*see* paragraph 728). There is no corresponding right of the insurer to terminate the policy. The insurer is only entitled to extraordinary termination namely in the case of non-payment of the renewal premium (*see* paragraph 235), non-gross negligent breach of the pre-contractual disclosure duties (*see* paragraph 241), the gross negligent breach of contractual duties to be observed prior to the occurrence of the insured event (*see* paragraph 266) or the breach of the duty not to change circumstances identified by explicit agreement between the parties as of relevance for the contract (§ 158 VVG).

V. Surrender Value

734. Whenever a life insurance contract is terminated by the policyholder or rescinded or avoided by the insurer before its maturity or an insured event has occurred, the insurer must pay the surrender value pursuant to § 169 paragraph 1 VVG. The surrender value is defined under § 169 paragraph 3 VVG as:

> 'the insurance's premium reserve calculated with effect to the end of the current insurance period according to the accepted actuarial rules using the bases of premium calculation, in the case of the termination of the insurance agreement the amount of the premium reserve resulting from a symmetrical allocation of the calculated acquisition and distribution costs for the first five insurance years'.

For example, where the policyholder pays an annual premium of EUR 1,000 and acquisition and distribution costs amount to EUR 2,500 the surrender value amounts to EUR 1,000 if the policyholder terminates the life insurance policy after two years (EUR 2,000 – EUR 2,500÷5 first insurance years x 2 years).

735. It is to be noted that according to § 165 paragraph 1 VVG the policyholder may, at any time from the end of the current period of insurance, demand that the insurance be converted into a paid-up insurance, insofar as the agreed minimum insurance cover is achieved. In that case the insurer uses the sum paid as a single premium for the life insurance and reduces the insured sum accordingly.

VI. Exclusions

A. *Suicide*

736. Pursuant to § 161 paragraph 1 VVG the insurer is not obligated to effect payment if the policyholder intentionally commits suicide before three years have elapsed since the conclusion of the contract of insurance.[446] The three years period does not apply if the act was committed while the policyholder was in a state of pathological disturbance of mind precluding his/her ability to freely determine his/her intent. Where the insurer is not obligated to effect payment, it must pay the surrender value plus surplus sharing (§ 161 paragraph 3 VVG).

B. *Killing by the Beneficiary*

737. Where the insurance has been taken out against the death of a person other than the policyholder, the insurer is not obligated to effect payment if the policyholder intentionally causes the death of the other person by an unlawful act (§ 162 paragraph 1 VVG). If a third party has been appointed as beneficiary, the appointment shall be deemed not to have occurred if the third party intentionally causes the death of the policyholder by an unlawful act (§ 162 paragraph 2 VVG).[447]

446. For the standard of proof, *see* OLG Hamm, 27 Sept. 2017 – 20 U 27/16, VersR 2018, p. 341.
447. Cf. OLG Saarbrücken, 28 Oct. 2016 5 U 31/16, zfs 2017, p. 343 (concerning the question of whether limited responsibility due to the lack of cognitive faculty of the beneficiary precludes intent).

Chapter 5. Pension Funds

738. As is the case in many other European countries, the German pension system consists of three pillars: state pension, supplementary occupational pension and private individual pension products.

§1. State Pension System

739. The first pillar is the mandatory public retirement insurance (*Gesetzliche Rentenversicherung*, hereafter 'GRV'), which is subject to the sixth book of the social law code (SGB VI). The GRV is part of the German system of social security that operates on a pay-as-you-earn mode. Participation in the state pension system is compulsory for all employees who earn not more than EUR 78,000 per year (western Germany) or EUR 69,600 per year (eastern Germany), respectively. Up to this income ceiling (*Beitragsbemessungsgrenze*) they contribute an ongoing percentage of earned salary. As of January 2018, the percentage amounts to 18.6. The amount to be paid is calculated on the employee's annual salary, which is automatically deducted by the employer and paid to the state, along with the same amount paid in addition by the employer to make a 50:50 contribution from both parties.[448]

§2. Private Occupational Pensions

740. The second pillar consists of occupational pension schemes, known as *betriebliche Altersvorsorge*, which is subject to the act to improve occupational pension schemes (*Gesetz zur Verbesserung der betrieblichen Altersversorgung*, hereafter 'BetrAVG'). The act, otherwise known as the occupational pensions act (*Betriebsrentengesetz*), was passed in 1974 with the aim of regulating occupational pension provision. The BetrAVG contains provisions for all types of pension scheme, such as direct pension promise, direct insurance, staff pension insurance, pension fund, benefit fund or pure defined-contribution schemes.[449] According to the 2017 statistics of the German Association for Occupational Pensions (*Arbeitsgemeinschaft fuer betriebliche Altersversorgung e.V.*) 18 million employees were active members of an occupational pension scheme, i.e., almost 60% of those employed and subject to social insurance contributions. Coverage is low, however, in small and medium-sized enterprises (SMEs) with less than 10 employees where only 28% are active members of an occupational pension scheme. About half of

448. For an overview of the state pension systems, *see* Ring, Grundzüge des Systems der gesetzlichen Rentenversicherung in Deutschland, JA 2018, pp. 87–95; for an overwiew of the taxation of company pensions and private pensions, *see* Bundesministerium der Finanzen (2017), Besteuerung von Alterseinkünften pp. 27–30, http://www.bundesfinanzministerium.de/Content/DE/Downloads/Broschueren_Bestellservice/2017-08-24-Besteuerung_von_Alterseinkuenften.pdf?__blob=publicationFile&v=15 (accessed 28 Mar. 2018).

449. For an overview of the company pension schemes, *see* Seel, Betriebliche Altersvorsorge – Eine Übersicht über die wesentlichen Rechtsgrundlagen, JA 2012, pp. 207–213.

those earning less than EUR 1,500 per month neither has an active occupational pension membership nor a private pension (*see* paragraph 750).[450]

I. Direct Pension Promise

741. Direct pension promises (*Direktzusagen*) by the employer are usually funded via book-reserve accruals. The employer promises the employee to pay an agreed amount upon retirement. The pension scheme contributions to book reserves reduce the employer's taxable income. While contributions and interest are not considered taxable income to the employee, benefits are taxed as deferred income when received (EET-system). In recent years, larger German companies set up contractual trust agreements (CTAs) to protect pension claims in the event of an employer's insolvency.[451]

II. Direct Insurance

742. Under a direct insurance (*Direktversicherung*) scheme, the employer takes out an individual or group life insurance policy in favour of its employees and pays contributions to the contract. The employee is the beneficiary in terms of § 159 VVG (*see* paragraph 725) and has a direct entitlement to the benefits accrued under the contract against the insurer. Contributions of up to 4% of income ceiling (*see* paragraph 738), i.e., EUR 3,120 (Western Germany) and EUR 2,784 (Eastern Germany) plus a fixed contribution limit of EUR 1,800 are exempt from taxes (§ 3 no. 63 EStG) and from social security contributions (§ 1 Nr. 9 ordinance on social security compensation (*Sozialversicherungsentgeltverordnung*, hereafter 'SvEV')).

III. Staff Pension Insurance

743. According to § 232 VAG the staff pension insurance (*Pensionskasse*) is a legally independent life insurance undertaking, the purpose of which is to provide cover for a loss of income due to old-age, invalidity or death and:

- which provides a funded insurance scheme,
- does not, as a general rule, provide benefits until the actual loss of income takes place
- in the event of death, may only provide benefits to surviving dependents, though a death grant, which may not exceed standard funeral costs, may be included for third parties who have to bear the costs of a funeral,

450. *See* http://www.aba-online.de/en/docs/attachments/01030ada-bdd5-460a-839f-992afe7c0749/20170330-BRSG.pdf (accessed 28 Mar. 2018).

451. For further details, *see* Granetzy/Wallraven, Ausgewählte Rechtsfragen der betrieblichen Altersversorgung im Konzern, NZA 2017, pp. 1231–1237.

- affords the insured an independent claim to benefits from the *Pensionskasse* or provides benefits in the form of a pension liability insurance.

744. The *Pensionskasse* may be operated by one or more enterprises. These pay contributions to the staff pension insurance, which funds the pension benefits later paid to the employees. Staff pension insurance schemes guarantee legal entitlement to their benefits and are monitored by the BaFin. The *Pensionskasse* must observe the 'prudent person' principle in accordance with § 234 paragraph 2 in conjunction with § 124 VAG, i.e., all assets must be invested in such a way as to ensure the security, quality, liquidity and profitability of the portfolio as a whole.

745. Staff pension insurance schemes are basically exempt from corporation tax (§ 5 paragraph 1 no. 3 KStG) and trade tax (§ 3 no. 9 GewStG). Contributions by the employer to the scheme are basically considered to be part of the employee's compensation package and therefore subject to wage tax (*see* § 40b EStG).

IV. Pension Funds

746. Pension funds (*Pensionsfonds*) are defined under § 236 VAG as a scheme with legal personality which:

- offers funded occupational retirement provision for one or more employers for the benefit of employees,
- is not permitted to guarantee the level of benefits or the level of future contribution required to provide a given level of benefits in respect of all benefit cases provided for as opposed to insurance contracts,
- affords employees an independent claim to payment of benefits from the pension fund, and is obliged to provide the retirement benefits as a life annuity.

747. Like staff pension insurance and direct insurance, pension funds guarantee legal entitlement and are subject to approval by the BaFin (§ 236 paragraph 4 VAG). Pension funds must be formed either as a joint-stock company or a mutual pension fund association (§ 237 paragraph 1 VAG). According to § 238 VAG pension funds are obliged to maintain own funds free of all foreseeable liabilities in an amount not less than the solvency margin, which is determined in relation to the total volume of business. They also must observe the 'prudent person' principle in accordance with § 237 paragraph 2 in conjunction with § 124 paragraph 1 VAG

V. Support Funds

748. Support funds (*Unterstuetzungskassen*) are separate legal entities mainly set up as a registered association (*eingetragener Verein*) or as limited liability company ('GmbH'), occasionally as foundation (*Stiftung*).[452] Employees have no legal entitlement to benefits from the support fund (§ 1b Abs. 4 BetrAVG). However, they may generally claim against the enterprise. Should the company become insolvent, the promised benefits are safeguarded by the Pension Guarantee Fund (PSV) (§ 14 BetrAVG). Support funds are not subject to supervision and are not required to comply with any investment criteria. As social welfare institutions, support funds are exempt from corporation tax (§ 5 paragraph 1 no. 3 KStG) and trade tax (§ 3 no. 9 GewStG).

VI. Pure Defined-contribution Schemes

749. Under the afore-listed benefit schemes, the employer is liable to pay a defined benefit amount to the employee. One advantage of defined-benefit amount is planning certainty. However, the pensions are usually relatively small to begin with, since employers, life insurers, *Pensionskassen*, *Pensionsfonds* or *Unterstuetzungskassen* have to make reliable calculations. In addition, significant restrictions apply to the investment of the capital, with only limited investments in real assets possible. In an attempt to eliminate the (perceived) disadvantages and to facilitate occupational pension schemes in SMEs the legislator, with effect as per 1 January 2018, has added the pure defined-contribution scheme to the list of possible scheme types. The act to strengthen occupational pensions[453] includes numerous changes not only to the BetrAVG but also to labour, social and tax law, which cannot be addressed here in detail.[454]

750. In the case of the defined-contribution scheme, the employer is liable only to pay the contributions to the sponsoring body but is not liable to pay a defined benefit amount. A condition for availing of the pure defined-contribution scheme is a corresponding collective agreement. The parties to the collective agreement must agree to occupational retirement provision in the form of the pure defined-contribution scheme and they must participate in its implementation and management.

---

452. C.f. Otto, in: Blomeyer/Rolfs/Otto, Gesetz zur Verbesserung der betriebl. Altersversorgung, 6th ed., C. H. Beck 2015, Kapital A n. 190.
453. Act to strengthen occupational pensions ('Gesetz zur Stärkung der betrieblichen Altersversorgung und zur Stärkung anderer Gesetze'), BGBl. 2017 I p. 3124.
454. For further details, *see* Wenning, Occupational pensions – Act on the pure defined-contribution scheme passed, https://www.bafin.de/SharedDocs/Veroeffentlichungen/EN/Fachartikel/2017/fa_bj_1707_Betriebsrenten_en.html (accessed 28 Mar. 2018).

§3. PRIVATE PENSION SCHEMES

751. The third pillar of the German pension system is made up of the private pension sector, which incorporate a varying range of individual pension investment plans. These can be set up through banks and insurance providers (*see* § 1 paragraph 2 pension provision agreements certification act (*Altersvorsorgevertraege-Zertifizierungsgesetz*, hereafter 'AltZertG')) to increase the pension entitlement when the employee reaches pension age. The main private German pension plans include, but are not limited to, the *Riester Rente* and the *Ruerup Rente*. These two plans differ with regard to the way of support the individual receives from the state. Moreover, while only individuals included in the state pension system as well as civil servants, judges, soldiers, their spouses and disability pensioners are eligible to the *Riester Rente*, anybody can conclude *Ruerup Rente* contracts.

I. *Riester Rente*

752. The so-called *Riester Rente* plan was introduced in 2002 by the AltZertG, named after the former Minster of Labour and Social Affairs, Walter Riester. The Riester pension was a response to the demographic decline in the working-aga population that is threatening to undermine the pay-as-you-go state pension insurance system and ultimately leads to lower pensions for future retirees. The Riester pension scheme is supposed to compensate lower pensions.[455]

753. Under the AltZertG employees receive state subsidies up to a maximum of EUR 2,100 if they invest at least 4% of their previous year's income in a Riester plan certified by the BaFin. The BaFin will certify the plan only if the following conditions are met: The provider must be life insurers, banks, building societies or investment management companies. The savings scheme must provide at least an amount equivalent to the amounts paid in. Benefits cannot be paid out before the age of 62 (§ 1 paragraph 1 no. 2 AltZertG).

754. Benefits are paid out in the form of a life annuity, or in the form of a one-off payment of up to 30% of the annuity and partial annuity immediately thereafter (§ 1 paragraph 1 no. 4 lit. a) AltZertG). Furthermore, the capital subject to tax relief and already saved may be withdrawn during the saving period for the purchase or construction of an owner-occupied residential property located in Germany or for the acquisition of mandatory shares in a cooperative society for the own use of cooperative society apartments located in Germany (§ 1 paragraph 1 no. 4 lit. b) AltZertG).[456] Riester products are treated according to the EET-system. State grant aided capital tied up in residential property is taxed as a pension benefit.

---

455. Baroch Castellví, AltZertG, 1st ed., C. H. Beck 2012, Einleitung n. 1.
456. For further information, *see* Baroch Castellví, AltZertG, 1st ed., C. H. Beck 2012, § 1 ns. 17 et seq.

II. *Ruerup Rente*

755. The *Ruerup Rente*, named after the economist Bert Ruerup, requires a contract that provides for the payment of a life-long pension. Anyone can conclude a Ruerup contract, although it is intended primarily for self-employed persons. During the saving period, the contributions are tax deductible pursuant to § 2 paragraph 1 AltZertG in conjunction with § 10 Abs. 1 Nr. 2b EStG under the following conditions: The contract of insurance or fund savings plan must have been certified by the Federal Central Tax Office (*Bundeszentralamt fuer Steuern*). The benefits are paid out as an annuity at the earliest upon reaching the age of 62. One-off payments and early withdrawals are not allowed.

756. Benefits are liable to tax. The tax deductibility of the annual contribution is limited to (as of 2018) to EUR 23,712 for individuals and EUR 47,424 for couples. Currently 86% of this contribution assessment ceiling can be (it is scheduled to rise in 2% steps until 2025) transferred as special expenses. When the person retires, a certain percentage of the pension entitlement is taxable. In 2018 this is 76%, but is scheduled to rise to in 2% steps until 2040 (§ 24a EStG).

Part VI. Private Insurance: Social Security System

757. The German system of social security is based on five pillars: health insurance (*see* paragraph 679), long-term care insurance (*see* paragraph 683), pension insurance (*see* paragraph 739), unemployment insurance (§§ 24 et seq. SGB III) and accident insurance (*see* paragraphs 643, 653). Employees are generally 'automatically' insured in all five branches of social security upon starting a job. They cannot opt out of this system by making an arrangement or signing an agreement with the employer. In general, employees – with few exceptions – do not have to take care of insurance cover themselves. Health insurance is one of the exceptions. Employees need to decide from which of the more than 100 statutory health insurers/long-term care insurers they want cover.

758. The employer calculates the social security contributions, deducts the employees' contributions from their salary and pays the collected contributions to the competent social security institutions (e.g., German Pension Insurance (*Deutsche Rentenversicherung*), Federal Labour Agency (*Bundesagentur für Arbeit*)). The employer also registers employees with their chosen health insurer at the start of employment. Employers and employees each pay half of the amount of the health insurance contribution, long-term care insurance contribution, pension insurance and unemployment insurance. Contributions to the accident insurance are made by employers to the employer's institutions for statutory accident insurance and prevention (*Berufsgenossenschaften*).[457]

457. For details, *see* 'Die Techniker', German social security, https://www.tk.de/tk/social-security-in-germany/german-social-insurance/576890 (accessed 28 Mar. 2018).

Part VII. Insurance Intermediaries

Chapter 1. Law of Establishment and Supervision

§1. General Remarks

I. Insurance Intermediaries

759. Insurance intermediaries are subject to the GewO, VVG, HGB and BGB. While the GewO deals with the authorisation and supervision of insurance intermediaries, the VVG lays down their obligations towards the policyholder. Both the GewO and the VVG follow the same concept in that the term intermediary comprises insurance agents and insurance brokers (§ 34d paragraph 1 sentence 1 GewO, § 59 paragraph 1 sentence 1 VVG). §§ 84 to 92c HGB contain rules on commercial agents relevant for the relationship between agents and insurers, and §§ 93–103 HGB in conjunction with §§ 652 et seq. BGB deal with the relationship between commercial brokers and policyholders on the one hand and with the relationship between brokers and insurers on the other one.

II. Insurance Advisers

760. In addition to insurance agents and insurance brokers the GewO and the VVG establish rules for insurance advisers which are defined as anyone advising third parties on a commercial basis in respect of negotiating, amending or reviewing of insurance contracts, the making of claims and who represents the policyholder out-of-court vis-à-vis the insurer without receiving any remuneration from an insurer or being dependent on an insurer in any other way (§ 34d paragraph 2 GewO, § 59 paragraph 4 VVG).

§2. Law of Establishment

I. Authorisation of Intermediaries and Advisers

761. Like all commercial businesses insurance agents, brokers and advisers must notify the local trade authority (*Gewerbeamt*) of the commencement of its business pursuant to § 14 GewO. Before starting mediation activities they need, in addition, authorisation by the local IHK (§ 34d paragraph 1 and 2 GewO). Along with the completed application form, which can be downloaded from the local IHK's homepage, applicants have to prove:

- personal reliability by submitting the certificate of good conduct (*Fuehrungszeugnis*, § 30 paragraph 5 of the federal register of criminal and court records (*Gesetz über das Bundeszentralregister*, hereafter 'BZRG')) and an excerpt from the commercial central register (*Auszug aus dem Gewerbezentralregister*, § 150 paragraph 5 GewO); if the applicant's place of residence is abroad, he/she must submit documents from his/her country, which prove that he/she has the personal reliability to provide the requested service;
- that they are solvent by submitting an excerpt from the list of debtors (*Auszug aus dem Schuldnerverzeichnis*, § 882b ZPO) and an attestation from the bankruptcy court (*Bescheinigung des Insolvenzgerichts*) and a certificate from the tax authorities (*Unbedenklichkeitsbescheinigung*);
- professional qualifications by means of a successfully completed examination before the local IHK;
- that their activities are covered by professional liability insurance (*Vermoegensschadenhaftpflichtversicherung*).

Further details can be found in the ordinance on insurance mediation (*Versicherungsvermittlerverordnung*, hereafter 'VersVermV'). [458]

762. If the applicant is not a natural person but a legal entity such as a GmbH or AG, the application form has to be completed by the legal entity itself. All documents have to be submitted for all natural persons authorised to manage the company (e.g., certificate of good conduct, personal documents).[459] In addition, an excerpt from the local trade register has to be applied for in the case of legal entities. Where the applicant is a partnership, which as such is not capable of holding a licence (e.g., civil unlimited partnership,[460] registered unlimited commercial partnership,[461] limited commercial partnership,[462] registered professional partnership[463]), each of the managing partners requires the licence.[464]

763. The authorization is to be refused if:

- there are grounds to indicate that the applicant is not reliable to conduct business (§ 34d paragraph 5 sentence 1 no. 1 GewO); as a rule, the applicant is deemed to

458. BGBl. 2007 I p. 2007 in the version as amended on 29 Mar. 2017 (BGBl. 2017 I p. 626).
459. Schoenleiter, in: Landmann/Rohmer, Gewerbeordnung, C.H. Beck 77th supplement October 2017, § 34d n. 12.
460. *Gesellschaft bürgerlichen Rechts*, hereafter 'GbR', § 705 BGB.
461. *Offene Handelsgesellschaft*, hereafter 'oHG', § 105 HGB.
462. *Kommanditgesellschaft*, hereafter 'KG', § 161 HGB.
463. *Partnerschaftsgesellschaft*, hereafter 'PartG', § 1 PartGG.
464. Cf. VG Bremen, 2 Nov. 2011 – 5 K 3670/07, BeckRS 2011, 55620; Marcks, in: Landmann/Rohmer, Gewerbeordnung, C.H. Beck 77th supplement October 2017, § 14 n. 55.

lack reliability if he/she has been convicted in the last five years before application of a crime or of theft, embezzlement, extortion, fraud, breach of trust, money-laundering, falsification of a document, receiving stolen goods, profiteering or criminal insolvency (§ 34d paragraph 5 sentence 2 GewO);
- the applicant is in a precarious financial situation (§ 34d paragraph 5 sentence 1 no. 2 GewO); as a rule, this is the case where the assets of the applicant are subject to bankruptcy proceedings or he is registered at the debtor's list in terms of § 882b ZPO (*Schuldnerverzeichnis*) (§ 34d paragraph 5 sentence 3 GewO);
- the applicant fails to furnish proof of professional liability insurance cover (§ 34d paragraph 5 sentence 1 no. 3 GewO); the minimum amount covered is at present EUR 1,230,000 for each insurance claim and EUR 1,850,000 for all insurance claims totally in one year; or
- the applicant fails by means of the successful completion of an examination by the local IHK to provide evidence that he/she possesses the basic proficiency in insurance, particularly as regards needs and demands, types of product, scope of benefits and relevant legal provisions as well as customer advice, needed for insurance mediation (§ 34d paragraph 5 sentence 1 no. 4 GewO).

Where licence is sought by a legal entity, adequate evidence of the first three requirements can be furnished by a sufficient number of natural persons employed by the applicant who are entrusted with supervising persons directly engaged in the mediation of insurance and who may represent the applicant (§ 34d paragraph 5 sentence 4 GewO), e.g., persons who hold a commercial power of attorney (*Prokura*).

764. Not subject to authorisation are intermediaries who:

- perform their activities solely on behalf of one, or where insurance products are not in competition several insurers, and full liability is assumed for their activities by the insurer(s) ('tied'/'multitied' insurance intermediaries) (§ 34d paragraph 7 no. 1 GewO);
- mediate insurance part-time, the insurance is complementary to the supply of a good or service and either covers the risk of a defect (e.g., extension to a term of warranty when purchasing technical equipment), loss or damage of goods or damage or loss of luggage or other risks in connection with a journey booked with the intermediary and the premium for the period insured projected for the year does not exceed EUR 600 (§ 34d paragraph 8 no. 1 GewO);
- mediate in their capacity as a building society or as intermediaries engaged by a building society for building-society depositors insurance as a component of the building-society savings contracts under a collective agreement that is intended solely for securing repayment of amounts owed to a building society from loans granted (§ 34d paragraph 8 no. 2 GewO);
- mediate, as a complementary service to supplying a good or service in connection with loan and leasing agreements payment protection insurance whose annual premium does not exceed EUR 500 (§ 34d paragraph 8 no. 3 GewO).

765. On application, pursuant to § 34d paragraph 6 GewO the competent IHK may exempt an intermediary who mediates insurance as a supplement to the products or services provided as part of his/her principal activity from the obligation to obtain authorization, if he/she provides evidence that:

- s/he performs his/her activity as an insurance intermediary on direct behalf of one or several insurance intermediaries who have received authorization or of one or several insurance undertakings;
- s/he is covered by a professional liability insurance; and
- s/he is reliable and adequately qualified and is not in a precarious financial situation.

766. Insurance agents, brokers and advisers registered in a Member State of the EU or another signatory state to the EEA do not need authorisation for their activities in Germany (§ 34d paragraph 7 no. 2 GewO). They have to notify their home registration authority of their intention to do business in Germany which will notify the DIHK.[465]

II. Registration of Intermediaries and Advisers

767. Insurance agents, brokers and advisers, as pointed out before (*see* paragraph 761), are obliged to register with the local IHK immediately after taking up their activity. In the case of tied agents, the insurer is responsible for registering the tied agent with the tied agent's local IHK. When an intermediary has been registered with the local IHK, it will also be entered into the national register of intermediaries (*Vermittlerregister*), which is administered by DIHK. There is no obligation to register, however, for insurance agents, brokers and consultants registered in a Member State of the EU or another signatory state to the EEA and for intermediaries which are exempt from the authorization requirement (§ 34d paragraph 10 GewO).

768. According to the statistics of the DIHK, there were 173,584 insurance agents, 46,924 insurance brokers and only 317 insurance advisers registered in Germany as of 2 January 2018.[466]

465. Schoenleiter, in: Landmann/Rohmer, Gewerbeordnung, C.H. Beck 77th supplement October 2017, § 34d n. 135.
466. *See* homepage of the DIHK, https://www.dihk.de/themenfelder/recht-steuern/oeffentliches-wirtschaftsrecht/versicherungsvermittlung-anlageberatung/zahlen-und-fakten/eingetragene-vermittler – only available in German.

§3. SUPERVISION OF INTERMEDIARIES AND ADVISERS

I. Chambers of Commerce and Industry

769. The local IHKs, where the intermediary is registered, are responsible for supervising insurance agents, brokers and advisers and can revoke their authorization (§ 35 GewO). In this regard it is important to note that § 51 VAG requires insurers to respond to complaints about insurance intermediaries who mediate their insurance products. The insurers must inform the competent local IHK of repeated complaints that can be of significant importance for assessing the reliability of an intermediary. The IHK then may initiate administrative offence proceedings against intermediaries, e.g., for breaches of the VersVermV. Under § 144 GewO for the mediation of insurance or reinsurance policies without authorization, fines of up to EUR 5,000 may be imposed.

II. Federal Financial Supervisory Authority

770. The BaFin does not supervise insurance agents and brokers. § 48 paragraph 1 VAG, however, requires insurers to only cooperate with insurance agents and brokers who have been authorized by the IHK. In the case the intermediaries do not need authorisation (*see* paragraphs 764, 766) or are exempt from authorisation (*see* paragraph 765), the insurers are only allowed to cooperate with them pursuant to § 48 paragraph 2 VAG if they are reliable, solvent and sufficiently qualified to mediate the insurance product in question. Details of what insurers have to observe when cooperating with intermediaries are set out in BaFin Circular 10/2014 (VA) – Cooperation with Insurance Intermediaries, Risk Management in Distribution.[467]

771. If insurers fail to comply with these obligations they commit an administrative offence (§ 332 paragraph 3 no. 3 VAG) and are subject to fines up to EUR 50,000 (§ 332 paragraph 5 VAG). It follows from these provisions that the BaFin is allowed to monitor insurers' distribution activities, which includes, e.g., supervision of the contractual agreements between insurance intermediaries and insurers and questions related to commissions.[468]

772. § 48b paragraph 1 VAG constitutes a ban on special remuneration and the sharing of commissions between the insurance agent and the policyholder, i.e., a ban on direct or indirect benefits in addition to the payment agreed on in the insurance contract. Only benefits which are deemed to be of little value are permitted according to § 48b paragraph 2 VAG, specifically those of EUR 15 or less per insurance

467. Available in English at https://www.bafin.de/SharedDocs/Veroeffentlichungen/EN/Rundschreiben/rs_1410_versicherungsvermittler_va_en.html?nn=8249098.
468. *See* https://www.bafin.de/EN/Aufsicht/VersichererPensionsfonds/Aufsichtsregime/Vermittlerwesen/vermittlerwesen_node_en.html.

contract and calendar year. It will also be possible to use intermediary commissions, e.g., for continuously improving performance or reducing the premiums of mediated contracts (§ 48b paragraph 3 VAG).

773. It is to be noted that policyholders can direct their complaints regarding insurance intermediaries to BaFin. The complaint process is free of charge to private costumers. BaFin assesses the matter and decides whether additional authorities (e.g., IHK, local trade authority, foreign supervisory authorities) need to be involved or the complaint needs to be passed on to one or more authorities in whole or in part. If BaFin takes action and pursues the complaint, it may contact the insurer and request a statement or communicate with the local IHK. The IHK and perhaps the local trade authority then decide what measures are to be implemented, including whether it is necessary to initiate trade prohibition proceedings.[469]

774. The situation is different with 'tied' intermediaries, whose reliability BaFin can assess on its own initiative. If the intermediary is considered unreliable, BaFin can order the insurer to terminate any collaboration with the intermediary and to delete the registration in the register of insurance intermediaries and consultants.[470]

469. *Ibid.*
470. *Ibid.*

Chapter 2. Insurance Intermediaries (Including Insurance Advisers) and the Insurance Contract

§1. Insurance Agent

775. An insurance agent is an intermediary who is contracted by an insurer or insurance agent to arrange or conclude contracts of insurance on a commercial basis (§ 34d paragraph 1 sentence 2 no. 1 GewO, § 59 paragraph 2 VVG). An insurance agent may act on behalf of one or more insurers, may be employed by the insurer and paid a regular salary, or self-employed and paid by the insurers on commission.

I. Obligations

776. The advisory and documentation obligations of the insurance agent towards the policyholder set forth in § 61 VVG are in general identical with the obligations of the insurer towards the policyholder under §§ 1a, 6 paragraph 1 to 3, 6a, 7a, 7b and 7c VVG (*see* paragraph 288). Unlike the insurer (*see* paragraph 294), however, the insurance agent is not obliged to provide advice during the term of the insurance agreement. If the insurance agent fails to provide adequate advise, both the insurer (§ 6 paragraph 5 VVG) as well as the agent (§ 63 VVG) are jointly liable for damages towards the policyholder.[471] Since the insurer uses the agent to fulfil its advisory and documentation obligations, the insurer is responsible for the agent's fault as for fault on its own part (§ 278 BGB).[472] Unless there is a separate agreement, e.g., on the commission between the policyholder and the insurance agent (*see* next paragraph), there is only a (pre-) contractual relationship between the policyholder and the insurer.

II. Remuneration

777. Unless it is a 'Netto-Police' the insurance agent receives a commission (*Provision*) for his mediation services from the insurer. 'Nettopolicen' are insurance policies with respect to which the premiums do not include commission for the mediation of the insurance contract. In this case insurance agents receive their remuneration on a fee-based compensation from the policyholder.[473] However, insurance agents must expressly inform policyholders on the effects of such separate agreement, e.g., that the policyholders remain obliged to pay the commission even if they

471. Cf. OLG München, 22 Jun. 2012 – 25 U 3343/11, VersR 2012, pp. 1292, 1295.
472. *Ibid.*
473. Cf. OLG Hamm, 23 Aug. 2017 – 20 U 38/17, VersR 2018, p. 222.

have terminated the insurance contract shortly after its conclusion.[474] If the insurance agents failed to inform the policyholders there is a presumption that the policyholders would have not concluded a 'Netto-Police'. The policyholder is thus entitled to refuse payment or to demand repayment of the compensation.[475]

778. According to §§ 92 paragraph 2, 89b paragraph 1 HGB, the insurance agent is entitled to demand an indemnity from the insurer after termination of the agency contract that amounts up to not more than three years' worth of commissions (or annual remunerations). There is no such claim if *inter alia* the insurance agent has terminated the agency contract, unless the conduct of the insurer gave justified grounds for doing so, or the insurance agent cannot reasonably be expected to continue his activities on account of his age or of illness (§ 89b paragraph 3 no. 1 HGB). Moreover, there is no claim for indemnity if the insurer has terminated the agency contract and there was a compelling reason for such termination owing to culpable conduct on part of the insurance agent (§ 89b paragraph 3 no. 2 HGB).

III. Power of Attorney

779. Insurance agents are authorized to act on behalf of the insurer. The scope of their authority is primarily determined by the agency agreement. However, the (minimum) scope of the insurance agent's power of attorney, which pursuant to § 72 VVG cannot be restricted vis-à-vis the policyholder, is defined in the VVG. According to § 69 paragraph 1 no. 1 to 3 and paragraph 2 VVG the insurance agent is authorized to:

- take receipt of applications for the purposes of concluding a contract of insurance and its revocation, as well as declarations made prior to the making of a contract and other declarations made by the policyholder;
- take receipt of applications for the renewal of or amendment to a contract of insurance and its revocation, termination, rescission and other declarations relating to the insurance agreement, as well as any information to be provided by the policyholder throughout the policy period;
- passing on to the policyholder any insurance policies or renewal policies drawn up by the insurer; and
- to accept payments which the policyholder makes in connection with the arranging or conclusion of a contract of insurance.

If the insurance agent is authorised to conclude contracts of insurance, the agent is pursuant to § 71 VVG also authorised to agree amendments or extensions to existing contracts and to make declarations of termination and withdrawal on behalf of the insurer.

474. *See* BGH, 5 Jun. 2014 –IIIZR557/13, VersR 2014, p. 877, para. 24; BGH, 12 Dec. 2013 –IIIZR124/13,VersR 2014, p. 240, para. 27.
475. *See* OLG Hamm, 23 Aug. 2017 – 20 U 38/17, VersR 2018, pp. 222, 224.

780. § 69 to 72 VVG apply *mutatis mutandis* to an insurer's employees who are acting as insurance agent.

IV. Attribution of Knowledge and Responsibility

781. Prior to the reform of the VVG 1908 the courts found that insurance agents are the insurer's eyes and ears (*Auge und Ohr*).[476] § 70 sentence 1 VVG has codified the jurisprudence and states that, whenever the knowledge of the insurer is of relevance in accordance with the VVG (e.g., regarding disclosure of material risks), the knowledge of the insurance agent shall be equivalent to the knowledge of the insurer. This rule does not apply to the knowledge of the insurance agent gained when not engaged in his activity as agent and not connected in any manner to the contract of insurance in question (§ 70 sentence 2 VVG).[477]

§2. Insurance Broker

782. As Insurance broker qualifies an intermediary who is mandated to arrange or conclude contracts of insurance for a client on a commercial basis without having being contracted to do so by an insurer or an insurance agent (§ 34d paragraph 1 sentence 2 no. 2 GewO, § 59 paragraph 3 VVG). In addition, the broker may, by mutual agreement, advise third parties who are not consumers with regard to the agreement, change or review of insurance contracts in return for a fee (§ 34d paragraph 1 sentence 4 GewO).

I. Obligations

783. Insurance brokers typically arrange insurance cover with insurers. They assist clients in the choice of their insurance by presenting them with alternatives in terms of insurers and products.[478] As the insurance agent (and the insurer), the insurance broker owes documentation towards the policyholder. According to the BGH the insurance broker, like other professional advisers, has a fiduciary duty to the policyholder[479] and must provide best advice.[480]

784. The scope of the broker's obligation to advice must be distinguished from the corresponding obligations of the insurance agents (and insurers) to act in the best interest of the policyholder.[481] Insurance brokers are pursuant to § 60 VVG

476. C.f. BGH, 14 Jul. 1993 – IV ZR 153/92, NJW 1993, pp. 2807, 2808.
477. For details, *see* Doerner, in: Proelss/Martin, VVG, 30th ed., C.H. Beck 2018, § 70 n. 6 et seq.
478. Cf. OLG Köln, 26 Feb. 2016 – 20 U 102/15, NJOZ 2016, pp. 908, 909.
479. Cf. BGH, 22 May 1985 – IVa ZR 190/83, NJW 1985, p. 2595 ('treuhaendleraehnlicher Sachwalter').
480. Cf. BGH, 22 May 1985 – IVa ZR 190/83, NJW 1985, p. 2595; OLG Hamm, 30 Apr. 2012 – 18 U 141/06, NJW-RR 2013, pp. 38. 39.
481. *See* OLG Saarbruecken, 26 Apr. 2017 – 5 U 36/16, RuS 2018, pp. 110, 111.

obliged to base their advice on an adequate number of insurance contracts and of insurers available on the market, so that they can make a recommendation on which insurance contract is meet the needs of the insurance customer at best. This rule does not apply if the insurance broker makes express reference to a restricted range of insurers and contracts.[482]

785. In contrast to the relationship between the policyholder and the insurance agent, there is a contract between the policyholder and the insurance broker which is usually concluded for an indefinite period and can be terminated by the policyholder at any time without notice.[483] The broker obliges her-/himself not only to provide advice prior to the conclusion of the insurance contract but also to adjust the insurance coverage in accordance with the needs of the policyholder with regard to the risks to be insured during the insurance period. In practice, insurance brokers make sure that claims are fairly handled and, if necessary, provide out-of-court support to their clients in making a claim against the insurer.[484]

786. It is to be noted that according to § 34d paragraph 1 sentence 8 GewO insurance brokers are entitled to provide legal advice to third parties, who are not private costumers, in agreeing to, amending or appraising insurance contracts in exchange for separate remuneration. Insurance agents that give the policyholder the impression that they are brokers (so-called Pseudomakler) are treated like insurance brokers.[485]

II. Remuneration

787. Unless otherwise agreed the broker receives by custom a commission ('courtage') not only for the mediation of the contract but also for the management and the monitoring of the policies from the insurer. The commission expenses are included in the insurance premium which the insurer receives from the client. There is a general ancillary contractual duty on the part of the insurer to correspond with an insurance broker who has been engaged by the policyholder and to pay commission.[486]

788. Alternatively, the broker and the policyholder may agree on a fee-based compensation or that the commission is to be paid by the policyholder ('Netto-Police'). In the latter case with regard to endowment policies (*see* paragraph 712) the payment provisions often included a clause that the payment arrangements continue to apply even if the policies are cancelled. According to case law such a clause

482. For details, *see* Doerner, in: Proelss/Martin, VVG, 30th ed., 2018, § 61 n. 62 et seq.
483. Cf. BGH, 29 May 2013 IV ZR 165/12, VersR 2013, pp. 841, 842; BGH, 22 May 1985 – IV a ZR 190/83, VersR 1985, p. 930; OLG Hamm, 30 Apr. 2012 – 18 U 141/06, NJOZ 2010, pp. 601, 603.
484. Cf. BGH, 14 Jan. 2016 – I ZR 107/14, NJW-RR 2016, p. 1056, paras 14 et seq.
485. Cf. OLG Hamm, 30 Apr. 2012 – 18 U 141/06, NJOZ 2010, pp. 601, 602 (with further references to case law).
486. Cf. BGH, 29 May 2013 – IV ZR 165/12, VersR 2013, pp. 841, 842.

is valid.[487] Unlike insurance agents, insurance brokers, in general, must not expressly inform the policyholder on the effects of such clause.[488]

III. Power of Attorney

789. There is no statutory power of attorney of the insurance broker. Therefore, whether and to what extent insurance brokers are authorized to act on behalf of the policyholder depends on the terms of their agreements. The same is true when a broker acts on behalf of the insurer. That is always the case where the broker provides services that would otherwise be handled directly by the insurer, such as premium payments and claims handling. According to a landmark decision by the BGH dated 14 January 2016, loss adjustment done by an insurance broker on behalf of an insurer is illegal according to § 3 RDG.[489] In this case the insurance broker mediated an insurance contract between a liability insurer and a company for dry cleaning (policyholder). A customer of the policyholder claimed damages for his ruined shirt. The insurer had granted a loss adjustment authority to the broker for this type of claim. The broker made use of this authority and offered to settle the claim on the current market value basis. The BGH held that loss adjustment is a legal service in terms of § 2 paragraph. 2 RDG, and therefore needs authorization unless the services may be provided in connection with another activity which is ancillary to a profession or activity. [490] The BGH then found that while claims management for the policyholder is ancillary to the profession as an insurance broker, this is not the case where the broker acts as loss adjuster for the insurer.[491]

§3. Insurance Adviser

I. Obligations

790. In principle, insurance advisers, as insurance agents and insurance brokers owe advise and documentation towards the customer/policyholder. The scope of the adviser's obligation to give advice, however, must be distinguished from the corresponding obligations of the insurance agents and insurance brokers. Like the insurance broker the adviser develops concepts for the customer/policyholder with regard to risk-adequate coverage, may select suitable insurers and represent the

487. *See* e.g., BGH, 12 Dec. 2013 –IIIZR124/13,VersR 2014, p. 240, para. 11; BGH, 20 Jan. 2005 – III ZR 251/04, BGHZ 162, pp. 67, 72 (with further references to its case law).
488. *See* e.g., BGH, 12 Dec. 2013 –IIIZR124/13,VersR 2014, p. 240, para. 16; BGH, 14 Jun. 2007 – III ZR 269/06, VersR 2007, pp. 1127, 1128 et seq.
489. BGH, 14 Jan. 2016 – I ZR 107/14, VersR 2016, p. 1118, paras 13 et seq.
490. *Ibid.,* paras 37 et seq.
491. *Ibid.,* para. 34.

customer's/policyholder's interests towards insurers.[492] In contrast to insurance brokers and insurance agents, who, in principle, receive the commission for the conclusion of the contract from the insurer, the insurance adviser receives the remuneration from the customer/policyholder.[493] Unlike the insurance broker contract the agreement between the adviser and the customer/policyholder is not concluded for an indefinite period of time but on an one-off basis. According to the OVG Berlin-Brandenburg the legal representative of an insurance broker company – i.e., the managing director of a GmbH – may not be at the same time the legal representative of an insurance adviser company.[494]

II. Remuneration

791. In the case of the customer concludes an insurance contract after the consultation of the insurance adviser, the insurer must give account to the fact that while the insurance mediation costs are generally calculated into the insurance premium, the insurance adviser is prohibited from receiving the remuneration from the insurer, and the policyholder has to pay for the insurance adviser's service. To compensate for paying the insurance adviser, § 48c VAG instead provides that the policyholder must receive credit from the insurer in the amount of insurer's costs for insurance mediation. This results in a lower premium for the policyholder. The policyholder is therefore in the same position as if he/she agrees on a 'Netto-Police' (*see* paragraph 777). If the credit received by the policyholder is greater than the costs paid for the adviser this means that using an adviser might result in a cost benefit for the policyholder.

III. Power of Attorney

792. There is no statutory power of attorney of the insurance adviser. Therefore, whether and to what extent the adviser is authorized to act on behalf of the policyholder depends on the terms of their agreement.

492. Cf. BVerfG, 5 May 1987 – 1 BvR 981/81, BVerfGE 75, p. 284, 294; for details, *see* Schoenleiter, in: Landmann/Rohmer, Gewerbeordnung, C.H. Beck 77th supplement October 2017, § 34e n. 9 et seq.
493. Schoenleiter, in: Landmann/Rohmer, Gewerbeordnung, C.H. Beck 77th supplement October 2017, § 34e n. 26 et seq.
494. OVG Berlin-Brandenburg, 31 Mar. 2017 – 1 N 41.15, BeckRS 2017, 106878.

Part VIII. Reinsurance, Co-insurance, Pooling

§1. Reinsurance

I. Regulation of Reinsurance Contracts

793. Since the abolition of § 779 HGB in the course of the reform of the VVG 1908 there has been no legal definition of the term reinsurance under German law. § 779 HGB provided that reinsurance means the insurance of the risks assumed by the insurer. According to Article 2 paragraph 1 lit. a) Directive 2005/68/EC[495] reinsurance means 'the activity consisting in accepting risks ceded by an insurance undertaking or by another reinsurance undertaking'.

794. Pursuant to § 209 VVG contracts of reinsurance are not governed by the VVG. They are subject of the provisions of the HGB and the general rules of the BGB including the provisions on standard terms and conditions if a clause qualifies as such in the sense of § 305 paragraph 1 sentence 1 BGB (*see* paragraph 160). There is no room for an application of the VVG by analogy. Where the VVG codifies general principles of insurance law which are applied to reinsurance these principles, in general, are binding by virtue of § 346 HGB. Pursuant to this provision due consideration must be given to prevailing commercial customs and usages concerning the meaning and effect of acts and omissions among merchants.[496]

795. There has been hardly any case law on reinsurance which allows the assumption that the parties often arrive at an amicable arrangement or have submitted their dispute to arbitration.[497] In practise the parties agree on ad hoc arbitration, and the arbitration clause often states that the arbitrators must have served on the board of directors of an insurer or a reinsurer (or in an equal position) for a certain period of time.[498]

495. Directive 2005/68/EC of 16 November 2005 on reinsurance, O.J., 9 December 2005, L 323/1.
496. For details, *see* Pamp, in: Oetker, HGB, 5th ed., C.H. Beck 2017, § 346 n. 6–29.
497. Schwepcke, in: Langheid/Wandt (eds), Münchener Kommentar zum VVG, 2nd ed., vol. 3, C.H. Beck 2017, 110. Rückversicherungsvertragsrecht no. 24.
498. Sieg/Schaloske, in: Brook, Insurance & Reinsurance, 1st ed., Sweet & Maxwell 2012, pp. 141, 156.

II. Regulation of Reinsurance Activities

796. Domestic reinsurers have been subject to insurance supervision by BaFin under the VAG since December 2004 (*see* § 298 paragraph 2 VAG). Reinsurers having their registered office in another EU Member State or in a state party to the Agreement on the EEA, which conduct business in Germany under the freedom to provide service (Article 56 TFEU), are primarily subject to supervision by their home country. BaFin does, however, consult the foreign supervisory authority if it identifies breaches of general German legal principles (§ 169 VAG).[499]

797. Reinsurers from countries that are not Member States of the EU or signatories to the agreement on the EEA are subject to authorisation and must establish a German branch office if they wish to carry on reinsurance business in Germany. The requirements for the authorisation, application and the establishment of a branch office can be found in §§ 68 and 69 VAG. § 67 paragraph 1 sentence 2 VAG provides an exemption for insurance undertakings that wish to carry on solely reinsurance business in Germany. According to this exemption, the requirement for authorisation and the establishment of a branch office does not apply if reinsurers carry on solely reinsurance business in Germany through provision of cross-border services and if the European Commission has decided in accordance with Article 172 paragraph 2 or 4 of the Directive 2009/138/EC[500] that the solvency regimes for reinsurance activities carried out by undertakings in the relevant country are equivalent to the regime described in that Directive.

§2. Co-insurance

I. Concurrent-Insurance

798. Co-insurance may be offered in the form that coverage is horizontally divided among several insurers and each takes over a pro rata share of the sum insured or a certain amount. The policyholder has contracts with all participating insurers, each of which is liable to the policyholder for its percentage share of any claim made under the insurance. In the insurance certificate the individual insurers are listed by name with their shares. Co-insurance arrangements are initiated by brokers who have knowledge of the market and the insurer who is likely to be able to lead the risk. The broker develops the program for the client and makes sure that the terms agreed with a lead insurer, also apply to the contracts with the following insurers to avoid that the client is exposed to multiple sets of terms and conditions.[501]

499. *See* https://www.bafin.de/EN/Willkommen/Zulassung/Versicherer/Versicherungsunternehmen_node_en.html (accessed 28 Mar. 2018).
500. Directive 2009/138/EC on the taking-up and pursuit of the business of Insurance and Reinsurance (Solvency II), O.J., 17 January 2015, L 12/1.
501. For details, *see* Armbruester, in: Beckmann/Matusche-Beckmann (eds), Versicherungsrechts-Handbuch, 3rd ed., C.H. Beck 2015, § 6 n. 40 et seq.

799. The leading insurer, who is assigned to supervise the contract and to fulfil contractual obligations towards the policyholder, is authorized to receive notifications and declarations of intent by the policyholder on behalf of all insurers involved. In many cases the insurance policy includes leadership clauses, which provide that claims of the policyholder are only to be asserted against the leading insurer.[502]

800. The litigation leadership clause serves the limitation of costs with regard to a possible litigation for all parties concerned. The policyholder only has to sue the leading insurer with reference to its share of risk. A judgment against the leading insurer has a binding effect for the co-insurers in the amount of their respective share. The litigation clause, thus, constitutes an acknowledgement by the co-insurers under the condition precedent that the leading insurer loses the legal dispute. The facts determined by the judgment are also binding for the co-insurers. Though the policyholder cannot enforce the judgment against the co-insurers, the enforcement of his claims becomes, however, far easier.[503]

II. Layer Coverage

801. Another form of co-insurance is where the risk is not spread horizontally but vertically by various different amounts. The separate 'coverage levels' are called layers. As soon as the coverage of the first layer is exhausted, the coverage of the second layer takes effect. When the coverage of the second layer is exhausted, the coverage sum of the third layer is provided etc., so that there is full coverage with the exceeding contract following coverage provided by the preceding contract. Often both forms of co-insurance are combined in that several insurers take over one layer. Like under concurrent-insurance there are as many contracts as there are insurers (layers). From the viewpoint of the second, third or so on lawyer the coverage provided by the preceding layer(s) is like an excess.

802. Layered coverage contracts also require some sort of leadership clause to be established in the first (primary) lawyer. As is the case with concurrent co-insurance, the broker arranges the layer coverage, approaches for that purpose different potential lead insurers and ask them to pricing and terms. Most important is that all excess layers follow the first layer's form.[504] Some insurers have their own excess wording which typically consists of drop down clauses and difference in limits/difference in conditions clauses.

502. *Ibid.*, § 6 n. 44; Kretschmer, Reichweite und Wirksamkeit von Führungsklauseln in der D&O-Versicherung, VersR 2008, pp. 33, . 34.

503. For further information *see* Lange/Dreher, Der Führende in der Mitversicherung, VersR 2008, pp. 289, 290 et seq.

504. Halbach, in: Langheid/Wandt (eds), Münchener Kommentar zum VVG, 2nd ed., vol. 1, C.H. Beck 2016, § 77 n. 8.

III. Insurance Pools

803. Co-insurance pools involve at least two primary insurers and need to be distinguished from *ad-hoc* co-insurance agreements on the subscription market. The difference between co-insurance pools and ad hoc co-insurance agreements is that the former ones are set up to cover a multitude of unrelated risks that fall within a specific risk category, whereas the latter are established to cover a specific risk that is known to insurers at the time of concluding the agreement. After the expiration of the Regulation 267/2010/EC[505] on 31 March 2017 institutionally arranged co-insurance pools can no longer assume that there is compliance with competition law without carrying out a detailed self-assessment if the conditions of in terms of the Regulation 267/2010/EC are met.

804. Institutionally arranged co-insurance pools can be further divided into two categories: on the one hand there are pools that are founded not only to share the risk but also to bundle and potentially institutionalise more functions and activities in the provision of insurance. On the other one there are pools that are founded because there is no market or the market on its own does not possess sufficient capacities in order to cover the respective risks. In Germany two pools fall into this category, i.e., the 'Atompool' (*see* paragraph 553) and the pharma reinsurance pool (*Deutsche Pharma-Rückversicherungs-Gemeinschaft*, called 'Pharmapool'). The Pharmapool has been found in 1976 and has around 100 insurers and reinsurers as members.[506]

505. Regulation (EU) No 267/2010 of 24 March 2010 on the application of Art. 101(3) of the Treaty on the Functioning of the European Union to certain categories of agreements, decisions and concerted practices in the insurance sector. O.J., 30 March 2010, L 83/1.
506. For details, *see* VW 1997, p. 685.

Part IX. Taxation of Insurance

§1. Taxation of the (Re-)Insurance Company

805. Insurers and reinsurers are subject to the general German tax rules. They have to pay 15% corporate income tax with an additional 5.5% solidarity tax (*see* paragraph 149).

§2. Taxation of Insurance Contracts

806. Insurance contracts may be subject to insurance premiums tax and fire protection tax. The insurance premium tax is regulated in the insurance tax act (*Versicherungssteuergesetz*, hereafter 'VersStG') [507] and in the fire protection insurance act (*Feuerschutzsteuergesetz*, hereafter 'FeuerschStG') (*see* paragraph 814).

I. Insurance Tax Act

A. Tax Basis

807. Pursuant to § 1 paragraph 1 VersStG the insurance tax applies to the payment of an insurance premium. Premiums include all types of payment which must be made to the insurer in order to establish and continue the insurance relationship (e.g., contributions, advances, additional payments, charges and policy drafting fees and other ancillary costs) (*see* § 3 VersStG).

B. Insurer Established in the EU/EEA

808. Where the insurer is established in the EU or in the EEA, the obligation to pay the tax relates to risks situated in Germany pursuant to § 1 paragraph 2 VersStG. Whether or not the risk is situated in Germany is to be determined by the definition

507. Available in English at https://www.gesetze-im-internet.de/englisch_versstg/index.html (accessed 28 Mar. 2018).

in Article 2 (d) in conjunction with Article 25 subparagraph 2 of the Directive 88/357/EEC[508] and Article 46 subparagraph 2 of the Directive 92/49/EEC.[509]

C. Insurer Established Outside of EU/EEA

809. Where the insurer is not established in the EU or in the EEA, the tax obligation arises from the fact that the policyholder has his head office or habitual residence in Germany or if the insurance covers an object located in Germany when the contract was concluded (*see* § 1 paragraph 3 VersStG).

D. Rate and Calculation of Tax

810. Pursuant to § 6 paragraph 1 VersStG the general tax of 19% of the insurance premium is levied in addition to the actual premium. Special rates and calculation rules (§ 6 paragraph 2 in conjunction with § 5 paragraph 1 VersStG) apply to:

- fire insurance and insurance against business interruption by fire (22% on 60% of the premium);
- residential building insurance (19% on 86% of the premium);
- comprehensive household insurance (19% on 86% of the premium);
- insurance against damage from hail, storm, heavy frost, heavy rainfall and flooding, and for insurance against hail, storm, heavy rainfall or flooding taken out in agriculture and horticulture for glass used to protect produce of the soil (0.3 per mille of the sum insured for each year of coverage);
- marine hull insurance (3% provided that ship is registered in Germany, solely serves commercial purposes, and is insured against the perils of the sea).

E. Exemptions from Taxation

811. Exempt from tax are premiums to be paid for *inter alia* reinsurance, health insurance, life insurance, long-term care insurance, occupational disability insurance, fire damage supporting funds (up to 5,500 Euro), livestock insurance (if the sum insured is under EUR 4,000) and the insurance of cross border transported goods (*see* § 4 no. 1, 5, 9, 10 and 12 VersStG).

---

508. Second Council Directive 88/357/EEC of 22 June 1988 on the coordination of laws, regulations and administrative provisions relating to direct insurance other than life assurance and laying down provisions to facilitate the effective exercise of freedom to provide services and amending Directive 73/239/EEC, O.J., 4 July 1988, L 172/1.

509. Directive 92/49/EEC of 18 June 1992 on the coordination of laws, regulations and administrative provisions relating to direct insurance other than life assurance and amending Directives 73/239/EEC and 88/357/EEC (Third Non-life Insurance Directive), O.J., 11 August 1992, L 228/1.

F. Liability for Payment

812. § 7 VersStG distinguishes between the tax debtor and the tax payment debtor. The policyholder is the tax debtor (§ 7 paragraph 1 VersStG). The tax payment debtor is the insurer that has to declare it to the tax authorities and pay it on behalf of the policyholder (§ 7 paragraph 2 VersStG). If the insurer has no head office or a branch in the EU or in the EEA but has authorized an agent to receive the insurance premium, the latter one is the payment debtor (§ 7 paragraph 3 VersStG). In the case of co-insurance the co-insurers can designate in writing one of them to pay the tax for the other insurers as well (§ 7 paragraph 4 VersStG). If neither the insurer nor an agent authorised to receive the insurance premium has a residence, a registered office or a permanent establishment in the EU or the EEA, then the policyholder must pay the tax (§ 7 paragraph 6 VersStG).

813. The tax payment debtor must, within 15 days of the end of each tax return period, submit a personally signed tax return or a tax return transmitted by means of an automated process to the Federal Central Tax Office (*Bundeszentralamt fuer Steuern*, hereafter 'BZA') in which the debtor must calculate the tax which has arisen in the tax return period (self-assessed tax return), and pay over the tax which has arisen in the tax return period (§ 8 paragraph 1 VersStG). The tax return period is the calendar month. If the total tax for the previous calendar year amounted to no more than EUR 6,000, the tax return period is the calendar quarter. If the total tax for the previous calendar year amounted to no more than EUR 1,000, the tax return period is the calendar year.

II. Fire Protection Insurance Act

814. The scope of the FeuerschStG is limited to insurances against the risk of fire, i.e., fire/business interruption insurance, insurance of residential buildings and home contents. The fire protection tax is to be paid in addition to the insurance tax. The fire protection tax is identical with the insurance tax, i.e., 19% (*see* § 4 paragraph 2 FeuerschStG). The basis of assessment of the fire protection tax is the insurance premium without insurance tax. Unlike under the VersStG the insurer is not only the tax payment debtor but also the tax debtor (§ 5 paragraph 1 FeuerschStG). The tax amounts to 22% on 40% of the insurance premium for fire insurance and insurance against business interruption by fire and 19% on 86% of the insurance premium for residential building insurance and comprehensive household insurance.

815. Regarding the declaration and payment of the tax to the BZA, the rules in § 8 FeuerschStG basically follow § 8 VersStG. The tax return period is the calendar month. If the total tax for the previous calendar year amounted to no more than EUR 2,400, the tax return period is the calendar quarter. If the total tax for the previous calendar year amounted to no more than EUR 40, the tax return period is the calendar year.

Part X. Risk Management and Prevention

§1. Supervisory Law

816. According to § 26 paragraph 1 sentence 2 VAG, which transposes Article 44 paragraph 1 of the Solvency II-Directive[510] into German law, insurers and reinsurers must have in place an effective risk-management system comprising 'strategies, processes and reporting procedures necessary to identify, measure, monitor, manage and report, on a continuous basis the risks, at an individual and at an aggregated level, to which they are or could be exposed, and their interdependencies'. This broad notion of risk management is not limited to the insurance sector. It rather reflects the general understanding of risk management in a business in Germany.[511]

§2. Corporate Law

817. Prevention is part of the risk management in that it deals with the response to identified and evaluated risks. It includes precautionary steps to prevent the materialization of the identified risk as well as repressive measures after the risk has materialized which provide for compensation for financial losses. Insurance belongs to the category of repressive measures. There is an obligation for the members of the management board to ensure that there is sufficient, i.e., risk-adequate insurance cover. This obligation follows from e.g., § 93 paragraph 1 AktG and § 43 paragraph 1 GmbHG which state in conducting business, the members of the management board of a stock corporation or a limited liability company must employ the care of a diligent and conscientious manager. In more detail § 91 paragraph 2 AktG provides that the management board of a stock corporation must take suitable measures, in particular surveillance measures, to ensure that developments threatening the existence of the corporation are detected early. It is important to note that the obligation to ensure risk-adequate insurance cover does not always require taking out insurance. The management board has full discretion how to respond to risks.[512]

510. Directive 2009/138/EC of 25 November 2009 on the taking-up and pursuit of the business of Insurance and Reinsurance (Solvency II), O.J., 17 December 2009, L 335/1).
511. Cf. Spindler, in: Münchener Kommentar zum Aktiengesetz, 4th ed., C.H. Beck 2014, § 91 n. 50; Fleischer, in: Spindler/Stilz, Aktiengesetz, 3th ed., C.H. Beck 2015, § 91 n. 29; Laars/Both, VAG, 4th online ed., Nomos 2017, § 26 n. 1 et seq.
512. For details, *see* R. Koch, Geschaeftsleiterpflicht zur Sicherstellung risikoadäquaten Versicherungsschutzes, ZGR 2006, pp. 184, 197 et seq.

818. This discretion, however, is limited whenever risks have the potential to threaten the existence of a company. In such cases all available precautionary steps as well as repressive measures including the conclusion of insurance contracts are to be taken.[513] If the board members fail to do so, they are liable towards their company as can be illustrated by the judgment of the BGH of 26 November 1985.[514] In this case the former chairman of a riding club suffered a severe knee injury due to a kick out of a horse owned by the club during riding practice in the club's riding hall. He sued the club for damages and the club set-off its claim for damages against the former chairman for the failure not to have concluded horse keeper liability insurance during his chairmanship. The BGH found for the club on the grounds that the taking out horse keeper liability insurance would have been in line with the principle to act reasonable in the best interest of the club.[515]

513. *Ibid.,* pp. 184, 199 et seq.
514. Cf. BGH, 26 Nov. 1985 – VI ZR 9/85, NJW-RR 1986, p. 572.
515. *Ibid.*, 574.

Selected Bibliography

General Books on Insurance Law

Beckmann/Matusche-Beckmann (eds), Versicherungsrechts-Handbuch, 3rd ed., C.H. Beck Muenchen 2015.
Wandt, Versicherungsrecht, 6th ed., Vahlen Muenchen 2016.

Article by Article Commentaries on the VVG and on Selected Model Terms and Conditions

Bruck/Moeller, Großkommentar zum VVG (edited by Baumann/Beckmann/K. Johannsen/R. Johannsen/R. Koch), 9th ed., DeGruyter Berlin.
vol. 1: Introduction, §§ 1–32 VVG, 2008.
vol. 2: §§ 33–73 VVG, 2010.
vol. 3: §§ 74–99 VVG, 2010.
vol. 4: Liability Insurance (§§ 100–124 VVG, AHB, ProdHM, UmweltHM, USV, AVB-AVG), 2013.
vol. 5:Legal Expense Insurance (§§ 125–129 VVG, ARB), forthcoming 2018.
vol. 6/1: Transport Insurance (§§ 130–141 VVG, DTV-Gueter, DTV-VHV), 2016.
vol. 6/2: Transport Insurance (DTV-ADS, Flusskasko, Wassersportkasko), 2015.
vol. 7: Property Insurance (§§ 142–149 VVG, AFB, VGB, VHB, ABU/ABN, AMoB, AMB, ABMG, ABE, AHagB, TierV), 2012.
vol. 8/1: Life Insurance (§§ 150–171 VVG, ALB, ALR), 2013.
vol. 8/2: Occupational Disability Insurance (§§ 172–177 VVG), forthcoming 2018.
vol. 9: Accident Insurance (§§ 178–191, AUB).
vol. 10: Health Insurance (§§ 192–208 VVG, MB/KK, MB/KT), forthcoming 2018.
vol. 11: §§ 209–216 VVG, Co-Insurance, International Private Law, 2013.
vol. 12: Motor insurance (PflVG, AuslPflVG, KfzPflVV, AKB), 2018.
Langheid/Rixecker (eds), Versicherungsvertragsgesetz, 5th ed., C.H. Beck Muenchen 2016.
Looschelders/Pohlmann (eds), Versicherungsvertragsgesetz, 3rd ed., Carl Heymanns Koeln 2017.
Proelss/Martin, Versicherungsvertragsgesetz: VVG, 30th ed., C.H. Beck Muenchen 2018.

Selected Bibliography

Rueffer/Halbach/Schimikowski (eds), Versicherungsvertragsgesetz, 3rd ed., Nomos Baden-Baden 2015.
Schwintowski/Broemmelmeyer (eds), Versicherungsvertragsgesetz, 3rd ed., ZAP Verlag Bonn 2017.
Wandt/Landheid (eds), Münchener Kommentar zum VVG, 2nd ed., C.H. Beck Muenchen.
vol. 1: §§ 1–99, VVG-InfoV, 2016.
vol. 2: §§ 100–216 VVG, 2017.
vol. 3: Nebengesetze, 2017.

Article by Article Commentaries on the VAG

Brand/Baroch Catsellvi (eds), Versicherungsaufsichtsgesetz, 1st ed., Nomos Baden-Baden 2018.
Prölss/Dreher (ed. by Dreher), Versicherungsaufsichtgesetz, 13th ed., C.H. Beck 2018.

Index

The numbers here refer to paragraph numbers.

Index

www.ingramcontent.com/pod-product-compliance
Ingram Content Group UK Ltd.
Pitfield, Milton Keynes, MK11 3LW, UK
UKHW020135290926
15471UKWH00003B/502

9 789403 505206